BRITISH DEFENCE CHOICES FOR THE TWENTY-FIRST CENTURY

Also available from Brassey's

CLARKE
New Perspectives on Secutity

GOW
Iraq, the Gulf Conflict and the World Community

LONDON DEFENCE STUDIES
Published by Brassey's for the Centre for Defence Studies,
King's College London

NAVIAS
Going Ballistic
The Build-up of Missiles in the Middle East

CENTRE FOR DEFENCE STUDIES
Brassey's Defence Yearbook 1993

BRITISH DEFENCE CHOICES FOR THE TWENTY-FIRST CENTURY

Edited by
MICHAEL CLARKE and PHILIP SABIN

With a Foreword by
SIR MICHAEL QUINLAN

The Centre for Defence Studies

BRASSEY'S (UK)

LONDON * NEW YORK

Copyright © 1993 Brassey's (UK) Ltd.

All Rights Reserved. No part of this publication may be reproduced, stored in a retrieval system or transmitted in any form or by any means: electronic, electrostatic, magnetic tape, mechanical, photocopying, recording or otherwise, without permission in writing from the publishers.

First English edition 1993

UK editorial offices: Brassey's, 165 Great Dover Street, London SE1 4YA
orders: Marston Book Services, PO Box 87, Oxford OX2 0DT

USA orders: Macmillan Publishing Company, Front and Brown Streets, Riverside, NJ 08075

Distributed in North America to booksellers and wholesalers by the Macmillan Publishing Company, NY 10022

Library of Congress Cataloging-in-Publication Data
available

British Library Cataloguing in Publication Data
A catalogue record for this book is available from the British Library

ISBN 1-85753-088-8

Photoset in North Wales by
Derek Doyle & Associates, Mold, Clwyd.
Printed in Great Britain by BPCC Wheatons Ltd, Exeter

Contents

Foreword by Sir Michael Quinlan   vii
List of Contributors   ix
Glossary   xi

Introduction   xiii
MICHAEL CLARKE

DEFENCE AND FOREIGN POLICY

1 *Britain and the Future of NATO*   3
JOHN BAYLIS

2 *Britain, Alliances and Intervention*   21
MICHAEL CARVER

3 *Intervention – When, How and Why?*   33
STUART CROFT

4 *A Homeland Defence Option*   50
JOHN MORRISON

DEFENCE AND NATIONAL PRIORITIES

5 *Resources, Commitments and the Defence Industry*   73
RON SMITH

6 *Maintaining Balanced Forces*   90
PHILIP TOWLE

7 *Britain and Alliance Burden-Sharing*   102
MALCOLM CHALMERS

8	*The Implications of Broader Security Challenges* GEORGE ASHMORE	130

DEFENCE FORCE STRUCTURES

9	*The Shifting Trade-offs in UK Defence Planning* PHILIP A.G. SABIN	149
10	*Concentration of Effort and Complementarity* DAVID GREENWOOD	175
11	*The Future of the British Army* COLIN McINNES	198
12	*Britain and Nuclear Weapons* LAWRENCE FREEDMAN	220
	Index	242

Foreword

Sir Michael Quinlan GCB

It is by now a commonplace that the framing of British defence policy, and of a force structure and defence programme to underpin it, has come since the end of the Cold War to pose a range of problems both new and more complex, if less grave, than before. Public discourse on how to tackle these problems is understandably taking time to find coherence and direction. A good deal of the debate, not least in Parliament, still betrays basic incomprehension of what defence planning for a country like Britain can in practice be like in a world where security concerns have lost their old simplifying patterns. Demands are still heard for lists of commitments, or of threat scenarios, from which the size and characteristics of forces to be provided can be handily calculated, and a defence budget level derived as a dependent variable; and complaint is voiced if a constantly-changing world is not matched by a constantly-changing defence programme (as well as, from other interests, if it is). The key reality is that defence planning is pulled in divergent directions by three key forces:

- global political uncertainty, with the risk of unforeseen demands in unexpected places at relatively short notice;
- defence provision lead-times, which mean that such demands fall upon armed services typically shaped by decisions made a decade and more before, and re-shapable often only in a similar timespan;
- resource constraint, in personnel terms as well as in money.

With this triangle of tensions, it is not sensible to look for ready and comprehensive measurement of particular need, or for neat assurance in advance that it can be promptly satisfied. That was essentially true, for most of Britain's defence tasks outside the main East-West confrontation, even before the collapse of Communism. Now that that collapse has removed, or at worst reduced greatly in salience, the main measuring-rod for our defence provision, the truth becomes still more evident. Choice amid uncertainty is inescapable; and constant revisiting of choice with every shift of political circumstance is a recipe for little but instability of programme, and therefore for likely waste and unreadiness.

In this environment there may be a temptation almost opposite to the demand for certainty: to conclude that defence planning is largely guesswork and that because awkward events may prove almost any choice wrong, or at least imperfect, one choice is just as good or bad as another. Such a temptation may fuel a disposition – always strongly present in the UK setting, for reasons worthy in their own way – to let institutional preference and loyalty govern policy decision. But risks are not purely random, nor is their importance everywhere equal. The proper deduction from uncertainty is quite different. It points to thinking all the harder about what choices are available, understanding more clearly what they mean in capability and cost, and assessing more realistically how they relate to the shifting world of the future and to Britain's view of itself in that world. The basic choices reflected in the defence programme changes of 1990-91 were a sensible set; doubts about their aggregate durability reasonably related to concern not so much that unwise choices were made as that fewer choices were made than economic constraints and international realities were likely in the long run to require. As I write, further choices are being made known. The welcome remoteness of substantial direct military threat to or near the UK homeland underlines the fact that defence choices, and the defence budget allocation that partly impels them, have more of discretionary judgement about them than in the past; and that they can and should increasingly be seen within a framework of security interest more broadly interpreted, and served by a broader set of complementary instruments, than in military terms alone.

Reflection and discussion need to continue, and the process will be the healthier if it is deepened and stimulated from outside government by critical contribution not over-swayed by institutional habit or near-term political discomfort. The Centre for Defence Studies was established for just this purpose, and the essays it has brought together in this book are an apt and timely contribution to an important debate.

Michael Quinlan
July 1993

List of Contributors

Sir Michael Quinlan, GCB, formerly Permanent Under-Secretary at the Ministry of Defence; now Director, The Ditchley Foundation.

Michael Clarke, Executive Director at the Centre for Defence Studies, King's College London.

John Baylis, Professor of International Politics at the University of Wales, Aberystwyth.

Field Marshal Lord Carver, GCB, CBE, DSO, was Chief of the General Staff, 1971-73 and Chief of the Defence Staff, 1973-76.

Stuart Croft, Senior Lecturer in Security Studies, University of Birmingham.

John Morrison, is a UK government official. During 1993 he attended the Royal College of Defence Studies.

Ron Smith, Professor of Applied Economics, Birkbeck College, University of London.

Philip Towle, Fellow of Queens' College, University of Cambridge, and Deputy Director of the Centre for International Relations at Cambridge.

Malcolm Chalmers, Senior Lecturer, Department of Peace Studies, University of Bradford.

George Ashmore, is the *nom de guerre* of a defence analyst.

Philip Sabin, Senior Lecturer, Department of War Studies, King's College, University of London.

List of Contributors

David Greenwood, Director of the Centre for Defence Studies, University of Aberdeen.

Colin McInnes, Defence Lecturer, Department of International Relations, University of Wales, Aberystwyth.

Lawrence Freedman, Professor of War Studies, King's College, University of London.

Glossary of Abbreviations

ABM	Anti-ballistic missile
ACE	Allied Command Europe
AMF	ACE Mobile Force
ANZAM	Australia, New Zealand, America (Defence Agreement)
ARRC	Allied Command Europe Rapid Reaction Corps
AWACS	Airborne warning and control system
BAOR	British Army of the Rhine
CENTO	Central Treaty Organisation
CFCs	Carbofluorocarbons
CFE	Conventional Forces in Europe
CFSP	Common Foreign and Security Policy (of the EC)
CIS	Commonwealth of Independent States
CSCE	Conference on Security and Co-operation in Europe
CSO	Committee of Senior Officials (of the CSCE)
DPC	Defence Planning Committee
EC	European Community
EDC	European Defence Community
EFA	European Fighter Aircraft
EFTA	European Free Trade Association
EPC	European Political Co-operation (of the EC)
ERM	Exchange Rate Mechanism
ETP	Emergency Tour Plot
GDP	Gross Domestic Product
GNP	Gross National Product
GPALS	Global Protection Against Limited Strikes
HCDC	House of Commons Defence Committee
HMSO	Her Majesty's Stationery Office
IAEA	International Atomic Energy Agency
IPPR	Institute of Public Policy Research
IISS	International Institute for Strategic Studies
IRA	Irish Republican Army
IUKADGE	Improved UK Air Defence Ground Environment Programme

KT	Kiloton
LPD	Landing platform dock
LPH	Landing platform helicopter
LSL	Landing ship, logistic
MACP	Military Aid to the Civil Power
MBFR	Mutual and Balanced Force Reductions
MCMV	Mine countermeasures vessel
MIS	Management Information System
MOD	Ministry of Defence
MSF	Manufacturing Science Finance
NAFTA	North American Free Trade Association
NAO	National Audit Office
NATO	North Atlantic Treaty Organisation
NI	Northern Ireland
NVA	Former East German Armed Forces
OECD	Organisation for Economic Co-operation and Development
OOA	Out-of-Area
PGM	Precision-Guided Munitions
RAF	Royal Air Force
RM	Royal Marine
RN	Royal Navy
RUSI	Royal United Services Institute
RVs	Re-entry vehicles
SACEUR	Supreme Allied Commander Europe
SALT	Strategic Arms Limitation Treaty
SAR	Search and Rescue
SAS	Special Air Service
SBS	Special Boat Service
SDE	Statement on the Defence Estimates
SEATO	South East Asia Treaty Organisation
SIPRI	Stockholm International Peace Research Institute
SLBM	Submarine-launched ballistic missile
SSBN	Ballistic missile-carrying submarine
SSN	Nuclear-powered submarine
START	Strategic Arms Reduction Treaty
TA	Territorial Army
TASM	Tactical Air-to-Surface Missile
TNF	Theatre nuclear forces
UN	United Nations
UNPROFOR	United Nations Protection Force (in former Yugoslavia)
WEU	Western European Union

Introduction

Michael Clarke

Defence Challenges in a New Era

British defence policy has changed in many dramatic ways during the 20th Century, but as policy-makers face the next century, they probably have to address more fundamental and difficult choices than any of their predecessors. This is a bold claim since British defence policy is constantly under the microscope and previous governments have also had to implement major changes in the resources allocated to defence. If British history since 1945 has been dominated by the imperatives of readjustment to a post-imperial role, then it is not surprising that British defence policy should always have been in a state of transition and under constant and active scrutiny by the Treasury, with the government seeking to match concepts of 'threat' with those of 'commitment' and also with calculations of the available resources.

Nevertheless, it is clear that British defence policy is in a more critical phase as we approach the 21st Century than at any time since 1945. There are a number of self-evident reasons why the post-Cold War world creates dramatically new choices for British defence policy. The end of the Cold War has changed the requirements of British defence – though in ways which are not yet fully discernible. Certainly, Britain no longer has to reckon with the prospect of fighting for its survival in an alliance threatened by an opposing alliance of roughly equal military weight. The British homeland is now more physically secure from invasion than at any time in the 20th Century and, though it is possible to imagine longer term threats to British territorial integrity, the immediacy and intensity of the threat which the Warsaw Pact seemed to pose to Britain and its allies during the Cold War have all but evaporated. The threat of a nuclear attack against the homeland still remains, at least in so far as other powers have the capability to mount one, though such a calculation of threat has also to take into account the present lack of any credible motive to do so. But if the threats against which defence policy has to be measured have changed to an extent that would scarcely have been imaginable 10 years ago, it is not yet clear how Britain should assess the new challenges to its security interests. Though the prospect of general war in Europe has receded considerably, conflict and insecurity across the continent seem set to increase exponentially.

Renewed economic constraints are also a major consideration in British defence policy. It is in the nature of defence policies that there will always be an economic constraint; indeed it is arguable that at other times in the last 45 years the economic constraints on British defence policy have been more severe. But in a climate in which the public sector deficit is currently around £50bn a year (in an economy whose GNP is less than £550bn) *and* in which there is a general expectation of a 'peace dividend' after the Cold War, it is inevitable that defence expenditure will come under very severe scrutiny. Furthermore, British defence policy is at a crossroads because European unity and the transatlantic relationship are also at such a juncture. The dichotomy between defence and security matters on the one hand and economic and social issues on the other – a dichotomy enshrined in the functions of NATO as opposed to those of the European Community (EC) – suited British diplomacy very well and allowed the country to play a central rôle in NATO and the transatlantic relationship whilst nevertheless being ambivalent in its attitude to the EC. But though the rôles of NATO and the EC are still distinctively different, both organisations have a critical interest in the new politics of post-Cold War security in Europe, and debate over Britain's contribution to that security for the future is part of a broader argument about its approach to the further development of European Union.

Not the least of reasons why British defence policy is at such a critical stage concerns the new political configurations arising throughout Europe now that bipolarity has collapsed. For the Western powers, relations with 'the East' are no longer driven primarily by the defence relationship between the two blocs, and now take on multi-dimensional political aspects in a situation of rapid change and great uncertainty. At the very least, the range of calculations defence policy-makers now have to make in order to assess the state of European challenges to British security has increased dramatically as European security has taken on new political and economic dimensions. Sub-regional alliances are emerging; ethnic distinctions have again become politically important after being suppressed by the dynamics of the Cold War; political stability has become intimately linked to problems of economic reform within the new democracies of the East; and the bedrock of Western unity is no longer based on the shared perception of a common threat to the security of all Western nations, and cannot be taken for granted. Without such a foundation of shared threat, NATO nations will probably have to work harder at maintaining their unity than was ever the case in the Cold War – difficult though that often was.

All this is commonly acknowledged by most observers of British defence policy and provides an obvious point of departure for any analysis. There are also, however, some less evident reasons why the 1990s should be regarded as such a pivotal time for defence policy-makers. For the disappearance of a manifest threat to Britain raises some fundamental questions about the very purposes of defence for a country such as this. In particular it begs first-order questions concerning what is meant by defence.

If 'defence' is regarded as the ability simply to defend the realm (including its dependent territories) from external aggression, then British policy-makers can afford to be fairly relaxed about their task for some time to come. For the 'realm' has become a great deal smaller after the process of decolonisation, and there is now far less to defend it against, as a threat to the homeland has become impossible to imagine with any credibility. Throughout most of the Cold War British forces were dwarfed by those of the Soviet Union and its allies, and though there was a reasonable expectation that they would perform their NATO rôles well, no one pretended that British forces were anything more than minimally adequate for the massive military challenge they faced. In present circumstances, however, a significant proportion of British forces could be regarded as surplus to requirements, if their task is defined only as defence of the realm. In this scenario, the second-order questions involve calculations about the risk that British forces might nevertheless have to defend the realm in circumstances so far unforeseen, and the extent to which a war-fighting capacity has to be maintained as a hedge against an uncertain future. In this sense, the size and composition of the forces are less important than their ability to be reconstituted within a given time in the event of a manifest threat to Britain – though force size is itself related to an ability to reconstitute.

On the other hand, if the definition of 'defence' is that it has somehow to contribute to the *security* of the country, then the policy-making equations are altogether more complex. For what constitutes adequate security for Britain is a far more political and abstract question than what realistically threatens its homeland or the remaining dependent territories. On this assumption defence policy has to be seen as only one component in a package that also consists of foreign and international economic policy; indeed, in this formulation defence policy may be regarded as the servant of foreign policy.

In particular, a 'security' definition of defence raises a series of second-order questions concerning how widely British security interests should be defined. Do they still include the security of Britain's allies, who may now – in contrast to the situation of the Cold War – be threatened by forces which do not also threaten Britain? How far is it in Britain's national interests to use its defence policy to support general political stability in Europe, or even more, some concept of world order, when this might necessitate the employment of British forces in situations which seem peripheral to Britain's direct concerns? Above all, if defence is regarded in this light, then policy-makers will not have time to reflect at leisure on a relative surplus of forces, but will instead face the situation where competing claims are made all too urgently on British forces that were structured for a different political purpose.

Before 1989, British forces were measured against their ability to fight a war for survival, and the fact that since 1945 they have done almost everything *except* fight such a war was regarded as a creditable bonus to their essential rationale, which remained unchanged. But the question arises as to what extent forces still structured for general war are appropriate to deal with a widening range of lesser contingencies that may arise in several areas simultaneously in the post-Cold War environment.[1] The suspicion grows that forces designed to fight a general war will not have sufficient utility as policy instruments to promote European or international security when they are faced by the challenges of so many local conflicts; while forces designed more appropriately to meet the likely challenges of the next two decades will lack a general war-fighting capacity. In this respect, British forces may be asked to perform tasks more akin to those of the Victorian era – where world order was defined through an imperialist prism – than to anything they have been tasked with since the mid-1930s.

The conceptions of defence as 'defence of the realm' and defence as 'the promotion of British security interests' represent ends of a spectrum of possibilities on which the second-order questions can be arranged – with a good measure of overlap in many cases. And of course, policy-makers are not in the business of choosing extreme ends of any spectrum, but rather of having to compromise with existing policies to provide as broad a set of credible choices as possible. Nevertheless, the essential choice remains, which explains why British defence policy stands at a more important conceptual crossroads than is often appreciated. From 1945 to 1989 Britain's defence interests and security interests were synonymous and the most sensible – and cost-effective – way to pursue them was to prepare to fight a NATO-wide general war. The immediacy of the military threat to the West made this policy a simple imperative. But with the emergence of a post-Cold War world, Britain's defence and security interests are not now obviously synonymous; in fact, as the 'defence' task has become less intense and the 'security' task arguably much more so, it appears that the spectrum defined here is widening all the time and that Britain may have to move decisively in one direction or the other if its forces are to be capable of performing any strategic function effectively.

The Government's Response

The response of the government so far to the new strategic environment of British defence policy has been incremental and has proceeded along three parallel lines. The first may be described as the 'Options for Change' process and the so-called 'post-options' adjustments that have continued since then. On 6 February 1990, the government announced that it was initiating its Options for Change exercise, which continued to run until late 1991. Various cuts were made under this programme and were announced in separate statements as decisions were reached. The essence of the Options for Change exercise, however, was enshrined in two major statements to the House of Commons on 25 July 1990 and 23 July 1991, and in the *Britain's Army for the 90s* White Paper which accompanied the latter statement.[2]

In these statements the government made it clear that it intended to reduce the total number of Army personnel from 156,000 to 116,000 by 1995. Infantry battalions in particular would be reduced from 55 to 38, which would include two Gurkha battalions.[3] The Royal Marines, serving in an infantry role, would constitute the equivalent of three more battalions, creating a possible total of 41. Armoured and armoured reconnaissance regiments were to be reduced from 19 to 11, artillery regiments from 22 to 16. Engineering regiments and signals regiments were to be reduced from a combined total of 30 to 21. It was announced that other regiments would be reduced in size or amalgamated, in a further programme to be announced later. These reductions amounted to 23 per cent of the Army's manpower, though some 35 per cent among the infantry. The number of troops stationed in Germany would be reduced from 55,000 to around 23,000 as the four divisions (three in Germany) of the 1st (BR) Corps were to be reduced to two divisions (one in Germany) which would make up most of the UK's contribution to NATO's new Rapid Reaction Corps (ARRC).

The Options process also affected the Navy and the Air Force, though in a less structural way than the Army. The Royal Navy and Royal Marines were cut from a personnel establishment of 63,000 to 55,000, attack submarines were to be reduced from 27 to around 16, and destroyers and frigates were to be cut from a level of 'about 50' to 'about 40'. Nimrod maritime patrol aircraft were to be reduced by 15 per cent. The Royal Air Force was to be reduced from an establishment of 89,000 to around 75,000. Nuclear-capable Tornado/Buccaneer squadrons were to be rationalised from 13 to 8, all of which would be Tornado GR1/1A squadrons. The 11 air defence squadrons in Britain and Germany were to be reduced to 7 by retiring squadrons of older Phantom aircraft. Two air bases in Germany were to be closed and other supporting elements such as the RAF's helicopter force stationed there would be trimmed down. At the same time, UK-based civilian personnel in the Ministry of Defence were to be reduced from 141,000 to 120,000 and locally-engaged civilians from 31,000 to around 15,000. It was also made clear that the 340,000 members of the reserve and auxiliary forces were 'under consideration' pending further plans to restructure the Army. The UK mobile force – intended to be sent to Denmark in the event of hostilities with the Warsaw Pact – was to be abolished, while the immediate reaction forces for NATO remained under discussion.

Having established the broad outlines of the Options for Change package, the government then moved to the even more sensitive process of announcing which regiments were to be reduced or amalgamated. In *Britain's Army for the 90s* the difficult choices were spelt out in July 1991. Then on 10 December 1991 the government announced that it would cut the Territorial Army by 15 per cent, from 75,000 to 63,500, and that it would alter the terms on which the regular reserve was organised for the future.[4]

Clearly, the Navy and the Air Force were being rationalised while the Army was being restructured in such a way as to reduce the British Army of the Rhine and to curtail the growth in manpower expenditure which threatened to overload the defence budget. The government claimed that the Options for Change process was not a defence review and that it was 'strategy-led but resource-disciplined'.

From the very beginning, however, the Options announcements ran into a barrage of criticism in both Parliament and the wider military establishment. The House of Commons Defence Committee expressed most of the relevant arguments succinctly in two particular reports: *Defence Implications of Recent Events*, and its review of the *Britain's Army for the 90s* White Paper.[5] Most of the criticisms centred on the perception that the Options process was in fact almost entirely 'resource-led', being essentially a cost-cutting exercise, that it was not informed by any proper strategic

Table 1 PLANNED FORCE LEVELS

	Actual Level 1990	Mid-1990s Force Levels Options for Change	Mid-1990s Force Levels Current Plans
Royal Navy			
Nuclear-powered ballistic missile submarines	4	4	4
Nuclear-powered submarines	14	12	12
Conventionally-powered submarines	10	4	0[1]
Aircraft carriers	3	3	3
Destroyers/Frigates	44	About 40	About 35
Helicopter carrier[2]	0	1	1
LPD	2	2	2
LSL	5	5	5
MCMV	38	34	25[3]
RM Commando[3]	3	3	3
Sea Harrier	24	22	22
Army			
Infantry battalions	55	38[5]	40[5]
Armoured regiments[6]	13	8	8
Armoured Recce regiments	5	2	2
Artillery regiments[6]	20	15	15
Engineer regiments[7]	13	10	10
Army Air Corps regiments[8]	4	5	5
Royal Air Force[9]			
Tornado F3	92	122	100
Phantom	65	0	0
Hawk[10]	72	52	50
E-3D Sentry	0[11]	7	6
Tornado GR1/1a/1b[12]	148	112	112
Harrier	74	52	52
Jaguar[13]	40	40	40
Buccaneer	30	0	0
Nimrod	35	27	27
Support helicopters[14]	93	90	90[15]
Transport & tanker aircraft	94	93	90

Notes
[1] Future of Upholder under consideration.
[2] LPH will enter service later in the decade.
[3] MCMV numbers will fall below this figure for a period following the pay-off or redeployment of Ton and River Class minesweepers and until new vessels come into service.
[4] Excludes RM Commachio Group.
[5] After withdrawal from Hong Kong in 1997.
[6] Excludes training regiment.
[7] Excludes Military Survey, Military Works Force and Commando Engineer Squadron.
[8] Excludes sub-units in NI equivalent to an additional Regiment and RM Squadron.
[9] Establishments of squadrons and operational conversion units.
[10] Aircraft in Air Defence role only.
[11] Shackleton previously operated in the early warning role.
[12] Excludes aircraft at Tri-national Tornado Training Establishment.
[13] Excludes training aircraft.
[14] Excludes SAR, The Queen's Flight and advanced flying training aircraft.
[15] We plan to increase our capability in this area. Number will depend on decisions yet to be taken.

Source: Statement on the Defence Estimates 1993, Cm 2270, (London, HMSO, 1993), p. 89.

reassessment of British defence policy in the light of the end of the Cold War, and that it was being undertaken in secret without adequate consultation with those branches of the Services which would be most affected by the changes.[6]

Though the government insisted that Options for Change was an irrevocable series of decisions, it became apparent by the end of 1991 that the process was an ongoing one and that other adjustments would have to be made. In response to the manifest pressures on British infantry regiments as a result of their involvement in the crisis in the former Yugoslavia and their rôle in the United Nations Protection Force (UNPROFOR), the government announced on 3 February 1993 that two of the regimental amalgamations would not be implemented, thus saving two more infantry battalions to take the available total up to 40 (43 if the Royal Marines are counted in an infantry role).[7] The first major cuts of what had become known as the 'post-options' programme were announced in the 1993 Defence White Paper. The Army was to lose the Phase III development of the Multiple-Launch Rocket System but, otherwise, the Navy and the RAF began to feel the pressures of genuine restructuring. The Upholder class of four submarines was cut entirely, since there was now said to be no rôle for it to defend British north-western waters; the frigate and destroyer force was to be held at 'about 35' rather than 40; Mine Counter-Measure vessels were to be reduced from 31 to 25; and Navy personnel cut further from 55,000 to 52,500. The RAF would lose another Tornado F3 fighter squadron; its air defence missile system would not be replaced; and its personnel was to be reduced by 5,000 to 70,000.[8] Following the 'Options' exercise, the minor reversals made in February 1993, and then the first major 'post-Options' announcements, UK forces – as of mid-1993 – were due to reach levels shown in Table 1 by 1995.[9]

The second strand of the government's response revolved around the creation of the Allied Command Europe Rapid Reaction Corps (ARRC). NATO had begun to restructure its forces from mid-1990 and it was clear that within the new force structure – composed of immediate and rapid reaction forces, main defence forces, and augmentation forces – the most important element would be a rapid reaction corps which would become NATO's first major means of military response should the need arise.[10] In June 1991, at NATO's Copenhagen Summit, it was announced that Britain would command this Corps, contributing to it a new 1st UK Armoured Division (to be formed from the disbanded 1st BR Corps), the UK 3rd Division, based in Britain, and an airmobile brigade for one of the Corps' two other divisions. This represented a military and diplomatic coup for Britain but also a major commitment for the future. Leadership of the ARRC reconfirmed Britain's place as a leading member of the

European NATO countries and made the best use of Britain's proven ability to project military power efficiently. It also represented something of a safeguard for the Army since committing more than two divisions to a multinational force would help protect it from further pressures from the Treasury. On the other hand, such a high involvement in the ARRC, and in particular the responsibility of command, implied considerable commitments for British forces, not least for infantry regiments which were being stretched so thinly. The ARRC is due to become fully operational in 1995, at exactly the same time as the Options for Change review is due to be fully implemented.

The third element in the government's response was enshrined in the 1992 Defence White Paper which reconceived British defence policy as resting not on 'four-and-a-half' pillars but rather on three 'overlapping rôles'. The original pillars had been set almost entirely in the NATO context and were:

1. Defence of the homeland.
2. Maintenance of the strategic nuclear deterrent.
3. Maintenance of forces on the continent of Europe for the defence of NATO.
4. Protection of the Eastern Atlantic.
5. (The half role). Out-of-Area operations.

This conception, which had endured explicitly since 1974 and implicitly since before that, was now reconceived as three overlapping, but more all-encompassing, rôles which were carefully articulated:

1. To ensure the protection and security of the United Kingdom and our dependent territories, even when there is no major external threat.
2. To ensure against any major external threat to the United Kingdom and our allies.
3. To contribute to promoting the United Kingdom's wider security interests through the maintenance of international peace and stability.[11]

The 1992 White Paper made it clear that these rôles would require a range of forces and that they would have to be enacted in a much less certain international environment: indeed, it was explicitly stated that military operations under the third rôle 'could be conducted by NATO, WEU, the UN, or ad hoc coalitions under UN or CSCE auspices'.[12] The 1993 Defence White Paper developed this scheme by offering a Chapter on the methodology of analysing the defence programme which identified 46 separate military tasks that the forces presently perform, designated according to which of the three rôles they primarily served.[13] This development of three defence rôles clearly offers a different emphasis from previous official statements. But the articulation of the first rôle encapsulates the essential dilemma. At first glance the wording of the first rôle represents no more than a statement of sovereignty. If the defence forces have any rationale they clearly have to defend the homeland. But also implicit in the wording is the dichotomy between protecting the homeland and promoting the security of the United Kingdom, more broadly defined. The careful wording implies that the drafters understand — even if they cannot adequately address — the implicit contradiction that defence of the homeland, where there is no major external threat, and protection of the security of the country, may not necessarily be synonymous.

Questions for the 21st Century

In 1983 John Baylis edited an excellent collection of papers on *Alternative Approaches to British Defence Policy* which enshrined the range of choices open to defence policy-makers and performed a valuable service to all analysts of the subject.[14] This collection is inspired by the same motives and is intended to serve a similar function. But a decade after the Baylis book the range of credible alternatives has to be set in a wider and even more challenging intellectual context. All the papers in this volume suggest that more radical choices will have to be made — in whatever direction defence policy goes — than have so far been announced by government. Even a choice to maintain the existing range and size of British forces must now be counted a bold decision since such forces will be very expensive to maintain, and will have to provide tangible political benefits if they are to prove their utility and cost-effectiveness in a rapidly changing international environment.

This book is divided into three sections, each addressing a major set of questions facing British defence planners today. The first section considers the relationship between defence and broader questions of foreign policy. The second section considers defence as one of a number of competing national priorities, all jostling for scarce resources. The final section assesses force structure issues within the overall defence effort. In each section, four defence experts offer their own perspectives on the choices Britain should make in response to the dilemmas which it now faces.

In the first section, John Baylis considers the ways in which the European alliance context of British defence policy might evolve in the future. He argues that NATO is likely to remain the best organisation through which to co-ordinate a military response to security challenges, though it is less certain how this can be made properly compatible with other security organisations in Europe.

Lord Carver and Stuart Croft then develop this position on the assumption that there will be calls and temptations for British forces to serve foreign policy in a range of ways by intervening in conflicts both in and around NATO territories. Lord Carver concentrates on the difficulties of defining clear national interests in the post-Cold War world in ways that can be translated into feasible and efficient military operations. Stuart Croft sets the motivations for British policy-makers to intervene in the service of world order against the likely degree of operational difficulty in doing so. His attempt to articulate the dimensions of choice offers suggestions of the directions in which British defence policy would have to go if the motivation to intervene for humanitarian purposes develops in the coming years. Finally, John Morrison sets out the argument that defence can be defined in a way that does not necessarily tie it to the broader concerns of foreign policy. He argues that a homeland defence option is certainly feasible at a much reduced level of forces; its desirability depends on the assumptions that are made about the relationship of defence to Britain's broader external policy interests.

The second section considers defence as one of a number of competing national priorities. Ron Smith analyses the way in which defence expenditure trends are likely to constrain the choices of policy-makers. He thinks that a great deal of painful readjustment, both for the defence establishment and for defence industries in Britain, is probably unavoidable even if defence spending levels off in real terms from the mid-1990s. Philip Towle then develops the argument that the maintenance of forces balanced at roughly their present levels should not only remain a high national priority, but may indeed be something that Britain can offer to the international community as a tangible contribution to stability. Though he concedes that a war for survival is unlikely, he argues that forces generally structured as they are at present offer a way of exercising some enlightened self-interest while maintaining a core of flexible and efficient forces as a hedge against any contingency. Certainly, he argues, economic arguments should not be allowed to drive the capability inexorably downward.

Malcolm Chalmers, by contrast, argues that the end of the Cold War has provided an opportunity to conduct a radical review of the economic burden placed on Britain by its defence commitments. It could reduce the burden either by simply reassessing the present threat, free from the momentum of Cold War assumptions, or by sharing defence burdens more equitably with its European allies in an attempt to develop a more integrated defence policy among the West Europeans. Force levels and expenditure, he argues, could be safely reduced to a much lower base line than at present. Finally, George Ashmore analyses the priority given to defence as against other priorities that affect the well-being of the British state and people. On the assumption that 'security' applies more to people than to the abstractions called states, he argues that Britain's armed forces have a much reduced rôle in the provision of security for the British people and that other threats, both global challenges – such as those posed by environmental problems – and domestic problems – such as our failure to establish adequate health or education standards – should be addressed under the heading of British security.

The final section addresses questions of force structure. Philip Sabin takes account of the various trade-offs that defence planners now have to make and encapsulates their major choices according to five general dimensions: readiness versus reconstitution; independence versus integration; flexibility versus specialisation; mobility versus punch; and finally, quality versus quantity. He argues that although Options for Change sufficed for the short-term, the longer term will require more deeply structural changes as choices are inevitably made on each of the five dimensions. Another way of addressing these choices would be to make a single – and very radical – change in the direction of much greater rôle specialisation, and David Greenwood analyses the context in which rôle specialisation arguments have now to be set. Both the risks, and the attractions, of this alternative are great in the present environment. So too, may be the implicit degree to which all European NATO allies will move down the rôle specialisation road. NATO, he argues, will become less an integrated military command structure and more a 'coalition in waiting', in which members will offer their relative specialisms on an ad hoc basis in response to a given challenge.

Many of the key choices for Britain revolve around the future of the British Army, and this issue is examined in depth by Colin McInnes. He analyses the background to the Options for Change process and the way in which Britain adopted leadership of the ARRC. His conclusion is that the Army is poorly structured to address the challenges it is likely to face, and will require further structural changes if it is to perform the tasks implicit in the direction of the Options exercise.

Finally, Lawrence Freedman considers Britain's nuclear forces. The nuclear force structure is moving inexorably in the direction of a minimum deterrent based on the Trident force, which will probably see out its planned life. The government will be faced with the charge that this is contrary to nuclear non-proliferation, but it will have to measure this contradiction against the very different strategic environment in which the Trident force will exist. For good or ill, Britain's strategic nuclear force is – in stark contrast to the situation at several points during the Cold War – the most predictable element in its military structure.

Notes

1. There is an argument that since British forces during the Cold War were always able to improvise their essential war-fighting capacities to the lesser contingencies out-of-area, the present situation is really not new. But the critical difference in the 1990s is that most comparable out-of-area operations are likely to absorb much higher proportions of available defence resources and will require decisions to forgo other capabilities.
2. *Britain's Army for the 90s*, Cm 1595, (London: HMSO, July 1991).
3. In fact, three Gurkha battalions would continue to exist until the hand-over of Hong Kong to China in 1997, when they would be reduced to two. So from 1995–97 there would, on paper, be 42 battalions if everything was included.
4. See also, *The Future of Britain's Reserve Forces*, Defence Open Government Document, 1992.
5. House of Commons Defence Committee, *Defence Implications of Recent Events*, HC 320, London, HMSO, 1990; House of Commons Defence Committee, *Britain's Army for the 90s: Commitments and Resources*, HC 306, London, HMSO, 1993.
6. On this last point, see House of Commons Defence Committee, *Options for Change: Army – Review of the White Paper, Britain's Army for the 90s*, CM1595, HC 45, (London, HMSO, 1992), pp.80–85. See also, House of Commons Defence Committee, *Statement on the Defence Estimates 1991*, HC 394, (London, HMSO, 1991), for a range of criticisms of the whole process.
7. The amalgamations between the Cheshire and the Staffordshire regiments, and between the Royal Scots and the King's Own Scottish Borderers were rescinded.
8. Statement on the Defence Estimates 1993, *Defending Our Future*, Cm 2270, (London, HMSO, 1993), pp.9–14.
9. Though the Options for Change announcements were all designed to be implemented by the end of 1995 – save for the adjustments occasioned by the withdrawal from Hong Kong in 1997 – the 1993 announcements referred merely to the 'mid-90s' as the target for the implementation of the restructuring.
10. Technically, the Allied Command Europe Mobile Force could be the first unit to be deployed in a NATO operation, but it is very small. The ARRC provides the most immediately deployable forces of any appreciable military weight.
11. Statement on the Defence Estimates 1992, Cm 1981, (London, HMSO, July 1992), p.9.
12. *Ibid*.
13. Statement on the Defence Estimates 1993, *op. cit.*, pp.20–21.
14. John Baylis, *Alternative Approaches to British Defence Policy*, (London: Macmillan, 1983).

DEFENCE AND FOREIGN POLICY

1
Britain and the Future of NATO

John Baylis

The end of the Cold War has created a major dilemma for British defence planners. For the past 40 years one of the central planks of British defence policy has been the commitment to collective defence ideas, particularly those reflected in the North Atlantic Treaty Organisation. After a hesitant acceptance of a continental commitment in the years from 1948 to 1954, NATO became one of the main priority areas in British defence policy for the rest of the Cold War period. However, with the breaching of the Berlin Wall in November 1989, the dissolution of the Warsaw Pact, and the major nuclear and conventional arms control agreements of the late 1980s and early 1990s, the old system of European security collapsed. This meant that for Western governments, including Britain, one of the key questions to be answered in the 1990s was whether the Cold War institutions, like NATO, could be modified to meet the new post-Cold War environment or whether a wholly new approach to European security had to be devised. This Chapter sets out to consider this question by looking at the new security problems facing Britain and its allies for the remaining years of the 1990s and the alternative security frameworks available. In this context the strengths and weaknesses of NATO will be considered by analysing two alternative security frameworks based on the Conference on Security and Co-operation in Europe (CSCE) and the European Community.

Security in an Uncertain World

In the immediate aftermath of the Cold War, debates about European security tended to focus on optimistic assessments of the opportunities to transform the power-based, bipolar system of security into a new European order which would be characterised by co-operation, respect for human rights and non-coercion, and in which military power would cease to be the major driving force of security.[1] Many observers believed that the end of the Cold War would bring about not only the end of ideological confrontation (in Fukuyama's terms, 'the end of history') but also a new era in which the traditional security dilemma could be transcended.[2] The failure of the coup in the Soviet Union in August 1991 and the move towards democratisation in Eastern Europe seemed to justify the hopes of those who believed that a wholly new Kantian approach to international relations might be possible after the hard-nosed, Clausewitzean realism of the Cold War era.[3]

Alongside such promising trends, however, was a more pessimistic interpretation summed up in John Mearsheimer's article 'Back to the Future' in the journal *International Security*.[4] In Waltzian neo-realist terms, Mearsheimer warned that the stability and security of the Cold War era would be replaced by nationalist conflicts, ethnic disputes and xenophobic tensions which had been suppressed by the discipline of the bipolar Cold War system. It was not long before the violence associated with the disintegration of the Soviet Union and particularly Yugoslavia, the resurgence of neo-fascism in Germany and elsewhere in Europe, together with a faltering in the movement towards European unity, seemed to many to justify Mearsheimer's warnings.[5]

Appealing as these two extreme visions are to contemporary 'idealists' and 'realists', they would appear to be far too simplistic. The evidence of recent years suggests that Europe in the 1990s is likely to experience a wide range of co-operative and conflictual situations which will require a multi-dimensional approach to diplomacy and security. It is already clear that the major threats to security are likely to be complex and diverse, emanating more from domestic instability than from direct state-to-state aggression. In this context security has to be viewed in holistic terms: military approaches will have to be combined with a range of political, economic, social and even ecological approaches if the security challenges facing European states are to be dealt with effectively. While 'realists' are wrong to think predominantly in military power terms, 'idealists' are equally wrong to marginalise military considerations in favour of political, social and economic co-operative arrangements. Both are also mistaken in their respective predetermined pessimism and optimism about the future. Dogmatic predictions of either kind are likely to be of limited value in the uncertain world of the 1990s. This can be seen from the difficult problem of how to interpret the significance of events in the former Soviet Union. While the end of the Cold War has eroded perceptions in the West of a direct military threat from the East, it would be wrong to conclude that the disintegration of the Soviet empire poses no problems for future European security. A number of contemporary concerns remain which trouble Western governments.

The first stems from the fact that, despite the importance of the START and CFE agreements, the new republics, and especially Russia, remain formidable military powers with uncertain domestic futures. So far the Russian government has done everything possible to demonstrate its good faith and co-operative intentions to the West. The attempted coup in 1991, the increasing economic instability and the threat to reform from conservative factions, however, raise serious question marks about the political complexion of the Russia government in the longer run. Future governments of any political form are likely to have severe domestic difficulties and preoccupations but there can clearly be no guarantee that future governments will see Russian interests in the same way as the Yeltsin leadership of the early 1990s. It is conceivable that Russia can sustain friendly relations with Western states, overcome its severe economic and political difficulties and eventually become a member of the key Western European and Atlantic institutions. Equally this might not happen and with such military capabilities, even at reduced levels, it would be irresponsible of defence planners not to guard against the possibility of a hostile Russian state emerging during the 1990s. Clearly, if this were so, the threat would not be as great as in the past, given the disintegration of the Soviet Union and the Warsaw Pact and the withdrawal of Soviet forces from Eastern Europe. Russia, however, would still be a formidable military power which would require the continued development of credible Western military capabilities.

Linked to these concerns are the anxieties about nuclear proliferation amongst the four main former Soviet republics, Russia, Ukraine, Kazakhstan and Belarus. Future conflicts between the new republics or civil wars within these states could involve nuclear weapons which would have serious consequences for the rest of Europe. The old Soviet empire consisted of 104 nationalities, with 64 million people living outside their ethnic homelands. Eighty-nine nationalities are mixed into 'foreign' republics with no national homeland of their own. This situation is made worse by the fact that the vast majority of the borders between the former Soviet republics are contested. Events in Azerbaijan, Armenia, Moldova and Georgia in the early 1990s indicate the dangers of violence and hostility on a massive scale. As Booth and Wheeler have argued: '... the potential for ethnic and national conflicts abound, with the brew of border disputes, hopes for self-determination, nationalist desires to reunite kith and kin living in other republics and the ever-present danger of minority rights being abused'.⁶ Such conflicts might not directly threaten European security but it is unlikely that Europe would remain unaffected by them. There would be increased pressures for peacekeeping and peacemaking operations, with dangers of further involvement and instability created by a major influx of refugees.

A harbinger of these dangers has occurred with the crisis in the Balkans. The violent break-up of Yugoslavia has demonstrated all too tragically the fragility of multi-ethnic states re-emerging from long periods of authoritarian control. It has also shown that Europe is not free from old-fashioned territorial ambitions, the obscenities of 'ethnic cleansing' and the willingness by significant political groups to use military force to achieve political objectives, including the expansion of territory. There could be no greater demonstration of the continuing relevance of *realpolitik* thinking than the speech made by General Ratko Mladic, the Bosnian Serb Commander in November 1992. His belief that 'might was right' was evident in his claim that:

> Our army is a reality which no-one can deny. The existence of our Serbian republic can be disputed, but the existence of our army is indisputable. We have our territory, our people, a government and the attributes of a state. Whether people want to recognise this is up to them.⁷

The inability of the international community to 'roll back' the territorial gains of the Bosnian Serbs and the failure of the Owen-Vance plan illustrate the continuing utility of military force in the contemporary international system. The Yugoslav crisis has also demonstrated that ethnic and nationalist violence within states can have broader, more direct, implications for European security. Growing instability in the Kosovo region and in Macedonia raises the prospect that conflict could easily spread to Albania, Bulgaria and Greece given the traditional disagreements between these states.⁸ The involvement of a number of Western European states in United Nations operations in Bosnia in particular also creates the possibility that these states could be sucked more deeply into the crisis.

Although the problems of the former Yugoslavia are particularly intractable they are far from unique in Eastern and Southern Europe. As Van Evera has shown, there are also up to nine potential border disputes, which in the new, more relaxed atmosphere of the post-Cold War world might re-ignite hostilities between states.⁹ Amongst the most acute of these is the border region in Transylvania where an ethnic Hungarian population straddles the border between Romania and Hungary. In central Europe tensions are evident in the divorce of the Czech and Slovak federations. A considerable number of potential 'Yugoslavians' also remain throughout the former Soviet empire.

For Britain the risks stemming from these actual and potential instabilities are in some ways less direct than for many of its allies on the continent, many of whom share common borders with the states in Eastern, Central and Southern Europe. The fact that UK forces represent the largest contingent in the UNPROFOR II force in Bosnia, however, means that Britain shares all the risks of escalation of the Balkan conflict. Despite the early reluctance of British leaders to embrace the continental commitment, since the late 1940s Britain's security has been inextricably linked to that of the continent. This has been confirmed in the 1990s with the government's determination to play a central role in NATO's new Rapid Reaction Force, set up to provide security in the post-Cold War environment.

Given the prevailing contemporary uncertainty and the importance of European stability for Britain's vital security interests, the key question is whether NATO remains the most appropriate framework for defence policy or whether greater emphasis should be placed on either a CSCE-based collective security system or a European defence community centred on the EC. Each of the alternative arrangements will be considered before looking at the case for and against maintaining the Atlantic system.

A CSCE-Based European Security System

A CSCE-based system of collective security owes its inspiration to the League of Nations in the inter-war period. Its chief advocate in the period from 1954 until 1973 was the Soviet Union. From the Soviet perspective the key problem of European security stemmed from the absence of peace treaties at the end of the Second World War and an anxiety about the revisionist intentions of West Germany. A European Security Conference was seen as the vehicle for securing a more formal recognition of the status quo, including a recognition of existing borders and reinforcing the predominant position of the Soviet Union in Eastern Europe. The West, however, was reluctant to provide the Soviet Union with the legitimacy it sought and focused instead on the insecurity which emanated from the imbalance of conventional forces in Europe. By the early 1970s a quid pro quo allowed the Soviet Union to have its Conference on Security and Co-operation in Europe while the West achieved its desired talks on Mutual Balanced Force Reductions (MBFR), to consider scaling down conventional military forces across the continent.

Despite the success of the CSCE between 1973 and 1975

(highlighted by the Final Act in August 1975) and the Helsinki process which continued throughout the late 1970s and 1980s, it was only in the 1990s that the CSCE was taken seriously as a major forum for European security. Following the democratic revolutions of 1989 the CSCE was promoted, initially by the new Eastern European governments, as a pan-European security framework which would provide new ideas and a fresh start for the creation of a new European order. Although this enthusiasm for a CSCE-based system was eroded somewhat as a result of the attempted coup in the Soviet Union in August 1991, as Adrian Hyde–Price has argued, it 'remains a powerful and, in many ways, an attractive vision of security in post-Cold War Europe' as far as some observers are concerned.[10]

The prospects of such a pan-European system being developed were enhanced by the adoption of the Paris Charter for a New Europe by the CSCE summit in November 1991 which attempted to institutionalise the CSCE process. The Paris Charter established regular meetings of government leaders and foreign ministers, with a Committee of Senior Officials (CSO) to prepare for the ministerial meetings. At the same time it was agreed to set up a Secretariat and an Office of Free Elections in Prague; a Conflict Prevention Centre in Vienna; and an Assembly of Europe. This institutional structure is to be supplemented by less formal ad hoc meetings on issues like human rights and 'unusual military activities'. An Emergency Mechanism was also established at the Berlin meeting of the CSCE foreign ministers in the summer of 1991, designed to allow the CSCE to play a rôle in what was then still a civil war in Yugoslavia.

Supporters of a CSCE-based system of European security argue that the organisation has reacted dynamically to the instabilities of the post-Cold War environment and is capable of further development into a broad collective security system for Europe as a whole. This would involve the development of a CSCE 'Security Council' and the acceptance of 'commonly-agreed standards and normative values' which, if broken, would lead all members to impose a wide variety of sanctions from diplomatic and economic pressure to military intervention.[11]

Whether, in practice, the CSCE is capable of moving in this direction is far from clear, however. The experience of the League of Nations in the inter-war period is not promising in this respect.[12] Already the need for unanimity has prevented the CSCE from becoming involved in various disputes. It seems doubtful that a system of majority voting will be sufficient to cement a body as diverse as the CSCE to enable it to take decisive and swift action in a situation of great crisis. Despite the modification to the unanimity principle agreed at the Berlin and Prague foreign ministers' meetings in June 1991 and

February 1992, the steps taken do not as yet go far enough. With a membership of 51 states, a system of qualified majority voting is needed if the CSCE is to be able to respond quickly and resolutely to the kind of security problems facing Europe in the 1990s.

Difficulties arise in two further areas. First, at present the CSCE has no means available to impose effective sanctions on those who break the rules. In the Yugoslav crisis some progress has been made to establish institutional links between the CSCE, the EC, NATO and the UN. Military forces have been used to help protect convoys carrying humanitarian aid. This is not the same, however, as using NATO forces to impose a peace settlement by direct involvement in the fighting. Peacemaking is altogether more problematical than peacekeeping. If the CSCE is to play a more effective rôle in dealing with contemporary security problems such as those posed by the Yugoslav crisis the question of enforcement will need to be resolved. In this context, as will be argued later, NATO is probably the only institution capable of providing the kind of forces which will be needed.

Linked to this is the second major difficulty which concerns the involvement of the CSCE in conflict situations which are not clearly state-to-state disputes. Given the traditional reluctance of international organisations to intervene in the domestic affairs of individual states, it is far from clear that the CSCE will be capable of ignoring state sovereignty and involving itself in issues relating to human rights or ethnic conflict. Increasingly it is these kinds of hostilities which are likely to arise in the post-Cold War Europe. It is one thing to recognise that military force will be necessary in future to protect minority groups, but quite another to envisage a collective security framework which will be capable of such action. At the very least the CSCE will need to develop a new code of conduct enshrining principles dealing with the respect for minority rights and the impermissibility of changing internal and external borders by force.

Given these problems it is perhaps not surprising that British governments have been reluctant in recent years to support proposals for transforming the CSCE into a fully-fledged collective security arrangement. This is not to argue that the CSCE has no value in dealing with contemporary conflicts. Britain clearly has an interest in promoting its activities in the fields of conflict prevention, arms control, crisis management and peacekeeping operations. The CSCE also provides a useful forum for building confidence and for continuing the process of dialogue and consultation on a wide-range of security issues, especially with the former Soviet republics and the Eastern European states. Further modifications of the CSCE along the lines suggested will also improve the contribution it can make to maintaining security and stability in Europe. As a collective security apparatus, however, the CSCE has major limitations.

A European Defence Identity

Given the scepticism about collective security arrangements, most West European governments have focused their main attention on collective defence systems which have a rather more successful history.[13] Apart from NATO the most likely framework for collective defence arrangements is the Western European Union (WEU) either within, or linked to, the European Community (EC). During the Cold War there were periodic attempts to develop a West European defence identity. The most ambitious of these plans occurred between 1952 and 1954 when the French Prime Miniser, René Pleven, promoted the idea of a supranational European Defence Community (EDC) which would be responsible to a broader European Political Community (EPC). The failure of the French National Assembly in August 1954 to ratify the EDC Treaty killed off the plan and blighted moves towards developing an effective European pillar within NATO, or as an alternative to NATO, for the next 35 years. Periodic attempts to develop the WEU which emerged from the Brussels Treaty of 1948 and the Paris Agreements of 1954 (following the EDC crisis), made only limited progress in the 1970s and 1980s.

With the end of the Cold War, however, there has been renewed interest in the WEU. For some observers, particularly in France, it is seen as the body which can provide the EC with the defence arm that it at present lacks. Supporters argue persuasively that with the end of the Warsaw Pact and the erosion of the Soviet threat NATO is likely to become increasingly redundant. As the American presence declines, as it is bound to do, the Europeans will have to assume more responsibility for their own defence. In this context, given the impetus towards greater European union with the 1986 Single European Act, the French government argued, after the events of 1989, that the WEU should become the defence arm of the EC.

For some, these arguments were reinforced by the Gulf War in 1991 and in the subsequent Yugoslav crisis.[14] In the Gulf conflict the failure of the West European states to develop a unified response led to calls from supporters of greater integration for institutional arrangements in the EC to help achieve a common foreign and security policy (CFSP). With the violent disintegration of Yugoslavia the successes and failures of EC diplomacy were seen by the same supporters as further evidence that a CSFP was necessary. The success of the EC in brokering the Brioni Peace Plan in July 1991 demonstrated the growing diplomatic significance of the Community. At the same time, however, the inability of the EC to stop the fighting in Bosnia during 1992 and 1993 reflected the limitations of its power. Despite the disagreements between European states about how to respond to these setbacks (reflected in the Maastricht Treaty of February 1992) the federalists continued to urge the need for greater progress towards an integrated political, economic and defence union in Europe.

Two further arguments have been put forward for a West European defence identity. First, at a time of great international uncertainty, created in part by the end of the Cold War, Community interests might be threatened outside Europe. Events in the Middle East and North Africa, in particular, supporters argue, might well necessitate military intervention to protect vital European interests. Europe could not necessarily rely on the United States or the United Nations to respond on its behalf.

Secondly, with German unification and what some see as the inevitable erosion of the utility of NATO, a more cohesive European defence identity would help to anchor Germany more effectively into the Western community.[15] Not only is this important as reassurance to Germany's neighbours in the East and the West but it would provide reassurance for Germany itself. German security since 1949 has been closely tied to the United States. Those who argue for a common European foreign and defence policy point to the loss of NATO's legitimacy with the end of the Cold War and declining US interest in Europe as evidence of the need for a framework for German security. With the constitutional restraints on Germany preventing the development of nuclear weapons and the deployment of forces outside Germany, it is argued that some effective substitute for the special relationship with the United States will be necessary if Germany is to be reassured and contained.

Britain's reaction to the idea of a more cohesive West European defence identity in recent years has been rather ambivalent. On the one hand the government has supported the enhancement of the WEU which occurred in the late 1980s and early 1990s and accepted that more emphasis should be given to the notion of a more distinct framework for European defence co-operation. At the same time, however, there has been a determined rearguard action to thwart largely French-inspired moves to combine the WEU with the EC. For Britain the WEU was better suited to acting as a bridge between the Atlantic Alliance and the European Community than as the defence arm of the Community itself. NATO, however, had to remain the primary institution of European security, at least in the short and medium term.

The scepticism of the British government about transferring major responsibilities for European defence to the EC and the WEU is understandable given the uncertainties of the contemporary era. There are a number of basic objections to promoting the EC as the primary institution of European security. First, there is the argument that such a defence organisation within the EC is unlikely to prove viable. Critics rightly point to the failure of the European Defence Community in the early to mid-1950s which demonstrated that without a supranational political authority there is little chance of harmonising the defence policies of the West European states.[16] The evidence of differences during the Gulf war and the Balkan crisis reinforces this view. A strong case can also be made that the establishment of the Franco–German Corps in 1992 was rather stronger on symbolism than real military potential. In the context of the debate about Western intervention in Bosnia in early 1993 the constitutional problems regarding the use of German forces demonstrated the weaknesses inherent in French and German plans to expand their joint corps into a 'Euro-corps'.

A second criticism concerns the contemporary difficulty of both widening and deepening the European Community at the same time. Plans to extend membership to a range of formally neutral and non-aligned states in many ways runs counter to the idea of establishing a distinct military framework for the Community. Whether these states would wish to join the EC if it involved military as well as political and economic union is far from clear. Linked to this is the problem of Turkey. Despite attempts to join the EC, Turkey remains outside the Community. A Western European defence identity without Turkey, a member of NATO and located in a region of such strategic importance, would certainly weaken European security arrangements. Given these difficulties, at least for the moment, neither the European Community nor the Western European Union appear to provide a credible framework for effectively co-ordinating the defence policies of member states.

NATO and the Continuation of Collective Defence

It does not, of course, follow that because CSCE-based or EC-based security systems have serious weaknesses a continuing focus on NATO is necessarily the way forward. Indeed, a powerful case can be made that NATO is an institution of the Cold War era which is out of touch with the more co-operative trends of recent years and with the erosion of the Soviet threat is likely to fade away. With its emphasis on the military balance between East and West, NATO is regarded by some as a dinosaur in the 1990s which has little to offer in an era of inter- and intra-state conflicts and security defined in social, political, economic and even ecological terms, as well as in military terms.[17] Viewed in this way the continuing emphasis on NATO may help to undermine, rather than enhance, security and cause nervousness especially in military circles in Russia and the former Soviet republics. At a time when the struggle for power in the new Russia has yet to run its course, the continuation of NATO after the Warsaw Pact has been dissolved may well encourage conservative forces who regret the decline of Soviet power and Western domination of the international scene. In this sense, critics argue, NATO is counterproductive. It undermines the process of reassurance which is so vital at a time of uncertainty and instability as East and West attempt to build a new, more co-operative relationship.

These are clearly concerns that have to be borne in mind. At the same time, however, they have to be balanced by the fact that NATO undeniably continues to perform an important security rôle, especially for Britain. One of the key objectives of British foreign and defence policy throughout the period since 1945 has been to 'entangle' the United States in the security of Western Europe. The 'myth' of the 'special relationship' has been used by British governments of Left and Right to supplement British power and protect British interests during an era of significant national decline. In this context NATO has played an important role in maintaining the 'special relationship' and giving Britain a privileged position in the Western alliance increasingly disproportionate to its actual political and economic power. The end of the Cold War threatens to undermine this privileged position and expose Britain's decline more cruelly than any event since Suez.

The continuation of NATO, however, provides the most effective institutional basis for maintaining an American military presence in Western Europe at a time of great tension and uncertainty. This is clearly of great importance for a European stability but it is also important for Britain in helping to maintain a close relationship with the United States and continuing a British rôle in the major debates about European security. A CSCE-based or EC-based security framework would undermine both British objectives and significantly erode British influence in Europe and the United States. In this context it is hardly surprising that the British government in recent years has been anxious to maintain the primacy of NATO and to secure, despite German opposition, a leading role in the new NATO Rapid Reaction Corps which has been developed to deal with the new security challenges.

Apart from helping to maintain an American military presence to contribute to stability in Europe, NATO also performs two other important tasks for Britain. One relates to the uncertainty over reforms in Russia. The other concerns the future rôle of a united Germany.

It was argued earlier that despite the profound changes that have occurred in East–West relations since 1989 those responsible for defence planning cannot ignore the possibility of the reform process in Russia going wrong. Nor can it be guaranteed that the SALT II and CFE Treaties will be fully implemented over the next 10 years. Should Russia slide further into economic, social and political chaos a new authoritarian government would not present the same kind of threat perceived by Western leaders in the past. Russia and the former Soviet republics will remain preoccupied by domestic problems irrespective of what government is in power. This does not mean, however, that such a government would be benign. Russia would remain the most formidable military power in Europe and might not be guided by defensive common security ideas. Military power might be seen in traditional terms as a national instrument to be used to reinforce strategic and political interests around the periphery of Russia.

In this context NATO would be the only institution capable of matching the military might of Russia, even in its attenuated form. Neither the CSCE nor the EC would be capable of the balance of power rôle that would be necessary in such circumstances. NATO is a tried and tested military organisation which even in its reformed state will be capable of high-intensity warfare should the occasion arise. It will also retain a reduced, but significant nuclear capability in the event of nuclear blackmail. Although such nuclear threats appear unlikely in the early 1990s the proliferation of nuclear weapons and ballistic missile capabilities means that defence planners cannot ignore such eventualities. Even if the worst does not happen in an era of continuing uncertainty, NATO continues to perform its traditional (and often unrecognised) task of providing psychological reassurance to its members. It was this reassurance which was of crucial importance in the dynamic political, economic and social evolution of Western Europe in the uncertain period after 1949. If Europe is to continue this evolution reassurance about security will have to be maintained.

NATO also continues to perform another vital rôle as far as Britain and other West European states are concerned. Together with the European Community it helps to provide an effective framework for maintaining a Western-oriented reunited Germany which is of crucial importance for the future stability of European security. In conjunction with the EC, NATO helps to tie the new Germany into a broader community which is reassuring both to Germany's neighbours and also to Germany itself. Without NATO, given the legacy of the past, Western European states would feel constantly nervous about German diplomacy and security policies. German governments themselves, without American backing, would also feel anxious about the self-denying ordinances of the post-war period and would therefore be more inclined to think about providing less-restricted military (perhaps even nuclear) capabilities for national defence. Given the limitations of both the CSCE and EC in security terms, it is unlikely that these two bodies could provide this mutual reassurance which is so important for the future development of a stable European security system.

It would be wrong to conclude from this brief description of the continuing utility of NATO that the Alliance still performs in the same way the traditional functions laid down by Lord Ismay. He claimed that NATO kept the Americans in, the Russians out and the Germans down.[18] In the post-Cold War era NATO has a much more positive rôle to play. It has to help maintain European–American relations at a time when some of the cohesion engendered by the Cold War has been lost. It has to help in the building of a new security relationship with Russia while maintaining the security interests of its members. And it has to provide a security community which will satisfy the new Germany and avoid anxieties in other West and East European states.

To achieve these objectives obviously requires a significant modification of the Alliance to meet the new challenges of the post-Cold War era. This process of adaptation has already begun. The creation of the North Atlantic Co-operation Council in the early 1990s was designed to link the Eastern European states to NATO and overcome the dangers of a power vacuum being created as Russia pulled its forces out of the region. This is likely to be taken a stage further in the next few years by the expansion of NATO to include Hungary, Poland and the Czech Republic. The increased openness of the alliance by encouraging visits by high-ranking Russian officers and other ex-Warsaw Pact military personnel to NATO headquarters has also helped to reduce suspicion of NATO. The importance of reassurance was clearly a major element in the adoption by the Alliance of a new strategic concept in November 1992. Designed to act as a blueprint in the new era, this acknowledged the fundamental changes which had taken place in Europe since 1989 and indicated the need for a wider, more political definition of security. The risks to security were now seen as arising less from calculated aggression against Allied territory, than from 'the serious economic, social and political difficulties, including ethnic rivalries and territorial disputes which are faced by many countries in central and eastern Europe'.[19] In political terms, it was argued that this meant an enhanced rôle for NATO in managing a wide range of unspecified military and political crises which might occur. In military terms this meant a need to prepare military forces for 'diverse and multidirectional risks', with 'fewer numbers of mobile multinational troops'.[20]

This attempt to transform NATO forces to meet the new risks threatening the stability of Europe, however, remains problematical. Despite the announced changes in military structure there appears to be a continuing uncertainty in the Alliance over whether to prepare for high or low intensity military operations. NATO force structures continue to retain armoured capabilities which would not be out of place in the old Cold War strategic environment. At the same time new force structures are being developed in the form of the Allied Command Europe Rapid Reaction Corps (ARRC) which is designed to provide the flexible military capabilities to meet the new challenges which are emerging. The Alliance, however, remains unclear how best to use its military forces to deal with the kind of low-intensity conflicts which are fast becoming the major problem of European security. In the Yugoslav crisis in the early 1990s NATO played virtually no rôle (initially because of an American unwillingness to become involved in the conflict). Unless NATO can demonstrate its ability to contribute to such crises it is likely to become increasingly irrelevant. What form such a contribution should best take, however, remains problematical. The dilemmas apparent in NATO planning are also reflected in contemporary British defence policy. Despite the fact that Britain provides the leadership of the new ARRC, the government's review of defence policy in the early 1990s, Options for Change, made no significant attempt to restructure British forces to meet the changed strategic environment. There was little attempt in particular to change the balance between infantry, armour, artillery and the air corps. As Colin McInnes has argued elsewhere in this volume:

> If the British Army envisaged fighting a similar war in the future to that it trained for in Germany for 40 years then this balance might be understandable. But it doesn't. Instead it foresees a variety of possible tasks mostly at the low–medium intensity level. In other words the Army's balance of arms reflects the requirement to be able to fight a high-intensity war in some strength, whereas the situations it is most likely to encounter are somewhat different.[21]

The question of whether to prepare for both high intensity as well as low to medium–intensity operations in Europe is a major problem for the British government, especially given the continuing economic pressures on the defence budget.[22] Should the priority continue to be given to maintaining both armoured and infantry forces or should the government accept the need for rôle specialisation which would, for example, leave the continental allies responsible for heavy armoured forces while Britain concentrated on more mobile and flexible rapid reaction forces? For a combination of political and strategic reasons there would appear to be strong motives for Britain to retain capabilities in Germany for both kinds of operation. This would involve maintaining the armoured division and rescinding even further the planned cuts in infantry regiments.[23] Although low–medium capabilities are likely to be of greatest utility, high intensity operations either in Europe or outside (as the Gulf conflict demonstrated) cannot be ruled out. If Britain is to play a key rôle in European security which remains its most important security interest, there is little to be said for rôle specialisation which leaves Germany and France to provide the armoured forces while Britain contributes only light forces for low intensity operations. Such a policy would not be consistent with leadership of the ARRC. If, as a result of economic pressures, this means reducing Britain's strategic nuclear deterrent and de-emphasising the global policing rôle, the price would appear to be worth paying, given the crucial importance to Britain of European security and stability.[24] The problem at present is that there appears to be no overall coherent strategic rationale for British force levels at either the national or Alliance levels.[25] Until this is achieved neither Britain nor NATO will have a clear basis for establishing defence priorities.

Apart from the need for clearer strategic planning, NATO faces another significant challenge during the rest of the 1990s. This involves the task of deciding what balance to strike between the political and military dimensions of policy. Clearly a great deal more can be done to provide reassurance to both the East European states and Russia. The political role of NATO in enhancing European security in the future is likely to be much more significant than in the past. There is, however, a limit to how far this can be taken without undermining the very essence of the Alliance. NATO's main function has been one of collective defence and this remains an important rôle in the post-Cold War era (including peacekeeping and peacemaking operations). Despite the political benefits of widening the membership of NATO to include the Eastern European states, and later pehaps even Russia, such a policy may, at least in the short term, significantly complicate the military transition which is already underway to reorganise NATO forces. Although the future development of NATO to enhance its political rôle must be continued, this should not be at the expense of undermining its military rôle.

Much more important should be the task of developing a new framework of European security involving a division of labour between different institutions, each contributing in its own way to the enhancement of security. The term 'architecture' which is often used to describe the desired co-ordination of various bodies implies an impractical degree of cohesion between interlocking institutions. Nevertheless it will be necessary for more effective links to be established between the CSCE, the EC, the WEU, NATO and the United Nations. Within the over-arching co-ordination of European security arrangements there will clearly be a rôle for the CSCE in providing an institutional framework for all European states (and the United States and Canada) to continue the dialogue about security which reflect the ideas and achievements of the Helsinki Final Accord. The new institutions for conflict prevention and crisis management established in the Paris Charter in November 1991 also have an important rôle to play in helping to deal with the contemporary instability in Europe. At the same time the EC can make a major contribution in dealing with the political, economic, social and even ecological dimensions of security. And, as the Balkan crisis has shown, the United Nations continues to perform useful functions in diplomatic and peacekeeping terms in dealing with intractable internal conflicts. The United Nations will also be crucial in providing the kind of legitimacy so necessary for armed intervention as both the Gulf conflict and the Balkan crisis have demonstrated.

Recent experience has also shown that effective security, peacekeeping and peacemaking arrangements require significant military capabilities which only organisations like the WEU and NATO can provide. The WEU represents an important forum for co-ordinating European defence policies, particularly in dealing with issues which come outside the terms of reference of NATO or which are peculiarly of interest to Western European states. It also seems likely that the task of developing a more effective defence identity, difficult as it is, will become more and more important during the 1990s. Given the nature of its focus and capabilities, however, it is clear that the WEU can only operate effectively if it is closely linked with NATO. Consultation within the context of the EC is of crucial importance but it seems premature at present (given the focus and contemporary difficulties of the EC) to make the WEU exclusively the military arm of the European Community.

In this context of overlapping institutions NATO continues to have an important rôle to play alongside the CSCE, the EC and the WEU. At present only NATO can provide effective military capabilities and thereby help to maintain the psychological confidence which has been so important in contributing to the dynamic development of Western Europe during the past 40 years. In the 1990s European security is likely to be shaped most by the future rôles of the United States, Russia and the new Germany, together with the way that crises are handled. While the other institutions have their part to play, NATO will continue to make a contribution to security in relation to these three states and contemporary instabilities which is unique, and, for the moment, indispensable. For Britain, therefore, NATO is likely to remain a key institution at least in the short and medium term which will allow governments to have a significant say in the major debates on European security which develop during the rest of the 1990s.[26] Despite the hard choices ahead for defence planners, NATO continues to provide a more effective collective defence framework for British security interests in an uncertain and turbulent world than any of the alternative structures so far available.

Notes

1. See for example R. Ullman, *Securing Europe*, (London: Adamantine Press, 1991).
2. See Francis Fukuyama, *The End of History and the Last Man*, (London: Hamish Hamilton, 1991). See also N.J. Wheeler and Ken Booth, 'The Security Dilemma', in John Baylis and N.J. Rengger, ed, *Dilemmas of World Politics: International Issues in a Changing World*, (Oxford: OUP, 1992), K. Booth, 'Redefining East–West Security', *International Affairs*, 6/1, 1990 and M. Chalmers, 'Beyond the Alliance System: The Case for a European Security Organization', *World Policy Journal*, 7/2, 1990.
3. See K. Booth and N.J. Wheeler, 'Contending Philosophies about Security in Europe', C. McInnes, ed, *Security and Strategy in the New Europe*, (London: Routledge, 1992).
4. J.J. Mearsheimer, 'Back to the Future: Instability in Europe after the Cold War', *International Security*, 15/1, 1990.
5. See for example the leading article in *The Sunday Times*, 18 April 1993 entitled 'The Shame and the Slaughter'.
6. K. Booth and N.J. Wheeler, 'Contending Philosophies about Security in Europe', *op. cit.*, p.22.
7. *The Independent*, 2 November 1992.
8. See Misha Glenny, *The Fall of Yugoslavia: The Third Balkan War*, (London: Penguin, 1992).
9. Stephen Van Evera, 'Primed for Peace: Europe after the Cold War', *International Security*, 15/3, 1990/1.
10. A. Hyde–Price, *European Security Beyond the Cold War*, (London: RIIA, 1990), p.214.
11. *Ibid.*, p.219. See also K. Birnbaum and I. Peters, 'The CSCE: a reassessment of its Rôle in the 1980s', in *Review of International Studies*, 16/4, 1990.
12. R.K. Betts, 'Systems for Peace or Causes of War? Collective Security, Arms Control and the New Europe', *International Security*, 17/1, 1992.
13. For the different views about European security see the Chapters by Len Scott, Frederic Bozo and Norbert Ropers in C. McInnes, *Security and Strategy in the New Europe, op. cit.*

14. See Frederic Bozo, 'French Security policy and the new European Order', *ibid.*, pp.205–6.
15. See Hyde–Price, *op. cit.*, pp.141–161.
16. See Len Scott, 'British Perspectives on the Future of European Security', in C. McInnes, *op. cit.*
17. See William Hopkinson, *Changing Options: British defence and global security*, (Cambridge: Cambridge University Global Security Programme, June 1992).
18. Lord Ismay, *NATO: the First Years 1949–54*, (NATO: 1955).
19. See S. Croft, 'NATO and Nuclear Strategy', in C. McInnes *op. cit.*, pp.117–24.
20. See Statement on the Defence Estimates, 1992, Cm 1981 (London: HMSO, July 1992).
21. See Colin McInnes's chapter, pp.211–12.
22. For an analysis of the economic pressures likely to affect British defence policy for the rest of the 1990s, see P. Sabin, 'British defence choices beyond "Options for Change",' *International Affairs*, 69/2 1993. On 4 April 1993 *The Sunday Times* claimed that the government was under pressure to cut defence spending by £4 billion over the following three years.
23. Given the Bosnian experience this would involve a moratorium on all amalgamations and disbandments of UK infantry battalions currently planned, in line with the recommendations of the Defence Committee, in *Britain's Army for the 90s*, HC 306, (London: HMSO, 1993). For reports on government plans to cut nuclear capabilities see *The Sunday Times*, 4 and 11 April 1993.
24. At present Options for Change is designed to maintain a range of balanced forces. Faced with growing financial pressures a policy of incremental 'salami slicing' designed to maintain this balance can only lead to increasing weakness across the board. On balance a policy of establishing priorities is preferable in maintaining the effectiveness of the most important defence capabilities. There is clearly room for cutting the number of warheads on the Trident force and cancelling the new stand-off nuclear missile. There is also probably a case for reducing Britain's amphibious capabilities and reviewing the carrier programme.
25. For a discussion of the vague nature of the new NATO strategic concept see S. Croft, 'NATO and Nuclear Strategy' in C. McInnes, *op. cit.*, pp.117–119.
26. 'Short term' implies the next two or three years and 'medium term', in the context of this Chapter, is taken to mean the remaining years of the century.

2
Britain, Alliances and Intervention

Michael Carver

Hamlet's Question

To intervene or not to intervene: that is the question:
Whether 'tis nobler in the mind to suffer,
The slings and arrows of outrageous fortune,
Or to take arms against a sea of troubles,
And by opposing end them?

Since 1945 British governments and their Chiefs of Staff have seldom had to face that question. They did over Korea and Suez, where the answer was 'Yes', and over Vietnam, where it was 'No'; but, over the wide field in which British forces have been committed ever since the end of the Second World War, intervention either was, or would have been if the question had been posed, automatic or at least semi-automatic. We either had an inescapable commitment, because we exercised sovereignty – or had done so until recently – or we had a treaty obligation. The latter might be either a Commonwealth commitment such as ANZAM (the Australian, New Zealand and American defence agreement), or through one of the anti-Communist alliances, NATO, CENTO or SEATO. There was also an undefined obligation, still lingering on as late as the early 1970s, to come to the aid of any member, or even ex-member, of the Commonwealth.

The dramatic changes in the Soviet Union and its attitude to the rest of the world and, since its break-up, that of its constituent parts, have transformed the situation. There is now no great Communist bogey demanding an unquestioned call to arms, whether to meet a physical attack by one of the Communist powers or Communist subversion in a country with which we had links or interests. Nor is a reversion to pre-1945 strategies any longer relevant. There is no major European nation, or group of nations, threatening to dominate the continent although there are some who see the European Community or Germany, or both together, in that light.

There are hardly any territories outside Europe over which Britain still exercises sovereignty or for the defence of which we are responsible. Once Hong Kong has been returned to China in 1997, the commitment will be even smaller. It is difficult to see how we could ever now escape from the commitment to garrison the Falkland Islands but, as long as it is maintained, it is not likely to lead us into hostilities with Argentina. There is no good reason to retain troops either in Brunei, where the Sultan has enough of his own, or in independent Belize, where a local arrangement to provide its security has been negotiated. It no longer makes sense to talk, as some sailors do, in terms of defending our trade routes or of power projection to secure our economic interests worldwide. The trade routes and economic interests are not ours alone. Their security is equally important to many other nations, and it is only in exceptional cases, such as the threat to Gulf oil supplies, that armed force is an appropriate method of securing them.

On the whole it is in the interests of the developed world to preserve the status quo and therefore to maintain peace; but there are many people, nations in themselves or groups within nations, who are not satisfied and who, for historic, cultural, religious or economic reasons, will seek change. They are not so interested in peace and, if they cannot obtain change in their favour by other means, will probably seek to do so by force. There are many well-meaning people who equate peace with justice; but, for those who seek change, the two are in conflict. Demographic factors exert strong pressures for change; environmental factors produce other pressures. The challenge to world order is how to adapt to and bring about changes without people killing each other. The pressure for 'intervention' by the armed forces of Britain is likely to be in resistance to change, in keeping or enforcing either the status quo or a transformation to a new political arrangement.

Except in Northern Ireland, and possibly the Falklands, such intervention is likely to be in association with other nations: in a United Nations force; in a coalition led by the United States as in the Gulf War; or in a European force, although the chances of the latter successfully engaging in major operations without US participation, which would inevitably involve American overall command, are slight.

Framework for Intervention

It is not sensible to consider the scale on which the British armed forces might be prepared for 'intervention' without discussion of the framework within which it would take place. That has two aspects: first, the general system designed to prevent conflict breaking out, or, if that fails, to limit it, so that the damage to one's interests is limited as far as possible; and, secondly, the structure of armed forces needed to serve that purpose. For many centuries Britain has relied on a balance of power in Europe as the system, and a military structure based on an alliance, in which we were prepared to make a substantial contribution at sea, but hoped to persuade or subsidise others on the continent to provide the land forces; although, in order to persuade them to do so, we had to provide some soldiers of our own, many of whom in the 18th and 19th Centuries were Irish. In the 20th Century it proved impossible to maintain a balance of power within Europe itself, even when we found ourselves committing all our resources of money and manpower to try to do so, as in the two world wars. We were forced to call on the New World to redress the balance of the old.

From 1945 to 1989 we continued to rely on a balance of power system, in which the United States, through the North Atlantic Alliance, balanced the huge military power of the Soviet Union. The military structure was provided by NATO. It is important to distinguish clearly between the Alliance and the military organisation. When the North Atlantic Treaty was signed in 1949, the Americans did not envisage establishing an integrated allied military command structure in Europe, because they did not envisage stationing troops permanently on the continent. The events of 1949 and 1950 in Europe and the Far East converted them to a greater commitment to Europe and, if their troops and nuclear weapons were to be firmly committed, they insisted on controlling the structure. In 1966 France withdrew from NATO but remained within the North Atlantic Alliance. Iceland has always been in that position.

Since Gorbachev's force-cutting initiative in 1989, we have not, in fact, relied on a balance of power system for Western Europe's security, which at present is not threatened by military action from those countries which used to form the Eastern European Communist bloc. Some changes have been made to the military structure of NATO, but they have not been fundamental. There has been some tinkering with the military structure, but no more than that. The main trend has been an attempt to bring together in a rather more integrated form the army and air force contributions of the European members, other than those of the nations on the periphery.

That attempt has run into two sources of dispute, which are interconnected. One is the degree to which it is desirable or necessary for the USA to remain committed to a European security system, and whether or not such a system should be linked to the European Community, or what is now confusingly referred to as European Union. Those who, like the British government, do not wish to see any weakening of the US commitment, fear that any attempt to reorganise NATO in any way that weakens US domination would encourage those influences in America which favour a diminution, if not an abandonment, of that commitment. They do not want the Yanks to go home, because they still fear a resurgence of a threat from Russia, or because, in the absence of the Americans, they fear that Germany, possibly supported however reluctantly by France, would dominate the continent, or because they fear that disagreements between different members of the European Community (or European Union) would inhibit decisive action to defend Europe's interests either within the continent or outside it. The major powers involved are influenced by these fears in different degrees and by others which arise out of them. The USA professes to want to see Europe assume a greater responsibility for its own defence and to be able to limit its own commitment; but it views with suspicion the emergence of a more independent Europe which might be less inclined to defer to American wishes, and particularly one which might gang up with Russia. As long as the North Atlantic Alliance exists, they resist the development of a structure which could take decisions and initiate action in the military field, but from which they would be excluded.

France and Germany see each other in the same light. Each wishes to make certain that the other could not pursue a separate policy, perhaps in collusion with Britain, perhaps with the USA, perhaps (in the case of French fears of Germany) with Russia. Each wishes to bind the other firmly into a tightly-knit community, not only so that neither could act independently, but in order that, before there is any enlargement of the Community, a machinery is established which can, as far as possible, ensure that policies affecting the Community, including those affecting security, can be decisively arrived at and implemented: that defence or security policies are coherent and politically directed. This is of some immediate importance, as the candidates nearest to acceptance are Sweden, Finland and Austria, whose electorates have become devotees of so-called neutrality. The British government is caught on the horns of a dilemma. It is keener than almost anyone else on enlargement and wishes to press ahead with it. It is not keen on deepening the European Community first, or indeed at all, and is resolutely opposed to the Commission or the European Parliament getting involved in defence. It realises that there is no question of the next three candidates joining NATO, and that they would have inhibitions about joining the Community if that involved a firm defence or military commitment. The UK government therefore seized upon the almost defunct Western European Union (WEU), based on the Brussels Treaty which preceded the North Atlantic Alliance. Ironically, France was keen, prior to 1989, to resuscitate and strengthen WEU as an embryo European defence organisation independent of the US, while Britain was lukewarm precisely for that reason. But when it appeared that there was a danger that such a rôle might be given to the European Community and its Commission, the British government changed its tune and began to favour WEU, provided that it did not rival NATO, build up a bureaucracy parallel to those of NATO and the Commission, and was not allotted any forces other than by double-hatting with NATO, which would retain its first priority. But Britain could not prevent the Maastricht Treaty from including a statement that the Community would develop a common foreign and security policy, possibly leading to common defence. At present WEU is supposed to be the organisation which will develop into the instrument through which the Community would implement any decisions by the governments acting together, which required the employment of armed forces without the co-operation of the USA or Canada, either within Europe or beyond it.

That concept has been confused by the formation of the Franco–German Army Corps, which is not associated with either NATO or WEU, but which both countries state could be made available to either. It is a political gesture intended to force the pace of the conversion of WEU into an organisation more closely linked to the Community or as a means of undermining it, if Britain or others prevent it from becoming linked. It is not surprising that candidates for membership of the enlarged Community complain that it is not clear what, if any, their military commitments might be; but, if it were clear, the immediate candidates would probably reject membership. Britain's answer is that membership of WEU would be voluntary. Not all members of the Community, nor all European members of the North Atlantic Alliance, are members. Looking at the future, one must ask: does Europe need its own security system? If so, what form should it take? Would it need a military structure, and, if so, what should that be? Finally, if Europe is to have a security system, what should it be expected to do?

To answer the last question first: its purpose would be to try to prevent conflicts of interest or emotion from erupting into actual fighting, between the nation-states of Europe, within them, or against their territory or vital interests from outside the continent. Military forces, both by deterrence and by their physical presence, can play an important part in the prevention of conflict; in containing or limiting it, if it erupts into fighting; and finally of defeating it or providing the basis of a political solution, whether or not that is a restoration of the *status quo ante*. If the result of action by military forces is to be security, there must be a political aim, and a solution which can be maintained without the continued use of military force. It is fatal to commit military force where there is no political aim that has some chance of solving the problem which caused the fighting. A controversial possible function of such a system could be to impose political solutions, favoured by the majority of Europeans, on the minority who, by their quarrels, were either disturbing the security of others or infringing the human rights of some of the people within their borders, as has happened in the former Yugoslavia: that is, peace-enforcement rather than peacekeeping. That would, in fact, mean the development of a European armed police force to impose, at best, the accepted law of the Community; at worst, the views of the majority on one or more recalcitrant members. One must be very cautious about moving down that road. Events in the former Yugoslavia, and in Somalia, have highlighted the dangers and difficulties involved in any intervention that is not genuine peacekeeping, that is, the monitoring and, if necessary, enforcement of an agreement, however reluctantly arrived at, between the parties in conflict. Any such intervention almost inevitably involves either taking sides in the conflict or gradually assuming responsibility for the maintenance of order; in other words, of government. Not only does that lack a legal basis, but the intervention is liable to become unlimited in extent and time. That is true whether it starts as an attempt to protect humanitarian aid or as an imposition of a ceasefire or political solution. The history of the extension of the British Raj in India at the end of the 18th and the beginning of the 19th Centuries is an historical example.

Having decided what a European security system might be designed to achieve, let us return to the first question posed. Do we need one at all? Is there not already a security system which should operate to support the security of nations within Europe and also their interest in security worldwide – the United Nations? Since 1989, both the Gulf War and the events in the Balkans have reminded us that, now the previous Cold War deadlock in the Security Council has been removed, the UN has an important part to play. Whatever the shortcomings in its procedure and ability to act decisively, it is the one body to which all its members can appeal in the hope that it will, as far as possible, be impartial between the parties to the dispute. It is also the only generally recognised organisation which can confer legitimacy on the use of armed force, even if that sometimes involves stretching the interpretation of its articles fairly far. It was very important for Britain to base its action in the Falklands on a UN Resolution, as it was for all the participants in the Gulf War. However, it would be unwise for Europe to rely solely on the United Nations, and governments would certainly be reluctant to agree to the erection of an entirely new system and structure. The best answer is probably to develop, transform, or if necessary abolish, existing systems, and, if they have them, their military structures.

The Soviet system has been transformed and part of its military structure, the Warsaw Pact, abolished; but the component parts of the Soviet military forces, which were the reality behind the Warsaw Pact, still remain in considerable strength. The North Atlantic Alliance remains unchanged, and its military structure, NATO, marginally transformed, having absorbed the East German forces from the Warsaw Pact. Many people pin their hopes on the Conference on Security and Co-operation in Europe (CSCE). It has the advantage that it includes all European countries, including the ex-states of the Soviet Union west of the Urals, and also the USA and Canada. But this advantage carries with it the disadvantage of a membership of 52 nations, a requirement for unanimity and the lack of any executive machinery. It has done, and continues to do, valuable work in establishing confidence-building measures and standards of behaviour in the field of such things as human rights. It is developing further measures which should result in the reduction of the potential for military conflict between its members and in encouraging neighbouring states to conclude bilateral treaties in support of that. But just because of the importance it attaches to unanimity, it is desperately slow to act. It might be suggested that the CSCE should therefore be given a Security Council and a bureaucracy like that of the UN. Few would think that desirable, and there is clearly no question of providing it with a political assembly or a military structure.

The next question concerns whether the North Atlantic Alliance and NATO should be extended to cover either the whole of Europe west of the former Soviet Union, or even further, up to the Urals. Although some of the ex-Warsaw Pact countries west of the Commonwealth of Independent States (CIS) would welcome its extension to cover them, this is not favoured by any of the governments of the Alliance; and for good reasons. It would undermine the solidarity of the Alliance: few of its members would be prepared to extend its commiment that an attack on the territory of any of its members would be regarded as an attack on all; and it could be regarded by Russia, Ukraine and Belarus as a hostile alliance. To extend it all the way to the Urals would render it meaningless. Its cosmetic extension through the North Atlantic Co-operation Council, which has resulted in admitting representatives of former Warsaw Pact countries to what are no more than informal conversations, has helped to make the latter feel that they are no longer regarded as enemies, but cannot be regarded as providing more security than that. Nevertheless it is important that at least the North Atlantic Alliance, if not NATO, must remain in existence and a reality, until Europe can feel confident that the potential threat, posed by the very large nuclear and conventional arsenal which remains within the borders of the former Soviet Union, has been reduced to an extent that no longer requires the reassurance of US support, even if such reductions are limited only to the nuclear weapon field.

Next there is the European Community, with which the WEU is loosely associated. The Community itself is a form of security system. War between its members is almost inconceivable, and the more tightly linked the Community, the more difficult it would in practice become. The original aim of its founders was just that; and it provides other forms of security apart from the prevention of conflict between states. It has not prevented, or tried to prevent, internal conflict within member states. But there are obvious difficulties in extending it to all of Europe between the Atlantic and the Urals, or even from the Atlantic to the border of the CIS, although that could come in time.

The division of responsibility between the proposed European Union and the existing WEU is clearly nonsensical in the long term, if not also in the short term. Military structures should conform to political structures, for military action must be in pursuit of a political aim and be subject to political direction. In the North Atlantic Alliance, it was acceptable that this was not the case, although the North Atlantic Council was supposed to provide it. In reality political authority rested with the president of the United States. No military action could be taken without it. This was acceptable to other members, except de Gaulle's France, in the face of the overwhelming nature of the Soviet threat.

If neither the North Atlantic Alliance, nor the CSCE, nor the European Union, or its satellite the WEU, can provide a European security system, should Europe after all rely on the United Nations alone or establish an entirely new system? That stark choice is not necessary; we can make use of all these institutions. As long as the nuclear and conventional forces of the CIS, and particularly the former, pose a significant potential threat to their western neighbours, the American commitment to support European security must remain, and the North Atlantic Alliance should continue.

However, the NATO military structure, and especially its command system, should be progressively transformed until it is no longer dominated by the United States except in the nuclear field. It should not be concerned with security within Europe itself, west of the ex-Soviet borders; but it should concern itself, as it does not officially do now, with co-operation between the USA and Europe in securing their common interests outside Europe. There should be no inflexible commitment on either side, either in regarding an attack on one as an attack on all, or over co-operation in protecting common interests outside Europe.

As regards security within Europe, the future European Union, (or whatever the Community is called) should accept full responsibility for security within its membership. Within Europe, outside its membership, the system would depend on the CSCE acting as an agent of the UN. The CSCE would be the instrument for developing all possible methods of preventing conflict between the Atlantic and the Urals, and for the pursuit of all measures short of the use of armed force. If either the CSCE itself, or any of its members, wanted armed forces to be employed in whatever capacity, the CSCE or that member would appeal to the UN Security Council to pass a resolution calling on its members to take action and to provide the necessary military structure, including the command structure, to implement it. That might well be provided by the European Union with or without the addition of other nations. There are often reasons for including those who come from outside the area as likely to be more impartial.

So, finally, what sort of military structure should the European Union have? Although there is quite a strong argument for all its members accepting the same commitments in every field, one must realise that, at any rate for some time to come, different members, for a variety of reasons, may be unwilling to commit themselves in advance to provide military forces or to integrate them with other forces to an extent that would make it difficult or impossible to employ them independently or withdraw them. But there will be others, including probably the founder members of the Community, who for political, economic and military reasons will wish to integrate some or all of their forces to a greater degree than now, and to establish a command structure capable of exercising command and logistical support of all or some of those forces, and of those of any other members of the Union who decide to contribute forces to a particular operation. Such an operation might be NATO-commanded, in the case of a threat from one of the former Soviet states; an operation outside Europe in defence of European interests, probably under US command and under UN auspices; an operation within Europe, but outside the Union, either under UN auspices or at the request of CSCE; or possibly, an operation within the Union itself (most likely limited to peacekeeping or humanitarian purposes).

What sort of forces this would require is difficult to foresee at present. So much depends on what happens within the former Soviet Union and what success the CSCE has in changing the pattern of the armed forces which European nations feel they have to preserve. That, in turn, depends to a degree on what happens in the Middle East and North Africa. One of the most difficult areas is that of nuclear weapons. The last thing one wants is to encourage the European Union to develop its own nuclear force. The principal priority at present is to discourage proliferation and to develop and manage a reduction in the vast stockpiles held by the CIS and the USA. Europe should rely on the Americans to provide the continent with security against the threat of nuclear attack from *any* direction. It is not realistic to think of Europe, or of any nation within it, engaging in hostilities against a nuclear-armed nation without US support. The idea would be to move back to a version of the original Baruch plan by which the USA would hold nuclear weapons under trust for the UN as a deterrent to any other nation developing or using them. That would be difficult for Russia or China to swallow, but would in fact provide far greater security for all, including Britain: greater security than attempting to abolish nuclear weapons altogether.

Within the sort of framework outlined above, the problem for the British government is to decide how large a part it wishes to play: to find the optimum balance between the influence it will wish to exert and the cost. That has always been the case, and governments have always wished to exert the maximum influence at the least cost. Nuclear weapons were supposed to provide that, but have signally failed to do so, although there are some who still suffer from the delusion that they do. It is even less possible than it used to be to calculate the strength of armed forces required by relating it to the strength of a potential enemy or enemies, as the battleship strength of the Royal Navy used to be calculated. There is no separate threat against Britain, and we could not defend our islands, or most of our interests outside them, by ourselves. Since 1945 the strength of our armed forces has not been based on any such strategic calculation. The forces have been reduced, step by step, as their unit cost has risen and as ex-imperial commitments outside Europe have been shed, until their basic core rested on the contribution which was assessed as needed to persuade the USA that we were setting a good example in Europe and elsewhere in the world in sharing the burden of opposing Communism. Force levels were also affected by the desire to see that our influence in the North Atlantic Alliance was not eclipsed by that of the Federal Republic of Germany. By this means, Britain has succeeded in ensuring that its general security, and that of its interests worldwide, have been assured by the support of the USA, the Suez affair having been an unfortunate aberration. There are those, particularly in the Treasury, who think that the price we paid for that has been too high, and that our real interest lay in accepting a more reduced world status and concentrating our efforts on modernising our economy. They believe that the great change in our security situation, brought about by the reduction in – even the removal of – the threats against which we had been arming, provides a golden opportunity for us at last to get our priorities right.

It would be imprudent to go too far down that road until we can see more clearly how matters are going to develop within what was the Soviet Union. The government has made a first step in its Options for Change reductions. Those should be completed before further steps are undertaken. Within the sort of framework outlined above, there are major decisions to make. The first is the degree to which it will be necessary for Western Europe, whether within the North Atlantic Alliance or not, to maintain a capability to fight a major modern war in Europe, with all the forces, equipment and infrastructure that requires. The second is the degree to which Britain integrates its contribution for that purpose with other European nations, and with which and in what framework. The third is the extent to which that contribution can be regarded as available for operations outside Europe, as part of a European force or as a contribution to a United Nations or some other coalition; and, in the light of that, the need to maintain national forces in addition to the contribution to a European force. As far as the Army is concerned, the last will largely depend on how long the commitment to provide a garrison of the present size in Northern Ireland continues. It is not easy to decide whether contributions to UN or similar forces would be better made on an integrated European basis or nationally. There are arguments on both sides. Much will depend on how both the North Atlantic Alliance (and NATO if it continues) and the European Community (and its defence aspect) develop.

When the situation becomes clearer, and in any case before the end of the century, the British government must address these issues and seek a solution, based on devoting a proportion of Gross National Product to defence, which the country should be capable of maintaining without constant revision. It should then devise the best value for money it can get to provide the nation with the greatest possible influence and freedom of action in pursuing policies to further the nation's real interests and not its sentimental nostalgia. The nightmare of the Chiefs of Staff, intensified by the development of television and modern information technology, is that the government will give way to pressure to 'do something', only to be faced by angry demands that 'somebody must be blamed' if there are any casualties or if inflated hopes of success are not fulfilled. The Chiefs will always wish to be assured that, if they are to commit their forces, there must be as clear an aim as possible; that it must be achievable; and that, once achieved, it will not involve a permanent commitment from which there is no escape. They will also want to be assured that they will be allowed to use all the resources needed to perform their task as quickly as possible. They know that it is far preferable to be accused of using a sledgehammer to crack a nut, making certain that the nut is cracked effectively, than, for fear of such an accusation or from financial or other considerations, to trickle forces in step by step, until far more are committed in the end and success slips away into the bog. The contrast between the Gulf War and Vietnam is the best example of that, and nothing is more absurd than the attitude of a newscaster, interrogating Malcolm Rifkind, the Defence Secretary, as to why he was reluctant to employ combat aircraft to impose a no-fly zone in Bosnia when he was prepared to do so in Iraq, and apparently regarding it as immoral to engage in military action only when he thought it would succeed. Members of the armed forces at lower levels than their Chiefs may be keener on 'intervention', as giving them the rare opportunity to practise their profession in reality instead of eternally in make-believe.

Britain must abandon the imperial nostalgia which induces people to assume that wherever trouble breaks out anywhere in the world we have a moral duty to intervene. We must look to our real interests. That means that we must be able to choose where and when to intervene and on what scale. It will always be a political judgement; but there is one area where we have no choice, and that is the security of Europe, and certainly Western Europe.

What all this will mean in terms of force levels in all three Services, or how they should be organised, is not easy to predict. If events in the former Soviet Union, and in Europe generally, develop in such a way that there is no real threat from the East against the West, changes going well beyond those implemented in Options for Change are inevitable. In the interim, all three Services, and partcularly the army, should see that they are more easily adaptable to change than they are at present. That includes the ability to change up as well as down, and demands a fresh look at their reserve organisation.

3
Intervention – When, How and Why?

Stuart Croft

With the end of the Cold War, British military forces have an uncertain role. The United Kingdom faces no direct conventional threat to its territory. However, it is a member of the most powerful alliance in the world (NATO) and possesses – despite 'Options for Change' and other reductions – if not one of the largest, certainly one of the most efficient and sophisticated armed forces in the world built up in the context of the fear of the Soviet Union and Warsaw Pact. This Chapter concerns itself with asking if there is a rôle that can be found for this British relic of the Cold War, its powerful and efficient military forces. If a rôle could be found, might it be of such significance that it would justify further investment in the military in order to maintain and conceivably expand its capabilities in various ways? In short, might there again be a world rôle for Britain, or at least an expanded regional rôle, now that it is free of its Cold War responsibilities?

In the immediate aftermath of the collapse in Cold War structures with the revolutions in Eastern Europe during 1989 and the unification of Germany in 1990, the British government seemed unwilling to undertake a serious strategic review. 'Options for Change', it was felt by many, was an inadequate response to the fundamentally transformed international environment.[1] Within three years, however, the British government was being criticised for having cut its defence expenditure too far and for providing an inadequately structured military force.[2] How symbolic are these changes in attitude of a feeling that Britain ought to create a new rôle for itself in the world with its military forces? And how might that rôle appear?

This Chapter will look at the new possibilities for Britain in two respects. First, it will ask if there are incentives for Britain to work with other countries to create the framework for a global collective security system under the United Nations. Second, it will examine under what circumstances, if any, British armed forces could be committed in the interests of humanitarian intervention.

British Security Policy: A New World Rôle?

Collective security lay dormant in British political practice since at least the Italian invasion of Ethiopia in 1935 until arguably the Gulf War against Iraq in 1991. Between these wars British policy was dominated by collective defence rather than collective security, and in the post-Second World War period the limited collective security guarantee provided by the United Nations was supplanted rather than supplemented by specific security guarantees provided by NATO. Following the Gulf War and the end of the Cold War, collective security might again become a linchpin of British security policy, globally through the United Nations, and regionally through the Conference on Security and Co-operation in Europe (CSCE). Yet British governments under both Margaret Thatcher and John Major have been profoundly unconvinced about the merits of collective security.

The first clear use of British military force outside the United Kingdom in the post-Cold War era was in support of collective security. Under Security Council Resolution 678, the United Nations authorised collective military action against Iraq for its invasion of Kuwait on 2 August 1990. Iraq had provided a relatively clear-cut case of aggression, allowing the United Nations to accept the necessity for the use of force to restore international boundaries for the first time since the Korean War some 41 years earlier. Resolution 678, adopted on 29 November 1990, set a deadline of 15 January 1991 for the withdrawal of Iraq from Kuwait; within a matter of weeks, Iraq had been driven from Kuwait by a military combination with British forces alongside those from the United States, Saudi Arabia, Syria, France, Kuwait and Italy.

Despite the success of the military action against Iraq, British policy-makers have not been enthused with the concept of collective security. After all, was it not really the case that the defeat of Iraq had less to do with collective security, and more to do with a collection of national interests: access to oil; the bolstering of domestic, regional and global prestige; and national and personal antagonism towards Iraq generally and President Saddam Hussein personally? If the invasion of Kuwait had taken place elsewhere in the world, with a lesser combination of national interests, would the reaction not have been similar to the relative indifference displayed towards Indonesia's invasion of East Timor in 1975? Collective security implies that national security is indivisible wherever it might be threatened; but for British policy-makers, the world is too uncertain a place for reliance on collective security. As Defence Secretary Malcolm Rifkind stated: 'I am struck by the contrast between the success of this period [since the foundation of NATO] and the defence and security failures of the inter-war years'.[3]

This cautious attitude placed British policy-makers onto the defensive for a period after 1989, for collective security was the focus of a good deal of political interest. During 1990 and 1991, as Communism collapsed in Europe and new leaderships came to power in the states of central and eastern Europe, many – such as Presidents Havel of Czechoslovakia, Gorbachev of the Soviet Union and Mitterrand of France – called for the replacement of collective defence through NATO and the Warsaw Pact with collective security in Europe through the development of the Conference on Security and Co-operation in Europe (CSCE), and they were supported by governments in Poland, Hungary, the Baltic states, Scandinavia and elsewhere. However, to many in Britain the creation of a collective security function for the CSCE, or overly emphasising the collective security function of the United Nations, looked very much like a rebirth of the League of Nations, an institution long discredited in British diplomatic circles for its association with appeasement. As Correlli Barnett has put it:

> Just as in the 1920s and 1930s, we are allowing ourselves to be swayed by a large and vociferous liberal lobby of romantic idealists who believe Britain should turn out diplomatically and militarily in a blue beret to prevent or sort out quarrels anywhere in the world.[4]

British supporters of collective security argued that the end of the Cold War had done much to re-establish the concept as one worthy of consideration.[5] The military power of the NATO countries is such that it could be put to the use of the United Nations in the interests of world peace. British forces would, in a sense, be a party to a global policing rôle. Such ideas have been met with little sympathy in official circles. One problem would certainly be the cost of such a rôle. A further problem would be the political difficulty of having British forces at the call of a United Nations Security Council that at any time might include China, Cuba and Yemen (after all, Resolution 678 was not supported by these countries). Perhaps an even more irreconcilable problem lies with the nature of many global conflicts. Very few have been of the Iraq–Kuwait type in the post-Cold War world. Many others have been concerned with civil unrest, be it in Somalia, Ethiopia, Sudan, Cambodia, Mozambique, Georgia or Moldova.

In any case, official debate in the period immediately after the end of the Cold War has been concerned less with a global collective security rôle through the CSCE, and much more with the need to maintain an emphasis on NATO as opposed to developing a primacy for a common foreign and security policy for the countries of the European Union based on the Western European Union (WEU). However, a counter-argument might suggest that the focus on institution-building or institution-maintenance has been misplaced. What may be needed in meeting the security challenges of the post-Cold War world may not be the rigidity of institutions, but rather more the freedom of ad hoc arrangements. This was, after all, one of the great lessons of the war against Iraq; and one of the problems with discussions over intervention in the former Yugoslavia during 1991 and 1992 was that of finding an institution in which the most concerned nations – the former Yugoslav states plus neighbours such as Romania, Greece, Albania, Italy, Hungary and Austria along with other involved countries such as Turkey and Germany – were all members or were sufficiently significant members to raise possibilities for solutions.

Collective security has been largely rejected in British policy-making and it seems difficult either to find a sufficiently influential constituency in Britain, or adequately powerful external factors, to see collective security providing a post-Cold War rôle for the military forces of the United Kingdom. Essentially, the concept of collective security does not seem to be in tune with the security threats and challenges of the post-Cold War period, with the important exception of the Gulf. However, the same may not be the case for humanitarian intervention.

Demands for Humanitarian Intervention

British military forces have long had a humanitarian rôle. During the 1990s the aid and assistance provided to Western Samoa in the aftermath of major destruction by two cyclones was a clear case. Other examples included delivering supplies to Turkey after an earthquake and to Bangladesh after flooding.[6] However, the concept of humanitarian intervention is rather different. Instead of providing simply logistic support for the civilian population, humanitarian intervention requires the provision of the instruments of force to prevent or lessen human suffering.

This does not necessarily provide a sufficiently tight definition, for it is rare to find a case where humanitarian aid could be provided without some political gain to the provider. Indeed it is likely that without some combination of this sort there would be a lack of domestic legitimacy for any intervention, with claims either that the action was immoral or that the costs too heavily outweighed the possible gains to the nation. This should not be allowed to confuse the issue, however. In the provision of military force for philanthropic ends, national interests and humanitarian concerns can never be totally divided.[7] Were the United Kingdom to become involved in peacekeeping or peacemaking in Eastern Europe, it might primarily be in order to save life; however, in attempting to prevent the growth of disorder, such action might well be in the interests of the United Kingdom, because of fears that disorder in the East might adversely affect business confidence in, and possibly even the stability of, the societies of the European Community countries, should large-scale uncontrolled migration occur. In another example, humanitarian intervention in Somalia in 1992–93 might have far less impact on the interests of the United States, but could act to increase American influence in the region.[8] As the Foreign Secretary, Douglas Hurd, has said:

> Some problems – state-sponsored terrorism, for example, or the proliferation of ballistic missiles – may prick our skin more than our consciences. But, if we really want a world that is more secure, more prosperous and more stable, then humanitarian problems can be just as threatening and must be seen not only as a moral issue, but as a potential security threat as well. We help people because they are hungry and because if they are not fed well they will die. But it is also true that countries racked by famine or civil war will be unsafe neighbours in the world village.[9]

Nevertheless, even if humanitarian and national motivations are not obviously separable, it is clear that some missions carry more risk than others, and that some offer less tangible rewards to the intervening state. It is possible to consider a spectrum of motivations for intervention along these lines, ranging from action clearly in the interests of the state (with humanitarian benefits in terms of preserving life being undoubtedly of secondary importance), to interventions in which the preservation of life is the key motivation and in which benefits to the intervening state are intangible.

But why should states become involved in humanitarian intervention? The opposition to a deeper consideration of a rôle in wider humanitarian intervention for Britain is strong. Two lines of argument predominate. The first suggests that British military forces should only be used when British interests are directly affected. Simon Jenkins has suggested that calls for humanitarian intervention are part of a cynical exercise which should be condemned.

> Whatever grief is accessible to a television camera, in Beirut or Kurdistan or Sarajevo, it must be accessible to British troops. Britain refuses to help the two million Yugoslav refugees. It must therefore do something

promotable. Soldiers in action are politically glamorous. Immigrants are politically grim.[10]

The second argument focuses upon long-term costs. For Sir Edward Heath, were British troops to be sent back to Kuwait by the government, 'you won't get them out. We shall find ourselves landed with yet another commitment abroad where there are no direct British interests'.[11] These arguments are politically pervasive and persuasive. Each time British forces in Bosnia came under attack during the winter of 1992 the level of concern with the acceptability of the operation rose.[12]

However, for others, those who might be identified as holding a 'cosmopolitanist' view of international relations, rights of individuals should not be affected by national allegiance. For such people, the key issue for security analysis is not the security of the state, but the security of individuals.[13] Indeed in many cases, such thinkers would argue, it is the state that causes insecurity for individuals in many parts of the world. As Steve Smith has put it:

> Precisely because security exists alongside other forms of power, influence and domination, privileging security at the level of the state may allow these other injustices to continue. The central problem here is that mature anarchy may make states more secure, but lead to increased subjugation for distinct groups of persons. Put at its simplest, should not security be based on individuals rather than on states?[14]

Such thinking draws explicitly on Kantian philosophy, and suggests that all individuals lose when the rights of other individuals are infringed. On such a view, the reasons why Britain should consider the application of its military forces in limited circumstances to protect human life in situations where British national interests are not, under any definition, challenged are straightforward. Would it not be a moral act to use British military forces to prevent the loss of life in circumstances in which the cost to the United Kingdom (certainly in terms of loss of life) would be small? And in the face of appalling violations of human rights, how can Britain not act?[15] To put this into concrete terms, a failure to act according to 'cosmopolitanist' principles has led to the accusation that 'the British government's response to the suffering in Bosnia has been ... unworthy of a civilised nation in the late 20th Century ... [Britain's] political masters ... have proved callous and indifferent to the plight of the Bosnians ...'[16]

Such views may seem naive to some. However, these humanitarian issues have been placed on the international political agenda. In a period in which television coverage brings the full horror of modern warfare into the homes of the majority of people in the West, inevitably political constituencies pressing for military action are created. Newspapers, opposition groups in parliament, pressure groups and others insist that the government should be aware of a particular humanitarian tragedy, and call for action to save lives. However, perhaps more significant than the technology of the news media may be the existence of constituencies in countries like the United Kingdom and the United States which are deeply concerned about moral issues. After all, over one hundred years before the disintegration of Yugoslavia, Gladstone was able to mobilise massive public opposition to British government inaction in the face of Turkish brutality against an uprising in Bulgaria which, in part, had originated in Bosnia and Herzegovina.

Thus the existence of the humanitarian issue on the international agenda is clear. For Britain, there is relatively little scope for avoiding discussion over involvement in intervention. In part this is because Britain has no self-imposed or external constraints on military action of the type that affect German and Japanese decision-making in this area. In part, too, it is because there are very few countries with the capabilities for intervention, due to the size and structure of their armed forces: Britain, along with France, is one of the few states with the ability for action. In addition, it is difficult to avoid discussion over involvement in intervention due partly to the nature of the domestic political debate, in which moral values have played a part in the discussion of international issues dating back at least to Gladstone and Cobden. Further, with a 'privileged position in the international community' – a significant member of both the United Nations and the European Community, in NATO with 'more commands than either Germany, France or Italy', and as a member of the G7 – British decision-makers inevitably have to respond to the international agenda, including calls for humanitarian intervention.[17] However, this may be to place the issue in too negative a context. It may even be that there are direct benefits to the United Kingdom from involvement in humanitarian intervention in terms of international prestige and influence; one example could be the British rôle in the drafting and passing of Security Council Resolution 688 and the subsequent implementation of Operation Haven to create safe havens for the Kurds suffering from Iraqi persecution. Perhaps greater British activity in this area in the United Nations would generate broader support for British retention of a permanent seat on the Security Council, against the strong claims of other states both in the developed and developing world.

How, then, might criteria be created that would assist in decision-making over the desirability of humanitarian intervention? Clearly the nature of the motivation to become involved in an intervention will be affected by the character of that action. Some acts of military intervention will be easier to achieve than others. Intervention would be eased by the active participation of willing allies, particularly militarily-effective allies (and those able to offer complementary skills), and allies able to provide logistic support. Such a mission would need domestic and international legitimacy. Both the Tanzanian overthrow of Idi Amin and the Vietnamese intervention in Cambodia to oust Pol Pot and the Khmer Rouge in 1979 were, at least in part, acts of humanitarian intervention. However, they were not legitimised in the eyes of the international community and, particularly in the case of Vietnam, the actions were widely condemned.

In addition to the above, it is important to delineate different types of missions. Perhaps the least risky would be the forceable imposition of a blockade. More challenging would be the creation of a no-fly zone to prevent aerial attacks against unarmed or lightly-armed opponents of the regime, such as that imposed over Iraq from 1991. However, it is difficult to limit a commitment to this level. As Lawrence Freedman has noted in connection with the no-fly zones over Iraq and Bosnia:

> In both cases no-fly zones have been declared. In both cases the main struggle for power continues on the ground – where no-artillery zones and no-ethnic-cleansing zones have had almost no success at all.[18]

Of greater risk would be the deployment of ground troops. However, there is also a spectrum of risk in the provision of ground forces according to their function. The least risky option would be the provision of forces purely for moving food, medicines and other life-saving equipment, such as that in Bosnia during 1992–93. More risky would be a 'friendly occupation' whereby the local leaderships accepted the rôle of the intervening forces, as was broadly the case in Somalia in 1992. Finally, and most dangerous of all, would be a 'hostile occupation' where the indigenous forces opposed the actions of the intervening forces with all methods, such as in the war over Kuwait.

Finally, the ease or difficulty of a mission to bring humanitarian relief would be complicated by the nature of the indigenous political and military situation. Would the political leaderships accept intervention or not? What would be the military capabilities of the indigenous military forces? Would they have the technical capability (relatively high technology weapons with good training and logistics) to be able to inflict heavy casualties on the intervening forces? Would the terrain aid or hinder the actions of the intervening forces?

It is thus possible to draw up a checklist of the ideal circumstances for the United Kingdom to become involved in an intervention designed largely to alleviate human suffering. First, it would be in the context of an international effort, a coalition of nations including the United States, major West European allies and local states, and legitimised by the United Nations or an acceptable regional organisation. Second, the action itself would be very limited — perhaps focusing on blockading or imposing no-fly zones, and at most the provision of a few ground troops. Third, it would be in a context in which the indigenous political actors accepted the legitimacy of the intervention. Finally, the indigenous military forces would be lightly armed, and the terrain would assist the intervening forces and hinder any local resistance.

Needless to say, such a combination of circumstances would be very rare. In a confused world, more difficult and ambiguous circumstances naturally present themselves. However, these criteria provide a baseline against which other actions and operations might be judged. Combining the two main factors discussed, a small matrix can be generated, as follows:

TABLE 1   TYPES OF INTERVENTION

		MOTIVATION	
		National Interests	Humanitarian concerns
OPERATIONAL	Greater difficulty	1	2
EASE	Lesser difficulty	3	4

One difficulty in the representation of concepts by matrices is that there may be an assumption of a mathematical relationship between the variables. Needless to say, this cannot be the case with the above. The Boxes under motivation (national interests and humanitarian concerns) and under operational ease (greater difficulty and lesser difficulty) can only represent emphasis rather than absolute values. Therefore, issues in Box 1 and Box 4 will be related along a spectrum, rather than being absolutely distinct. However, this Table does assist in understanding the nature of decisions over the use of military forces. For example, in the post-Cold War period, British military forces had up to the end of 1992 been involved in four military conflicts: the war in Iraq over the future of Kuwait in 1991; the subsequent protection of the Kurds in Iraq; the supply of food and other materials in Bosnia; and the continuing conflict in

Northern Ireland. Each of these conflicts can be placed into the above matrix.

TABLE 2   BRITISH INTERVENTIONS, 1989–92

		MOTIVATION	
		National Interests	Humanitarian concerns
OPERATIONAL	Greater difficulty	Northern Ireland	Bosnia, 1992–93
EASE	Lesser difficulty	War against Iraq, 1991	Operation in Kurdistan

The value of this approach is that it clarifies the ease with which governments may be able to decide to use military force to intervene in local disputes. Box 1 (in Table 2 represented by Northern Ireland) illustrates an issue over which it will be difficult to obtain a satisfactory resolution through the imposition of a military intervention. However, it is also an issue over which the government will feel that it has relatively little choice as the problem impinges on what the government itself will define as the national interest. The decision to use military force will thus be relatively clear-cut. Both Boxes 3 (in Table 2 represented by the 1991 war in Iraq) and 4 (in Table 2 represented by the operation in Kurdistan) illustrate a situation in which there would be debate about the use of force although they are areas in which the costs of intervention ought to be relatively low given the lesser difficulty of the operation; (this, of course, does not imply that these missions were easy in themselves). Decisions in these areas are related to fine calculations of opportunity costs of action and inaction. The great problem comes with Box 2, represented above by Bosnia. These are difficult operational issues in which the primary interest is humanitarian. Intervention in such circumstances is likely to be highly contested within government.

Tables 1 and 2 give an indication of the range of possibilities, but given that many of the issues lie on a spectrum, by extending the matrix it is possible to include other conflicts and external interventions from the end of the Cold War period into the post-Cold War world. For example, one can include the wars in Afghanistan (from 1979), the Falklands (1982) and the Gulf War (1991); the American incursions into Lebanon (1982), Grenada (1983), Panama (1989) and Somalia (1992); Russian/Commonwealth of Independent

States' interventions in Moldova and Georgia (1992); the multinational escorting of United Nations convoys in Bosnia (1992); and the continuing conflict in Ulster.

TABLE 3   GLOBAL MILITARY INTERVENTIONS, 1979–92

National Interest – Humanitarianism

Greater Difficulty	1 Afghanistan Falklands	2	3	4
Moderate Difficulty	5 Northern Ireland	6 Kuwait Moldova	7 Lebanon Bosnia Georgia	8 Kurds
Lesser Difficulty	9	10 Grenada	11 Panama	12 Somalia

Clearly it is possible to disagree with some of the above characterisations. However, they are designed to be illustrative rather than authoritative.

Certain issues become clear with such a categorisation. Decisions to intervene over issues in Boxes 1 and 5 are relatively clear for governments, as they define direct national interests to be at stake. Similarly, it is difficult for governments to avoid involvement in issues illustrated by Boxes 2 and 6, although calculations of the opportunity cost will prove to be of greater significance. Interventions over issues in Boxes 9, 10, 11 and 12 are likely as the probability of success is very high and the costs low. Debate over humanitarian intervention therefore lies essentially in Boxes 3, 4, 7 and 8. These are the issues over which the direct gain to the nation appears least, and yet the risks seem high. An inability to point to tangible gains from intervention in these conflicts gives strong disincentives for governments to act. One can create hypothetical examples for Boxes 3 and 4: intervention to protect Palestinians protesting against Israeli policy in the West Bank and Gaza; full-scale military intervention to prevent fighting in the former Yugoslavia; the deployment of military force to prevent violence between Hindus and Moslems in a disintegrating India; the forcible disarming of the Khmer Rouge in Cambodia. All of these cases point to the practical limits to humanitarian intervention. These practical limitations are reinforced by international norms. Intervention was criticised by many states during the Cold War as a tool designed to limit the sovereignty of states. In all the examples placed in Boxes 7 and 8 in Table 3, there were grave concerns over the implications for the sovereignty of the states receiving the military forces. 'Cosmopolitanists' have long argued that the nature of international society was to place more emphasis on the security of states than upon the security of people. However, despite the collapse of Communism, the problems of conceiving of international intervention particularly in Boxes 3 and 4 illustrate the continued difficulties in changing that balance.

From the above analysis it appears that there are three categories of conflict into which British forces might be sent. The first, issues where the government declares essential national interests to be at stake (Falklands, Northern Ireland) is self-evident and, as a central part of defence policy, will not be considered further. The second would relate to the identification of issues such as those in Boxes 11 and 12 in which the United Kingdom might become involved. Given Britain's limited world rôle, these are likely to be in close association with allies. The third relates to issues illustrated by Boxes 7 and 8. For practical reasons as well as for legitimacy, such operations are even more likely to be collaborative. Common to both would be the identification of circumstances in which the British government decided to send forces to safeguard human life. However, for these options to be realisable, there are several requirements.

Central to the ability to provide forces for humanitarian intervention is the ability to deploy flexible forces. This has several implications for the United Kingdom. The first is that all three Services – Army, Air Force and Navy – need continued investment in logistics and in materials. If Britain is to be able to provide a capability for humanitarian intervention, no Service can receive priority over another, and reductions in the size of the Services need to be made in the knowledge that this will limit the ability of the United Kingdom to undertake certain types of mission. If flexibility is the key, stocks of one of the most valuable pieces of equipment for such operations, helicopters, may need augmenting. In addition, and given existing commitments, it has been suggested that the size of the British Army may need to be reconsidered if Britain is to maintain an ability to deploy ground troops as part of a humanitarian operation.[19] However, this may be overemphasised. One of the problems for the British Army in the early 1990s has been implementing cuts mandated by Options for Change which necessarily leave all units weakened while reductions and amalgamations are implemented. After 1995 these problems will be much reduced. In addition, after 1997 up to nine extra infantry battalions may become available by the withdrawals from Hong

Kong and Berlin, the possible ending of commitments to Belize and Brunei and, conceivably, reductions in the levels of forces in Cyprus.[20] Before altering the size of the British Army again, it is therefore important to be clear about the nature of the tasks the armed forces will be expected to perform from the late 1990s. In the light of reduced global commitments in the immediate future, an increase in the number of personnel in the armed forces from augmented Options for Change levels may not be appropriate, unless the United Kingdom were to reverse this trend and take on more long-term commitments.

Regardless of any changes to the structure and size of the armed forces, however, inevitably the most difficult circumstances would be when, in terms of Table 3, commitments in Boxes 5 and 7 had already been entered into, and pressure for another intervention grew. In January 1993, Defence Secretary Rifkind noted that British 'assets ... available for peacekeeping are limited', in response to opportunities for Britain to become involved in either the action in Somalia, or in the face of pressure to again deploy ground forces in Kuwait.[21] Emphasising this point, Foreign Secretary Hurd commented:

> Obviously, we cannot be everywhere and we cannot do everything. Our diplomacy is now undermanned compared to that of our main colleagues and competitors. Our armed forces are already overstretched ... We must make it clear that ... it is impossible to guarantee order and good government everywhere.[22]

Such points are important. However, they are perhaps overly negative. The size of a nation's armed forces is always limited, and the tasks that it may perform necessarily constrained; this is particularly so for a medium-sized country with a relatively weak economy, such as the United Kingdom. Given that British forces cannot 'be everywhere', it is the task of the government to decide priorities. In order to achieve that task, it is useful to have clear criteria.

It may be argued that Britain will not enter into an intervention as outlined above without allies; indeed, this was one of the criteria spelt out earlier in this Chapter. This further implies that there may be scope for burden-sharing with allies in which rôle specialisation may occur. Perhaps if NATO develops into a co-ordinating body for peacekeeping and humanitarian intervention this may be possible. However, it was suggested earlier that it may well be that ad hoc arrangements will be the order of proceedings, given that humanitarian missions will be viewed in different ways by different governments according to the circumstances. If this is the case, rôle specialisation will be impossible as it will be impossible to identify allies in advance, thus leading to a rationalisation of armed forces. So although further rationalisation, standardisation and interoperability procedures with a range of allies would certainly increase the ease of joint operations, the political difficulties of achieving this (short of a coherent and co-ordinated European common foreign and security policy) are great.

Conclusion

Humanitarian intervention may provide a rôle for British armed forces in the post-Cold War world. This Chapter has tried to set out ways in which those operations may be conceived. Of course, many will be dissatisfied with including criteria such as operational ease in a discussion about humanitarian intervention; if it is to mean anything, should it not mean the protection of people from military excess regardless of their nationality? Perhaps that is so, but it is difficult to believe that a domestic consensus in favour of humanitarian intervention could be maintained in the face of a significant loss of British life. Thus the enterprise must be limited, not only by state interests but also by domestic factors.

However, this is not to suggest that humanitarian intervention is not important. The concept, and the practice, are important for three reasons. The first is the most obvious. The prevention of genocide and the abuse of human rights are widely accepted to be essential norms in Western political systems. Inevitably there are constituencies that will demand that this be extended globally. This moralism, referred to earlier, has been supported by many political speeches; for example, by Douglas Hurd in stressing the British interest in 'a safer and more decent world'.[23] Second, humanitarian intervention may lead to the creation of some form of deterrent to other political leaders (perhaps in the former Soviet Union?) who might be tempted to follow the example of Slobodan Milosevic. Third, the failure of international institutions to achieve any tangible results in halting the violence against civilians in the former Yugoslavia or Iraq has had the effect of weakening the legitimacy of, and confidence in, both the European Community and the United Nations.[24] This may further reduce the credibility of international law which, for an international trading country such as Britain, would be very damaging. 'National interest in the maintenance of the rule of law is not an unaffordable luxury.'[25]

One area in which Britain might be able to play a rôle is in the creation of ad hoc coalitions and the generation of legitimacy for humanitarian operations from international organisations. The position of the United Kingdom as one of the Permanent Members of the United Nations Security Council has been an important factor in past issues, such as in the creation of a safe haven for Kurdish refugees. Indeed, the United Nations remains the only credible legitimising institution for humanitarian intervention. Many regions of the world lack functioning regional groupings. Europe, which possesses more than most, has yet to create an institution within which to legitimise and operate intervention: neither the CSCE, nor NATO, nor the European Community has had much success in the case of the former Yugoslavia. None of this is to suggest that Britain has some leadership rôle; but only that there may be scope for a positive influence.

However, the legitimacy of even the United Nations to sanction humanitarian intervention is not clear. Many were heartened by the passing of Resolution 688 legitimising the creation of safe havens in northern Iraq. However, that Resolution was passed on the basis of Article 2(7) of the United Nations Charter, which instructs the Security Council to take action when there are threats to international peace and security. Some may query whether the refugee crisis caused by Iraqi repression was such a threat; certainly China and India did not agree, as they abstained over Resolution 688, which may therefore be less of a precedent than is sometimes thought. In addition, the logic of this argument is that should a state be able to repress a minority and keep the effects entirely within its national borders, then the Security Council would have no mandate for intervention.[26]

Unless such issues are clarified and the United Nations becomes able to legitimise intervention under clearer definitions, the practice of external intervention in national humanitarian problems will continue to be haphazard, frustrating those arguing for a 'cosmopolitanist' approach. In such circumstances, states will be forced to make difficult decisions over whether and when to intervene by reference to national criteria. In such a world it is vital that a country such as the United Kingdom should be able to draw upon its own coherent set of criteria, one able to draw a wide measure of political support. The practice of British involvement in humanitarian intervention in 1991–93 provides a basis for thinking about such standards, but the intellectual and political task of generating widely applicable criteria has yet to be fully undertaken.

This Chapter set out to ask whether a rôle could be found for Britain's armed forces. The conclusion has been that there is such a rôle, much more in the area of humanitarian intervention than collective security. It then asked whether this rôle could justify continuing high levels of expenditure on the armed forces, including perhaps the reversal of some of the reductions brought about by Options for Change. The answer here is 'no'. The issue should be how to use existing military forces to improve the lot of people in parts of the world where violence is common, rather than to allow global disorder to influence the size of British forces. Douglas Hurd has commented that 'if boils keep on breaking out on the face of the world, our commitments could well increase – provided, that is, that we wish to maintain our position as a medium-large power with a developed sense of international responsibility'.[27] However, to become so dependent on global disorder is a recipe for delaying further the strategic review so necessary after the end of the Cold War. Correlli Barnett has argued that

> again a British government faces the old and as yet never solved problem of the disparity between the rôle Britain thinks it ought to play in the world, and the size of the armed forces which a sluggardly economy can pay for ... Now ... is surely the time to define in real hard-nosed terms the likely future direct threats to the security of the United Kingdom and what proportion of GNP we can really afford to spend on defence.

That such a review is required surely cannot be in doubt. In a rethink about British security priorities, however, humanitarian intervention should not be left out. There is a rôle for the alleviation of human suffering through the use of military forces, although for domestic and international reasons, that rôle is constrained. This Chapter has sought to argue that limits should be set on intervention, and that intervention should be based on strict criteria, the provision of which has been attempted here.

Notes

1. The author was one of those who made such criticisms in *British Security Policy* (London: Harper Collins, 1991), especially pp.201–16.
2. House of Commons Defence Committee, *Defence Implications of Recent Events*, HC 320, (London: HMSO, 1990).
3. Malcolm Rifkind, in a speech at the Centre for Defence Studies, 14 May 1992 published in *West European Union Press Review* No.90, 15 May 1992, p.2.
4. Correlli Barnett, 'Military illusions shattered again by harsh economic realities', *The Times*, 29 January 1993.
5. Malcolm Chalmers, 'Beyond the Alliance System', *World Policy Journal*, Spring 1990, pp.215–50.
6. See Statement on the Defence Estimates 1992 Cm 1981 (London: HMSO 1992), paras. 238–9, p.41.
7. The term 'national interests' is being used to denote the interests of the state as defined by the government in any particular case. It is a particularly unsatisfactory term analytically, but it is one which is frequently used.
8. See, for example, Mark Fineman, 'After the Marines: 4 US Majors Await Somali Oil Season', *International Herald Tribune*, 19 January 1993. Fineman

suggested that 'Four major US oil companies are sitting on a prospective fortune in exclusive concessions to explore and exploit tens of millions of acres of the Somali countryside. That land, in the opinion of geologists and industry sources, could yield significant amounts of oil and natural gas if the US-led military mission can restore peace to the impoverished East African nation'.

9. Douglas Hurd, 'Foreign Policy and International Security', *RUSI Journal*, December 1992, p.2.
10. Simon Jenkins, 'Playing at soldiers in Bosnia', *The Times*, 25 November 1992.
11. Heath is quoted in, Colin Brown 'Major to conduct review of Bosnian operation', *The Independent*, 22 January 1993.
12. See, for example, Michael Evans, 'Big artillery burst greets UK troops in Bosnia war zone', *The Times*, 16 November 1992; David Fairhall, 'British troops under fire after breaking Serb siege', *The Guardian*, 20 November 1992; Adam LeBor, 'British troops fired on by Muslims and Serbs', *The Times*, 4 December 1992; and Adam LeBor, 'British troops take cover as Croats and Muslims battle', *The Times*, 19 January 1993.
13. The leading proponent of this view in the United Kingdom is Ken Booth. See, for example, his 'Security in Anarchy: Utopian Realism in Theory and Practice', *International Affairs*, Vol.67, No.3, 1991 and 'Security and Emancipation', *Review of International Studies*, Vol.17, No.4, 1991.
14. Steve Smith, 'Mature Anarchy, Strong States and Security', *Arms Control: Contemporary Security Policy*, Vol.12, No.2, September 1991, p.335.
15. For an insight into the appalling nature of the war in the former Yugoslavia, see the report of Tadeusz Mazowiecki for the United Nations. See Mazowiecki, 'A Massive Violation of Human Rights', *International Herald Tribune*, 30 November 1992.
16. Jane M.O. Sharp, 'Intervention in Bosnia – the case for', *The World Today*, Vol.49, No.2, February 1993, pp.29–30.
17. See Sharp, *op. cit.*, p.30.
18. Lawrence Freedman, 'When the sky isn't the limit', *The Independent*, 19 January 1993.
19. See House of Commons Defence Committee, *op. cit.*
20. See, on this point, Michael Dewar, 'The Military Overdraft', *The Guardian*, 29 January 1993.
21. Christopher Bellamy, 'British Army stretched to fulfil UN missions', *The Independent*, 21 January 1993.
22. Quoted in Nicholas Wood, 'Hurd lays down limits on British role in the world', *The Times*, 28 January 1993.
23. From a speech at the Royal Institute of International Affairs reported in 'Hurd's Troubled World', *The Times*, 29 January 1993.
24. For a critique of the EC's role, see Michael Brenner, 'The EC in Yugoslavia: A Debut Performance', *Security Studies*, Vol.1, No.4, Summer 1992.
25. 'Forces for Peace', *The Times*, 26 January 1993.
26. See Christopher Greenwood, 'Is there a right of humanitarian intervention?', *The World Today*, Vol.49, February 1993, pp.34–40.
27. Douglas Hurd, *RUSI Journal, op. cit.*, p.3.

4
A Homeland Defence Option

*John Morrison**

> Oh! what a snug little island,
> A right little, tight little island!
> (Thomas John Dibdin)

Introduction

Generalisations are dangerous, but it is fair to say that over the past four decades Britain – unlike the US – has not benefited from a deep, continuing and wide-ranging analysis of the nation's basic defence and security needs. There has of course been both political wrangling and academic debate over the UK's need (or not) for nuclear weapons, but a perhaps surprising consensus on other aspects of defence policy. Discussion has in the main focused on the form of Britain's contribution to collective defence through NATO, rather than questioning the value of collective defence as such. This consensus has survived the fall of the external Soviet empire, the unification of Germany, the fragmentation of the Soviet Union and the disappearance of the Warsaw Pact threat – a process which effectively took only three years, from Gorbachev's December 1988 speech to the United Nations announcing unilateral force reductions to his December 1991 resignation.

A future historian looking back on this period might well expect that fundamental changes of such magnitude would have stimulated a correspondingly major Western reponse. By 1991 even the most cautious politicians and defence planners had been forced to accept

---

* The author is a UK official who is currently a student at the Royal College of Defence Studies. This article, which is based on research towards a course thesis, is intended as a purely personal contribution to a wider debate on defence policy; it does not in any way reflect official Ministry of Defence or UK government policy.

not only that the traditional threat from the East had disappeared, but that it would never reappear in its previous form. The former Soviet Union, bereft of its former allies and racked by increasingly severe internal problems, was clearly in no condition to engage in military adventures outside its borders. Once this had become apparent, surely NATO nations would have to reconsider the basis of their defence structures and policies? The United Kingdom in particular had, by European standards, accepted a disproportionately high defence burden for decades; was this not the opportunity to rethink the very *raison d'être* for Britain's armed forces?

In the event, there was no such fundamental review of Britain's defence needs. The Options for Change exercise was carried out in 1990, at a time when there still appeared to be a residual external threat to NATO, and thus amounted to 'less of the same', with commitment to NATO remaining at the heart of UK defence policies. This cautious response was not confined to the UK; the December 1991 Maastricht summit gingerly committed itself to developing a Common Foreign and Security Policy '... including the *eventual* framing of a common defence policy that *might in time* lead to a common defence' (emphases added). Not until the 1992 Defence White Paper[1] was UK defence policy finally redefined in terms of three defence rôles rather than four defence pillars, but the second rôle – insurance against any major threat to the United Kingdom and its allies – was still seen as primary, and '... to be discharged through the collective security provided by the North Atlantic Alliance'.[2] NATO was to '... continue to be the focus of our peacetime planning and training'.[3]

This continuing UK government stress on the primacy of NATO meant that more radical defence policy options were not – indeed could not be – seriously considered. Nor did the parliamentary opposition encourage a wider debate; after its 1987 poll defeat Labour had no wish to be stigmatised again as the party of 'weak defence'. The public debate was therefore couched on both sides in terms of force sizes and numbers within a continuing commitment to NATO, rather than exploring Britain's fundamental defence requirements. Our future historian would have been struck by the contrast with the pragmatism of the 15th Earl of Derby a century earlier:

> I do not believe that it is possible for us to lay down any formula or general rule which shall bind us in our foreign policy for all time and on all occasions. We must deal with the circumstances of each case as it arises.[4]

or Joseph Chamberlain's forthright statement a little later to the

German ambssador that:

> The policy of this country for many years has been a policy of isolationism – or at least non-entanglement in alliances.[5]

Instead, Britain's Alliance rôle was taken by almost all as unquestionable, despite the fact that as late as the 1930s such an explicitly binding and apparently open-ended commitment would have been seen as an aberration. In the public debate, no serious consideration was given to the idea that Britain's long-term security needs might be better met by a more explicitly national defence policy which sought to move away from political and military commitment to NATO or a successor European security organisation. Such a policy could range from the strict formal neutrality of Sweden or Switzerland to a 'semi-detached' membership of NATO of the type France has maintained since 1964.

This Chapter looks at one of these options, which falls in a largely neglected area of the security spectrum, described by Michael Clarke as 'defence isolationism'.[6] Having identified four defence policy options for the UK – Business as Usual, Differential Alliances, A Common European Defence Policy and Broad Internationalism – Clarke notes:

> The United Kingdom is one of the few European powers for whom a defence isolationist policy is a feasible option. Such an option assumes that the UK is prepared simply to defend its homeland to the best of its ability in any future war. This could be pursued through defensive strategies, limited offensive strategies, retaliatory strategies, or mixtures of all three. It does not necessarily imply isolationism in other senses. UK security policy might still be highly internationalist, but the defence component of it territorially limited.[7]

It is interesting, however, that having identified this option, Clarke does not explore it futher. This Chapter seeks to do so, but using the term 'homeland defence' rather than 'isolationism', with its pejorative overtones. In doing so, it attempts to answer two questions:

> *Could* Britain adopt a defence policy based on homeland defence? In other words, are there any objective reasons why such a policy would pose unacceptable risks to UK national security?
> *Should* Britain adopt such a policy? Are there wider political or economic considerations which require UK defence commitments (and hence military forces) to be extended beyond those needed for purely national defence?

After a brief review of the historical background to British defence policy, the Chapter considers Britain's vital interests and how these might be threatened in the 1990s and beyond, in order to establish the worst case which UK defence policy needs to allow for. It goes on to consider the forces needed to meet Britain's essential security requirements. Having set this irreducible baseline, it then looks at the wider European and global contexts to consider the options open to the UK should it wish to contribute to broader security structures.

The Way We Were

In the 18th and 19th Centuries, Britain's foreign and defence policies were based on two main imperatives. The first was the need to ensure that the continent of Europe was not dominated by an unfriendly power or coalition; alliances were therefore shifting and tactical, and large armies raised when necessary. The second was the need to maintain Britain's trading advantage and access to raw materials across the oceans. This led to a maritime strategy which in due course became interwoven with commitment to an empire whose continued existence was taken for granted. What need had Britain for enduring continental alliances when it ruled the seas and its worldwide empire provided the grandest alliance of all? This view persisted well into the 20th Century despite Britain's relative political and economic decline, and in two World Wars troops came from all parts of the empire to fight on Britain's behalf.

But after 1945 such comforting assumptions were no longer possible. Britain, economically exhausted by the war, could no longer count on a fast-crumbling empire; while its world status resulted more from the temporary weaknesses of others than its own long-term strengths. Faced by a growing Soviet military threat and the realities of a bipolar world, successive British governments quite reasonably saw the country's security as guaranteed only by a firm commitment to a US-dominated NATO. In once-isolationist America, neutrality or non-alignment was now seen not only as impractical but as positively unethical: as John Foster Dulles put it in 1956:

> These [NATO] treaties abolish, as between the parties, the principle of neutrality, which pretends that a nation can best gain security for itself by being indifferent to the fate of others. This has increasingly become an obsolete conception, and, except under very exceptional circumstances, it is an immoral and short-sighted conception.[8]

Since the establishment of NATO in 1949, successive British governments have effectively subscribed to this view. In the face of a manifest Soviet threat, security was to be found through participation in a deliberately 'entangling alliance', with each member committed to mutual defence against external aggression.

Whether the Soviet Union ever had any intention of attacking the West is still a moot point, but the combination of an aggressive ideology and massive military forces was seen as uniquely threatening. NATO also brought political benefits, not least by locking West Germany into a collective Western security structure. For its part, the Soviet Union (not, it must be said, without reason) felt encircled and menaced by the forces of America and its allies. A self-reinforcing cycle of mistrust was created in which each side felt threatened by the other's military developments and so compelled to respond to them, while those reactions were in turn seen as threatening by the other side.

So much is commonplace. But in retrospect the Cold War can be seen as having had a pervasive and still enduring effect on Western political and military thinking. The division of the world into opposed armed camps meant that 'the threat' became the dominating factor in both sides' defence planning. It was implicitly assumed that the adversarial relationship between the United States and the Soviet Union – and hence between NATO and the Warsaw Pact – would persist indefinitely. The former subtleties of great-power relationships in Europe were seen as something best left to the historians, and politicians adopted – or at least professed – a Manichean certainty. The pervasive stress on the Soviet Union's military strengths meant that the Warsaw Pact's internal weaknesses tended to be discounted. While some Western observers accepted the possibility that the Soviet empire could collapse from within, few saw that as something which would come soon or need affect the realities of defence planning.

In the UK, the political realities of the two-party system militated against any fundamental reconsideration of defence policy. In elections, the Tories predictably presented themselves as the party of strong defence, while Labour – whether in or out of office – strove mightily to stress that their defence credentials were equally sound. Furthermore, events ensured that radical thinking about defence was effectively discouraged. Following the Falklands conflict, the term 'defence review' had (with no small help from the Services) become largely discredited. After 1982 the consensus in official UK defence circles was that such reviews were at best risky and at worse thoroughly dangerous; the forces pointed out *ad nauseam* that had John Nott's proposed cuts in the Navy been implemented they would have prevented the recapture of the Falklands. The British defence establishment was thus predisposed against any explicit review of Britain's fundamental defence needs, as being both risky and unnecessary. This attitude was if anything reinforced by the wholly unexpected UK involvement in the Gulf War, when Britain found itself participating in a type of conflict it had never anticipated;[9] the range of possible future military commitments appeared to have been extended rather than reduced.

In part, this reluctance to get down to the basics of defence reflected the lack of a clearly formulated British security policy integrating the country's political, economic and military objectives. Over the previous half-century the United Kingdom had lost an empire and control of the seas; in the absence of these driving imperatives it had become a wholehearted supporter of the NATO Alliance, yet without formulating any wider concept of where its true security interests lay. Not for Britain the explicit self-interest of the French or the hesitations and reservations of the smaller NATO members such as Norway, Denmark or Belgium. Thinking on defence became compartmentalised, and a generation of UK defence planners grew up feeling little need to look beyond the apparently eternal certainties of a looming (and apparently ever-increasing) Warsaw Pact threat and wholehearted NATO membership. In consequence, many found it hard at the end of the 1980s to accept the abrupt disappearance of a planning imperative which had existed for some 40 years; only when the Soviet Union itself broke up did some accept that the traditional threat had finally evaporated. Even then, many argued that a threat from the East could still reappear one day, with the West at some point in the future finding itself faced by a resurgent and antagonistic Russia. Before considering the feasibility of a British defence policy based on homeland defence, it is therefore necessary to consider first the nation's basic security requirements and then the ways in which these are – or might be – threatened in the foreseeable future.

Britain's Vital Defence Interests

Every government accepts the fundamental obligation to defend its people against invasion, attack or lesser threats, and to maintain whatever military forces are needed to that end. It may also have external commitments or vital interests which demand some form of military response. But an important distinction must be made between these primary defence interests and the mechanisms by which they are defended. Participation in an alliance may be desirable, but in the last resort any alliance is only a means to an end, not an end in itself. In 1993, Britain's primary defence interests may be defined as:

- Protection of the United Kingdom, its surrounding waters and airspace against attack of all types.
- Protection of the nation against internal subversion and terrorism.

- The similar protection of its dependent territories against external and internal threats.

Some would add Britain's treaty obligations and commitments to the list, but these have reduced greatly over the years and it is questionable whether any still constitute *primary* defence interests. It can also be argued that the UK needs to defend itself against international developments such as a threat to external trade or the supply of vital resources such as oil; whether these would necessarily require a British military response will be considered later.

Threat – What Threat?
Traditionally, military threats have been seen as having two components: capability and intention. Country A may have the military capability to attack Country B, but this does not amount to a threat unless A is perceived to have malign intentions towards B; otherwise Canada would be manning its border with the US and Britain fortifying the Channel Islands against France. Conversely, it matters little if a country would like to attack another if it lacks credible military means to do so. A Third World leader such as Gadhafi or Hussein can mouth threats against the UK, but neither Libya nor Iraq are in any position to mount a credible military attack against the UK itself. The Soviet Union's unique status as a perceived threat over four decades depended on its possessing both the capability of mounting an attack against the West and intentions which were perceived as at best ambiguous and at worst wholly malign.

For the foreseeable future, or the 'realistic policy-planning horizon' (phrases which themselves of course beg many questions), Northern Irish terrorism will constitute the only threat to the territory of the UK itself which calls for a significant military response. Other forms of terrorism (whether domestic or international), drug trafficking or international crime may lead to calls on the armed forces, but these remain essentially police matters. Russia of course retains the theoretical capability to launch a 'bolt from the blue' nuclear strike against the UK, but even in the most frigid years of the Cold War such an independent strike was never regarded as credible. Instead, the threat to Britain was seen as part of that to NATO as a whole: a Warsaw Pact attack against Western Europe which would begin at the conventional level but almost inevitably escalate to nuclear warfare. No-one now argues that a much weakened Russia could undertake such an adventure; even if it had the will to do so. Belarus, Ukraine and the newly independent republics of central and eastern Europe have provided NATO with its own form of defensive glacis.

Looking beyond central Europe, it is equally hard to identify military threats to essential UK interests. The commitment to defend the Falklands against attack remains, but there are no signs that Argentina will regain either the intention or the capability to undertake such an adventure. The other dependent territories do not face credible threats; while it could be argued that Hong Kong is a possible exception, that commitment will disappear in 1997 – and in any case the territory could never have been defended against a determined Chinese thrust, nor subsequently regained by force of arms.

But even if the traditional threat to NATO has gone, it can reasonably be argued that Britain has wider interests in maintaining peace and stability in Europe and ensuring that the international political and economic order is not jeopardised. This is a key theme of the 1992 Defence White Paper, which however makes it clear that the UK is not prepared to give an open-ended commitment to acting as a world policeman:

> The participation of British forces in any particular operation will depend on the precise circumstances. The forces required to meet these requirements will be drawn from those with other rôles.[10]

Collective security through NATO thus remains the cornerstone of British defence policy. Even if Britain itself is not subject to any external military threat (Northern Ireland being regarded as an internal security problem), it is officially asserted that NATO as a whole continues to have a basic requirement for joint defence. But this inevitably begs the question 'defence against what?', and here the Defence White Paper is rather vague. While hoping for enhanced security, the Defence Secretary's introduction to the 1992 Defence White Paper sees defence as a necessary insurance policy in a world of risks and uncertainties:

> Nevertheless there will remain nuclear and other powerful weapons in the former Soviet Union. Should, against our hopes and expectations, the reform process not succeed, we cannot be sure who will control these. There are new instabilities in central Europe, as recent tragic events in Yugoslavia show. Outside Europe, proliferation of dangerous weapons continues with unstable regimes acquiring ballistic missiles and nuclear and chemical weapons capabilities along with other advanced weapons such as submarines. The tenth anniversary of the Falklands conflict is a cogent reminder of the risk of unexpected conflict.[11]

But while the world may have become a more uncertain and dangerous place since the collapse of bipolarity, it does not necessarily follow that the risks to NATO – and even less the UK –

have grown commensurately. Indeed, it is hard to envisage any significant external threat to NATO countries arising over the next 10–15 years which would require the UK to maintain defence forces at currently planned levels.

Some would argue that this is unimportant: that it is NATO's structures and mechanisms rather than its military forces which provide stability, and that NATO's rôle is as much to ensure peace within Europe as to protect against external dangers. It could, for example, be suggested that without this established forum for mediating differences, Greece and Turkey might have come to blows before now, as they nearly did in 1987. This may be true; but even if NATO is a politically useful organisation, that provides no justification for the maintenance of military forces at any particular level. Much the same holds true for arguments based on the need to maintain American involvement in NATO, and here the question must be: 'to what end?' In the later part of the Cold War era there was a nagging European fear that the US might progressively disengage from Europe, ultimately removing the strategic nuclear umbrella which was seen as an essential element of flexible response. But in the absence of a Warsaw Pact threat, and with growing emphasis on a European security dimension, the rationale for a substantial and continuing American military presence in Europe is no longer self-evident.

The interim conclusion is therefore that neither the UK nor NATO face external military threats which would call for British armed forces of the present size and type. Indeed, much of the recent debate on UK defence policy boils down to the question 'what should we do with the forces we have?' rather than 'what do we need forces for?' – or, as Hopkinson puts it, '... we can now attempt to find a rôle more nearly related to that of which we are capable'.[12]

This seemingly back-to-front line of argument must be based on the assumption – whether implicit or explicit – that there are political, economic, ethical or moral imperatives which justify the expense of maintaining forces well beyond those needed for the defence of the UK itself. It implies that a British defence policy based narrowly on the country's national interests would somehow be 'wrong'.

Is Homeland Defence Immoral?
During the Cold War, the Dulles view of neutrality effectively held sway. At its crudest, this was that those who were not for NATO were against it, with neutral and non-aligned states seen as at best misguided and at worst as playing into the hands of the Soviet Union. But even in a bipolar world, some European countries' neutrality was accepted – Sweden and Switzerland by tradition and Austria by

treaty. With Western encouragement, Yugoslavia and Romania made capital out of their ambiguous political positions, while for three decades France has demonstrated that membership of NATO does not necessarily require a formal commitment to its military structures.

It can therefore reasonably be maintained that neutrality or homeland defence are not in themselves unacceptable on moral or ethical grounds. In this context there are, however, two related arguments against the UK's adopting a homeland defence position, and these need to be addressed briefly. The first is that such a change of status would weaken NATO fatally, leading to its collapse. But even the Alliance partners have accepted that NATO cannot continue indefinitely in its present form and that change has become inevitable. The second (and more cogent) argument is that by adopting a homeland defence policy the UK would be abrogating its moral obligation to help maintain international peace and order. But, as will be argued later, homeland defence need not mean a retreat from the world. It would still be open to Britain to participate in peacekeeping or peacemaking operations in Europe or beyond – but it would choose to do so as a participant in an ad hoc coalition rather than as a member of a pre-existing alliance.

Britain's Minimal Defence Forces

Before considering such options, however, it is worth considering the military capabilities the UK would need for its own purposes – that is, in direct defence of its national territory and domestic security (the current commitment to defend the Falklands will be addressed later). These would constitute the minimal defence forces needed for a policy of homeland defence.

> **The Army:** In the absence of a political solution in Northern Ireland, the army's internal security commitment to provide Military Aid to the Civil Power (MACP) will continue. The Northern Ireland commitment calls for a professional army with adequate logistic support but its numbers could be reduced from the 116,000 envisaged for the mid-1990s to some 70–80,000. The troops would need to be equipped only at light scales, with no requirement for heavy armour or artillery and hence a much reduced procurement programme.
>
> **The Royal Navy:** This would be confined to an essentially coastguard rôle, tasked with protecting Britain's territorial waters and its rights and activities in the surrounding seas; the main requirement would be for surface vessels up to – but not larger than – frigates. It is debatable whether any underwater capability would be required, but if it were it could be discharged by a small number of conventional submarines. The

Royal Marines (with the exception of the SBS) would no longer be required.

The Royal Air Force: This would be the air equivalent of a coastguard navy, and indeed a reshaped Fleet Air Arm might provide all that was needed. If the RAF were maintained, existing aircraft would be adequate for the policing rôle; in the absence of an air threat to the UK there would be no need for an advanced fighter aircraft such as EFA.

Special Forces: There would be a continued requirement for both the SAS and SBS for both the internal security and counter-terrorism rôle, with suitable logistic support from the RN and RAF.

The Nuclear Deterrent: With no direct nuclear threat to the UK, there would be no requirement for a *national* nuclear deterrent capability. Strategic and tactical nuclear weapons, together with their dedicated platforms and supporting infrastructure could be scrapped.[13]

The commitment to defend the Falklands – the only dependent territory which could realistically be faced by an external military threat – introduces a complicating factor. If this were to be regarded as absolute and open-ended, then significantly larger and more capable naval and air forces would be required to permit rapid reinforcement in time of crisis. The ideal solution would be to negotiate a binding political settlement with Argentina which would remove any credible military threat to the islands. Failing that, it might be more cost-effective in the long term to pay the 2,000 Falkland Islanders a substantial sum – say £1,000,000 each – on condition that they emigrated. Assuming the great majority accepted the offer, the unconditional commitment to defend the largely uninhabited islands could then be allowed to lapse.

The Pros and Cons of Minimal Defence
British adoption of minimal defence structures as part of a policy of homeland defence would bring political benefits. The UK would be able to demonstrate that an advanced country could greatly reduce its armed forces without endangering its essential interests. The scrapping of nuclear weapons would set a particularly virtuous example and no longer require the UK to maintain implicitly that its requirements for nuclear defence are somehow greater than those of Ukraine or Kazakhstan.

In economic terms, minimal defence could provide very substantial savings. The UK intends to reduce the 4.2 per cent of GDP which it devoted to defence at the beginning of the 1990s to around 3.2 per cent by 1995–96. Minimal forces would permit further reductions in the defence burden to (at most) the 2.0–2.1 per cent of GDP spent by Canada, Denmark or Italy. This would cut the defence budget from its present £24,520 million to around £10 billion a year. However, as the Options for Change exercise has shown, the savings would not accrue immediately. Force reductions would require redundancy payments, major procurement programmes would have to be ramped down, and defence industries might have to be given short-term help to avoid damagingly high levels of local unemployment.

Apart from the reductions in UK defence procurement, there would also be an impact on defence exports. At present these have reached some £5 billion a year and are estimated to support some 100,000 jobs.[14] Major defence industries such as tank, combat aircraft and warship production could not survive on export orders alone, and such platform manufacturers would gradually disappear. But platforms constitute a reducing proportion of a weapon system's overall cost, and electronics, propulsion systems, component and sub-equipment manufacturers, as well as a wide range of smaller companies, should continue to prosper; export sales of well over £1 billion a year should still be achievable.

A policy of homeland defence of the UK and the maintenance of minimal armed forces thus appears to provide substantial political and economic benefits. But many would argue that these would be outweighed by the penalties. Above all, the UK would no longer be capable of participating in the collective defence of Europe (except in so far as it was busy defending its own bit of the continent). This is indeed an important point which is addressed in detail later; but other objections seem less compelling.

Sacred Cows and Red Herrings
There can be no doubt that with the advent of minimal forces the status of Britain's armed forces would decline, and that many prestige military institutions would have to be eliminated or rationalised. This would provoke the usual outcry, despite the fact that sentimentality is generally a poor basis for policy. Britain's international status would suffer: at present the UK's permanent seat on the UN Security Council is to a considerable extent justified by its possession of nuclear weapons, the size and capabilities of its armed forces and its willingness to involve itself in international peacekeeping activities. It would be hard if not impossible for a Britain with minimal forces to justify its seat; but it is any case debatable whether the UK will be able to justify its 'Big Five' status for much longer. The supposed 'special relationship' with the US would wither, but in practice would no longer be needed. Nor would it be necessary to support a large UK intelligence community whose cost, though never made public, must be substantial.

In short, the answer to the first question posed in this paper – *could* Britain adopt a policy based on homeland defence – must be 'yes'. In purely military terms, it would still be possible to defend the country's essential security interests without a binding commitment to NATO or any successor European security organisation. It is therefore necessary to expand the debate by moving on to the second question, and ask whether there are wider security considerations which require UK defence commitments (and hence its military forces) to be extended beyond those needed for purely national defence.

Homeland Defence in the World Context

This Chapter has suggested that NATO does not face external military threats which require its European members to maintain forces at current levels. But even if this were accepted, it could be argued that such forces will still be needed for three purposes:

- To maintain peace and stability within Europe by retaining the ability to intervene in domestic and international conflicts.
- To engage in peacekeeping and peacemaking operations under UN auspices on the periphery of Europe and further afield.
- To guard against the long-term possibility of a major external threat (usually assumed to be from a resurgent Russia) reappearing.

Intervention Within Europe
The first of these arguments would have been more convincing had the European Community, Western European Union or NATO shown themselves capable of intervening effectively to contain or resolve the civil war in the former Yugoslavia. Instead, the majority of politicians have shown themselves to be all too keenly aware of the limitations of military power in such circumstances. Some have suggested that the early deployment of substantial international forces might have imposed peace upon the warring factions,[15] but the opportunity, if it ever existed, soon passed. Throughout, the Western powers have been afraid of repeating the American experience in Vietnam and becoming bogged down in a protracted and increasingly costly conflict.

The failure to provide an early and decisive response to clear-cut aggression in the former Yugoslavia (the Serbs being the worst but by no means the only offenders) will inevitably condition European responses to any future civil war or international conflict on the continent. It is of course possible that European leaders might conclude that only early and decisive external intervention could bring the fighting to an end, and act accordingly. But it seems all too likely that they would draw the opposite conclusion: that any involvement in somebody else's war is a risky business which should if possible be avoided.

Operations on the Borders of Europe

Following the Gulf War, the second argument – that Europe must ensure stability in neighbouring regions – seems more compelling. But recent experience is here more of a hindrance than a help in charting a way ahead. A brutal dictator with regional ambitions, known to be armed with chemical and biological weapons and suspected of developing a nuclear capability, invaded and occupied an effectively defenceless neighbour and in so doing threatened Western oil supplies. This provided a clear *casus belli* and the resulting war was both justifiable – the civilised world against Saddam Hussein – and fought on an almost ideal battlefield. With the benefit of hindsight it can be said that the eventual outcome was never in doubt, with the coalition strategy being driven largely by the imperative of minimising non-Iraqi (and to some extent Iraqi) casualties.

It is unlikely that future peacekeeping or peacemaking operations on the periphery of Europe will be anything like as straightforward. Developments since the Gulf War have provided a better guide to the problems of protecting ethnic and religious minorities, thwarting the ambitions of authoritarian regimes, hindering the development of weapons of mass destruction and preventing regional conflicts. The Gulf War demonstrated the utility of military force in responding to unprovoked, overt and direct aggression by an unpleasant regime without powerful friends. The aftermath has shown all too clearly that it has only a limited part to play in resolving wider or more complex problems. Furthermore, the unprecedented unanimity of the UN Security Council may well turn out to have been a short-lived honeymoon; Russian or Chinese objections may hinder or prevent a decisive UN response to future conflicts.

It is sometimes suggested that the UK, in common with other advanced economies, has a vested interest in ensuring the maintenance of its vital supplies; oil and certain strategic minerals are most usually cited. This is true, but only in exceptional circumstances can such supplies be secured by military means; economic and diplomatic tools are generally more appropriate. Furthermore, there is no necessary linkage between dependency on external supplies and the maintenance of any particular scale or type of armed forces. Japan, which imports virtually all its raw materials and fuels, is both constitutionally and militarily incapable of intervening at a distance to protect those supplies. To suggest that Britain, which is economically weaker and has less at risk, should undertake more than Japan, smacks more of 'doing our bit' than a reasoned risk/benefit analysis.

Insurance Against Future Threats

The third argument – that NATO and the UK must maintain military capabilities against the possible re-emergence of a major threat in the longer term – appears the most convincing one, and is most often cited as justifying the planned size and shape of UK forces. It is pointed out that Russia (and to a lesser extent Ukraine) still retains very large nuclear and conventional forces, equipped with weaponry which will decay only very slowly. It is suggested that an authoritarian regime could emerge from Russia's present chaos, determined to regain great-power status and with nationalism reinforced by resentment against a West blamed for the destruction of the former Soviet Union. The imposition of strong central rule could permit the regeneration of the economy and the creation of a war machine that could once again threaten a much-weakened Western Europe. Some would argue that this risk alone justifies the maintenance of strategic forces capable of defending more than just the UK base, with military capabilities appropriate to a high-intensity conflict against an advanced adversary.

Proponents of this view can cite the period between the two world wars as demonstrating the folly of disarmament and the dangers of assuming that the world has truly changed. From 1919 to 1932 British defence policy was based on the Ten Year Rule,[16] and even when this was abandoned there was a reluctance to accept that conflict with Germany was a real possibility, let alone inevitable:

> In the British view there were truly no *états de mauvaise foi*. If Hitler resorted to coercion with his own people and acted ungentlemanly in his dealings with many foreign governments, discussions and incentives could change all of that. Even the most irascible politician could be placated if treated with respect. Conciliation, negotiations, and understanding would suffice, because it did not occur to most of the British public that any sane politician would deliberately choose war over peace.[17]

Many would argue that UK national security must never again be allowed to depend on such wishful thinking, or trust in the good intentions of others. Is it not worth maintaining substantial armed forces, a whole-hearted commitment to NATO and a sizeable long-term procurement programme as our insurance policy against the ultimate danger of an attack from the East?[18]

Yet however tempting this historical analogy may be, it is hard to maintain in any detail. In order for Russia once more to pose a threat to Western Europe (as distinct from menacing its immediate neighbours) it would single-handedly need to regenerate a large part of the military capabilities once possessed by the Warsaw Pact as a whole. To do so, it would have to accomplish an economic revolution which would permit it to devote some 20 per cent of GDP to defence without beggaring the country. Having somehow achieved this goal, it would then need to dominate or otherwise render *hors de combat* the Ukraine, Belarus and its former Warsaw Pact allies before it could reach Western Europe. While none of this can be ruled out as a possibility given enough time, any such achievement must now realistically be counted in decades rather than years. If so, a new Ten Year Rule (however unpopular its historical connotations) can be seen as a perfectly reasonable assumption for any NATO country.

Indeed, a policy of homeland defence would increase Britain's long-term options rather than reducing them. The UK would retain the option of building up its forces and recommitting itself to a European security structure (albeit with a reduced all-round capability) if it believed a long-term threat was developing. In the shorter term it could still decide to involve itself in ad hoc coalitions if it so chose, whether within Europe or as part of a UN operation elsewhere – just as neutral and non-aligned nations have for many years. But if it chose to do so on its own terms it could structure its forces accordingly rather than in a way designed to meet a now-vanished threat. It is therefore worth considering the military implications of retaining the option to operate overseas.

Beyond Strict Defence of the Homeland

It should be reiterated that a policy of homeland defence does not require either strict neutrality on the Swedish or Austrian model or a withdrawal from world affairs. A country which is not locked into an alliance can still participate in military adventures beyond its borders; the key feature is that it does so in a place, time and fashion of its own choosing. Britain could decide for a variety of reasons – political, economic or moral – that it wished to retain the capability of sending forces overseas to operate in conjunction with other countries (even with present forces, its ability to operate in isolation is very limited). Indeed the UK could, if it wished, continue defence expenditure at current levels for such reasons without a binding commitment to NATO, though this might be hard to justify.

But whatever the *quantity* of resources devoted to defence, the *nature* of the resulting forces would differ from those currently planned. There would be no requirement for tactical or strategic nuclear weapons. Naval capabilities would be reoriented to embargo and blockage operations and the transport and support of ground and air forces, instead of counter-ship and submarine operations in the North Atlantic. Ground forces would be optimised for internal security duties and low-intensity conflict, with little need for tanks and other heavy weapons. Air forces would not necessarily require the most modern aircraft, since they would generally be pitted against less capable enemies. Electronic communications would need to cater for operations with a wide range of potential partners rather than being tailored to mainly national requirements.[19]

Above all, Britain would need to accept that its contribution to international military activities should be complementary rather than comprehensive. The UK sent an armoured division to the Gulf because one was available; but that does not mean any future involvement need be of that type or on that scale. Only the US now has the full range of capabilities required for worldwide power projection, and it is highly questionable whether any major peacekeeping or peacemaking operation outside Europe could succeed without American involvement or support. A homeland defence policy would permit the UK to structure its forces in ways which would most effectively supplement those of potential military partners – particularly the US – rather than seeking to retain a complete range of military capabilities. Whatever the resulting mix, it is fair to say that it would inevitably differ substantially from that which was needed to meet the sophisticated Warsaw Pact threat.

Conclusion

From an historical perspective, the UK's wholehearted commitment to NATO over four decades can be seen as an aberration which was justified only by the unique circumstances of the Cold War. The disappearance of any credible threat from the East opened the way for a fundamental review of Britain's security requirements. Such a review might have been based on a dispassionate assessment of the nation's vital national interests, taking suitable account of its much reduced circumstances. Instead, the continuing response has been to cling to NATO as the one certainty in a changing world, with a vague commitment to move in due course to some new but as yet undefined form of collective defence. NATO capabilities are now centred on the Allied Rapid Reaction Force (ARRC), but its rôle and *modus operandi* are by no means clear. British defence forces are indeed being reduced, but through the traditional process of salami-slicing rather than basic restructuring. The UK is still seeking to retain a full range of military capabilities and, despite its economic problems, continues to spend more on defence than any other European member of NATO.

Alternatives do exist. This paper has focused on one of them: a policy of homeland defence which would concentrate on defending Britain's essential security interests. This would resile from binding commitments to collective security organisations, but would not necessarily require a formal declaration of neutrality. Rather, it would permit a range of options stretching from minimal defence to continued involvement in international peacekeeping and other operations. The common feature would be the abandonment of any attempt to maintain the full range of forces and military capabilities appropriate to a great power. By doing so, it would permit a reconciliation between the resources available for defence, the rôles to be undertaken and the forces needed to undertake those rôles effectively.

But it must be accepted that any British government is in reality unlikely to adopt a policy of homeland defence, since this would inevitably incur both domestic political attacks and international opprobrium. The short-term penalties of any such change would be seen as vastly outweighing any long-term benefits. Politicians, believing that the British public favours 'strong defence', will understandably calculate that it is safer to go on as before and to maintain their commitment to existing defence commitments and rôles, whether or not these are still appropriate to a fundamentally changed security environment. Exploration of more radical options will not be viewed as a vote-winner.

This approach holds two dangers. First, collective security structures in Europe – whether based on NATO or some successor organisation – may simply not prove viable in the post-Cold War era. 'Collective security', after all, requires the joint commitment of many nations. The UK may find itself committed to a type of communal defence which will become steadily less effective as other nations reduce their contributions and restrictions on exercises make it harder to preserve the worth of common military procedures. Secondly, UK domestic economic pressures are likely to result in further salami-slicing defence cuts, with British forces finding it ever harder to fulfil their obligations. Ultimately the country could end up with a navy, army and air force still theoretically capable of undertaking a full spectrum of military rôles, but in practice so under-resourced that it could not be confident of success in any of them.

In the last resort, any country's external policies, whether diplomatic, economic or military, must be based on national self-interest. That in turn calls for a clear understanding of what the country's real security interests are, and how much it can afford to spend on defending them. Defence policy should be only a subset of a wider, more complex and multidimensional security policy directed to maximising the safety and well-being of its citizens. The development of UK defence policy in recent times has shown little sign of deriving from such a fundamental analysis, and the resulting changes to force structures and rôles have been decremental rather than radical. As long as the commitment to collective security structures is seen as absolute, there will be little movement. An alternative policy of homeland defence would not increase the risks to Britain, but would open up new possibilities more appropriate to a country in reduced circumstances facing a world of greater uncertainties. It merits consideration.

Notes

1. *Statement on the Defence Estimates 1992*, Cm 1981, (London: HMSO, July 1992).
2. *Ibid.*, p.9.
3. *Ibid.*, p.9.
4. The Earl of Derby 1885. Quoted in John Baylis, *British Defence Policy: Striking the Right Balance*, (London: Macmillan, 1989).
5. Chamberlain 1888. Quoted in Baylis, *op. cit.*
6. Michael Clarke (ed), *United Kingdom Defence Policy in the 1990s*, (London: Centre for Defence Studies, March 1992), p.3.
7. *Ibid.*
8. Quoted in Richard Latter and Dietrich Schindler, *The Future of Neutrality in Europe*, Wilton Park Papers 41, HMSO, June 1991.
9. For example, the forces' climatic specifications for new ground and air defence equipments had been almost entirely geared to operation in the European theatre; fitness for desert conditions could only be justified if it would help exports.
10. Cm 1981, p.9.
11. Cm 1981, p.5.
12. G.W. Hopkinson, *Changing Options: British Defence and Global Security*, University of Cambridge Global Security Programme Occasional Paper, June 1992.
13. The argument that, within Europe, the UK and France have some sort of unique national requirement for nuclear weapons is less than convincing. A case can be made for Europe as a whole having some form of nuclear capability, but it is hard to argue that the UK has any greater *national* requirement for nuclear weapons than any other western European nation.
14. Cm 1981, p.61.
15. Jane M.O. Sharp, *Bankrupt in the Balkans: British Policy in Bosnia*, London: IPPR, 1993, p.7.
16. A directive to the armed services that they should frame their estimates on the assumption that they would not be engaged in a major war within the next 10 years.
17. Kalevi J. Holsti, *Peace and War: Armed Conflicts and International Order 1648–1989*, Cambridge Studies in International Relations, 14, 1991, p.236.

18. The retention of a UK nuclear deterrent when conventional forces are being cut substantially can only be logically justified by the assumption that such a renewed threat is a real possibility in the period up to 2025.
19. As part of this process, the requirement for highly secure (and hence expensive) electronic equipment, capable of operating in the face of the Soviet Union's sophisticated electronic warfare and signals intelligence capabilities, could be largely relaxed.

DEFENCE AND NATIONAL PRIORITIES

5
Resources, Commitments and the Defence Industry

Ron Smith *

When so much has changed, it is almost reassuring that some things stay the same. The Soviet empire may have disappeared, but at least the traditional tension in British defence policy between inadequate resources and excessive commitments remains. The Chancellor of the Exchequer's 1992 Autumn Statement increased the tension, subtracting almost £1.3 billion from the planned defence budget over the next three years. In this Chapter, the resources that are likely to be available to defence over the next decade are projected and the implications this will have for commitments and the defence industry are examined.

Any judgement about likely future resources inevitably requires making a forecast. Economic forecasting has recently acquired a justifiably bad reputation. Neither the Treasury nor most independent forecasters predicted the strength of the Lawson boom nor the length of the subsequent recession. Thus the exercise below should not be thought of as a prediction about what will happen, rather it is a structured numerical way of thinking about how the factors that shape the defence budget may interact.

Resources

To structure a discussion of the resources available, it is useful to think in terms of a series of questions. First, what priority will the UK

---

* This paper was written while I was visiting the Centre for Economic Forecasting, London Business School. I am grateful for advice from the Ministry of Defence on the statistics. All errors and opinions are my responsibility.

British Defence Choices for the Twenty-First Century

TABLE 1 ACTUAL AND PROJECTED DEFENCE BUDGET

	79-80	84-5	90-1	91-92	92-93	93-94	94-95	95-96	96-97	97-98	98-99	99-2000
Growth %	2.94	2.01	−0.53	−1.96	−0.84	1.89	3.75	3.51	2.50	2.50	2.50	2.50
Inflation %	16.68	5.08	7.99	6.91	4.25	2.75	3.25	2.75			3.00	2.90
Defence Share of GDP %	4.48	5.25	3.93	3.96	3.96	3.74	3.52	3.24	3.20	3.10		
At 1991-92 prices												
Defence Budget*	21260	25950	23302	23015	22830	21957	21474	20433	20689	20544	20378	20191
Personnel Costs	9062	9068	9408	9948	9450	9000	8550	8459	8255	7989	7704	7648
Armed Forces	4862	4905	5131	5480	5228	5046	4751	4696	4629	4533	4431	4431
Pensions	1063	1255	1503	1615	1433	1370	1298	1284	1256	1220	1181	1175
Civilians	3136	2908	2773	2853	2789	2584	2502	2479	2370	2235	2092	2042
Other Costs	3767	5005	4970	4839	4714	4611	4509	4291	4345	4314	4279	4240
Equipment	8432	11879	9448	9753	8667	8346	8414	7683	8089	8241	8395	8303
Equipment share %	39.66	45.78	40.55	42.38	37.96	38.01	39.18	37.6	39.1	40.11	41.2	41.12
Number of Personnel (thousands)												
Armed Forces	328.8	336.4	312.7	297.9	285	270	245	234	225	215	205	200
Civil Servants	276.2	206.5	173.1	168.7	165	150	140	134	125	115	105	100

* Defence Budget figures are in £m, and do not include overseas contributions to the cost of the Gulf conflict, totalling £524m in 1990–91 and £1,525m in 1991–92.

put on defence, in particular what share of GDP will be thought appropriate for it? Secondly, how well will the UK economy perform, in particular what will be the growth rate of GDP? Together these two judgements determine the real resources available to defence. The Autumn Statement contains the Treasury's answers to these questions to 1995–96 and I will make some guesses beyond then. Thirdly, how many will be employed in the armed forces and the civil service and on what terms? Finally, what will be required for expenditure on infrastructure and works? Having answered those questions, we are left with the amount available for spending on equipment.

Table 1 summarises some answers, based on the Treasury forecasts and my assessment. Money figures are all given in 1991–92 prices, with the effects of inflation having been removed using the GDP deflator. The detailed calculations are discussed in the Appendix, which also explains some of the numbers. To begin with, consider the share of output that the UK devotes to military spending, the best indicator of the priority attached to security, which is plotted in Figure 1. After rising in the early 1980s, it peaked in 1984–85 at 5.3 per cent, falling to 3.93 per cent in 1990–91. It is projected by the Treasury to fall to 3.24 per cent in 1995–96. I assume that the share then continues its fall, but more slowly, just going below 3 per cent in the year 2000.[1]

The size of the defence budget itself depends both on the share and

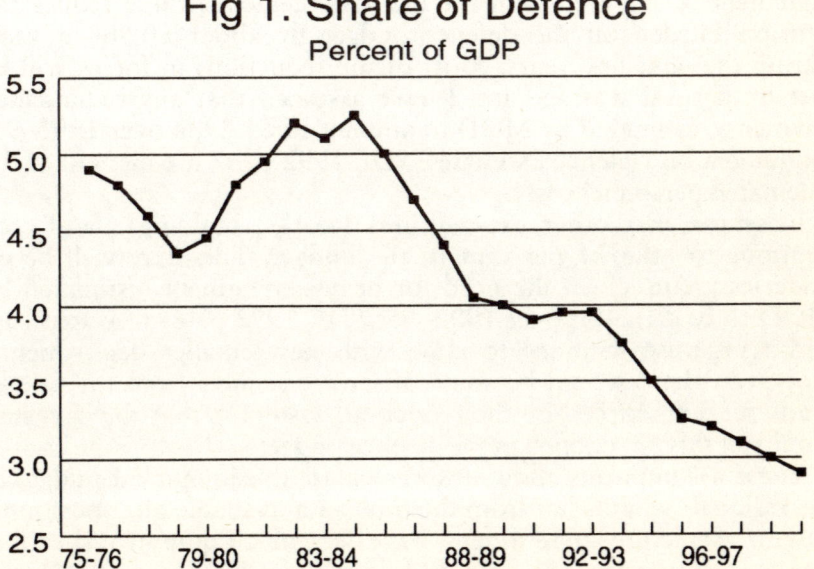

Fig 1. Share of Defence
Percent of GDP

on the level of output which the economy manages to generate. In real terms (i.e. correcting for inflation using the GDP deflator) the defence budget peaked in 1984–85 at £26bn (in 1991–92 prices), fell to £24bn in 1990–91 and on Treasury forecasts will fall to £20.4bn in 1995–96, a 15 per cent real reduction over the five-year period. If the economy grows at about 2.5 per cent a year thereafter, my assumption about the share would leave the real defence budget roughly constant at just over £20bn till the year 2000. An alternative, equally plausible, assumption would be that cuts in the second half of the 1990s matched those in the first half. That would give a real defence budget of £17.5bn in 1999–2000.

Even at the £20bn assumed for the late 1990s, the budget will be very tight and I assume that the Ministry of Defence balances the equation by continuing to cut personnel. In order to maintain a reasonable standard of equipment, further cuts of the same order of magnitude as those in Options for Change will be required. I assume that the numbers decline in line with the Options for Change targets for 234,000 in the armed forces and 134,000 in the civil service by 1995–96, and continue to decline thereafter, reaching 200,000 in the armed forces and 100,000 in the civil service by 2000.

Over the longer term real wages tend to grow at the same rate as the economy as a whole and I assume that this holds true for MOD personnel. This implies a reduction in real wages during 1992–93 in line with the policy on public sector pay announced by the Chancellor in the Autumn Statement. Pensions are tied to the pay bill in line with the new arrangements announced in the Autumn Statement. Compared with the old arrangements, these reduce the pension burden on the defence budget by about £0.5bn a year, during the next few years. Most of the reductions in forces will be met by natural wastage and I have assumed that any redundancy payments, estimated by MOD to amount to £1.29bn over 1992–95, (Statement on Defence Estimates, *SDE 1992* p.46) are met out of the calculated personnel costs.

I assume that other expenditures (works, buildings, land etc.) continue to take 21 per cent of the budget. This may well be an under-estimate, given the need for heavy investment (estimated by MOD to be £1.14bn over 1992–95, *SDE 1992* p.46) to restructure and reorganise facilities to cope with new smaller deployments. However, there would be some offsetting savings from the sale of land etc. that is freed by the reduction, assuming that the Treasury would let this be retained in the defence budget.

These assumptions allow us to calculate the equipment budget as the residual: what is left from the total sum available after personnel and infrastructure commitments have been met. Equipment spending (in 1991–92 prices) fell from £11.88bn in 1984–85 to £9.45bn in

1990–91, that is by just over 20 per cent in real terms. On the assumptions given above, it will fall a further 20 per cent to £7.68bn in 1995–96. This is almost exactly what was spent in 1977–78. Thereafter, on our assumptions, it will rise slightly as the pressure from personnel costs is reduced, reaching £8.3bn in 2000 and accounting for 40 per cent of the budget. Historical data and the central forecast for the equipment budget are plotted in Figure 2.[2] Alternative forecasts for the equipment budget are discussed below.

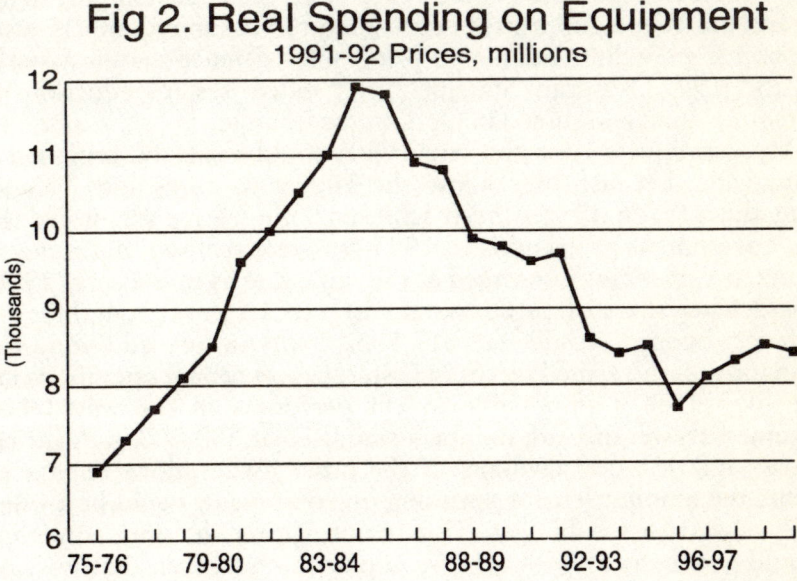

Fig 2. Real Spending on Equipment
1991-92 Prices, millions

The projections up to 1995–96 are as close as I can make them, using public data, to government assumptions, and it is clear that they embody some optimistic assumptions. My own assumptions beyond 1996, constant real funding and the ability to make large cuts in personnel, are also rather optimistic. It is not clear why the government's projections of the components of the budget, which have to be calculated as part of the public expenditure process, cannot be published rather than forcing defence firms and other commentators to try to reconstruct them. The most useful feature of a framework of this sort is not the forecasts themselves, but the way it permits the investigation of alternative scenarios, which helps indicate the robustness of policy in the face of alternative outcomes. I will examine two alternatives, one for the planning period, where I am using government assumptions, and one for the late 1990s, where I have made relatively optimistic assumptions.

In the first instance, suppose that the government instituted a pay freeze on both the armed forces and Ministry of Defence civil servants, maintaining their real pay at 1992–93 levels until 1995–96. This is potentially feasible since the government is running down the numbers of both and does not need to raise wages to encourage recruitment. Such a policy might, of course, cause some problems of morale, but were the government able to enforce a wage freeze on defence, equipment spending would be £8.5bn in 1995–96. This is over three quarters of a billion higher than our central forecast, but is still a lot lower than the 1990–91 figure. To get a substantially higher figure for the equipment budget requires assuming much faster economic growth, much higher priority for defence than is assumed in the 1992 Autumn Statement, or much faster reductions in personnel than is assumed in Options for Change.

My assumptions for the late 1990s could easily be criticised as unrealistic, because they allow the budget to come into balance, something that has rarely been achieved before. Suppose instead that the government projections to 1995–96 were realised, but that cuts in defence spending continued at the same rate as in the early 1990s. The defence share of output would drop to 2.5 per cent and the real defence budget would be £17.5bn. Suppose, in addition, that demands on the armed forces in Ulster, peacekeeping operations and the like made it impossible to cut personnel in the way I have assumed above. Instead, numbers stabilised at 230,000 in the armed forces and 130,000 civilians. If the other assumptions remain the same, the amount left for spending on equipment would be £4.6bn, 27 per cent of the budget. This is not a forecast, since something would give before the share of equipment was driven that low. But the calculation does indicate the sensitivity of the budgetary equation and the difficulties defence planners will face in balancing it.

There is another possible source of funding for defence, not projected in the Table. The Gulf payments could be regarded as a precedent. UK armed forces are professional and combat proven and in many scenarios would be more politically acceptable than troops from certain other countries. Thus it may well be that other countries would be willing to finance the use of British troops in certain multilateral contingencies. While this would be a matter of inter-allied rôle specialisation, rather than systematic development of a commercial mercenary capability, it might provide the odd billion to a hard-pressed budget. Of course, such operations would only help if they generated more finance than they cost. The Gulf conflict seems to have cost the UK slightly more than it received in contributions, (National Audit Office, 1992b).

There is also a range of risks. It should be emphasised that the figures for the budget and GDP up to 1995–96 are Treasury forecasts. These assume falling inflation, despite the significant devaluation that followed the departure from the Exchange Rate Mechanism, and very rapid growth in 1994–95 and 1995–96. While it is quite possible that the economy will exhibit a rapid non-inflationary rebound from the recession, and the Treasury has been predicting this for some years, poorer performance on growth or inflation could lead to a further erosion of the real defence budget and the amount available for equipment. For instance, the Treasury is forecasting that inflation will be just under 3 per cent a year from 1993 to 1996. Suppose instead that inflation was 5 per cent (a very respectable number by UK historical standards) and the government kept to its announced cash targets. As a result the defence budget would be over £1bn lower in 1995–96, at £19.2bn. Since we have assumed competitive wages and Options for Change force levels, equipment would take the brunt of the cuts, falling to £6.74bn, a 30 per cent cut over four years.

Of course, by getting better value for money, the MoD may be able to get more out of a smaller budget. There is evidence of efficiency gains in the fact that for the last couple of years, defence prices have gone up more slowly than other prices. In particular, the Ministry hopes to save £0.3bn over the next four years by contracting out various functions currently provided in-house. One imponderable in the projection is the effect of the New Management Strategy on the budget. If the devolution of power to budget-holders is more than cosmetic it could have important consequences. On the positive side, devolution to decision-makers offers the potential for large efficiency gains but, on the negative side, the new incentives may have unwanted consequences and there is some danger of loss of control of the budget, unless MOD Management Information Systems (MIS) are improved. The Public Accounts Committee and the National Audit Office (NAO) have commented on deficiencies of MOD MIS, and operation of the Defence Research Agency as a trading fund was delayed because the appropriate financial systems were not in place.

Under Treasury projections, not only is the defence budget going to be badly squeezed over the next few years but, on my projections, the worst of the squeeze will fall on the equipment budget, which by 1995 will be 40 per cent lower in real terms than it was a decade earlier. However, my rather optimistic assumptions imply that the budget could be back into balance by the end of the century. This would require real spending to stabilise at around 3 per cent of GDP, and the armed forces to be cut to 200,000, leaving equipment taking 40 per cent of a £20bn budget. Once more, it should be emphasised that these numbers should be regarded as providing a framework for thinking about the possibilities rather than firm forecasts. Things could be very different: security crises could require the UK to put a much higher priority on defence; economic crises could require even deeper cuts.

Policy, Planning and Programme

A defence policy geared to deterrence of the Soviet Union suggested certain rôles: nuclear deterrence, naval forces in the North Atlantic, ground and air forces on the central front, and defence of the home base. These rôles then provided a framework for the programme of forces and equipment that needed to be provided. These forces and equipment, although designed to meet a Soviet threat, were sufficiently flexible to be used in other theatres such as the Falklands and the Gulf. While precise specification of the programme was neither easy nor uncontroversial, it was a lot more straightforward before 1989 than it is now. With one important exception, it is now difficult to specify a definite threat that needs to be deterred or defended against. Thus the new rôles are necessarily vague: protection of the UK, insurance against any major external threat, and promoting the UK's wider security interests.

The exception, the one definite threat the UK faces, is internal: the continuing war in Northern Ireland. In the absence of political developments, which seem unlikely, any defence plan must make a commitment, primarily of the Army, to provide forces for Northern Ireland. The Ministry of Defence claims that, even with the forces envisaged in Options for Change, this commitment can be met. This claim has met with some scepticism and there remains considerable concern about the pressures that will be put on the Army and the Marines in the infantry role.

Forces may well need to be used in a number of other theatres, but such uses seem either less likely or more discretionary. For insurance purposes, it makes sense to maintain, in conjunction with our NATO allies, some military capability against the resurgence of a threat from the former Soviet Union. However, it seems unlikely that any of the successor states could mobilise the political or economic resources to mount a serious threat in the next decade. Other large areas of the world are actually or potentially unstable, including the former Warsaw Pact area, the Balkans, the Middle East and North Africa. British military forces will probably continue to be used as part of discretionary contributions to multilateral peacekeeping or peacemaking efforts in such areas. UK governments might also wish to deploy military forces to deal with problems associated with residual colonial responsibilities, such as the Falklands, Gibraltar and Hong Kong, were suitable forces available. Maintaining suitable forces for all these eventualities would be expensive.

Again with the exception of Northern Ireland, these general considerations provide very little guidance on the structure of the programme. The Autumn Statement says that the government's 'strategy is based on the ability to adapt to change both internationally and in NATO, the maintenance of force structures with the flexibility and mobility to respond to new circumstances, and the continuing pursuit of value for money'. The difficulty is that flexibility and mobility, particularly strategic mobility, are very expensive characteristics. Flexibility and mobility could be provided in the context of a common European defence programme, and this is discussed in Fontanel and Smith (1991), but at present there is little political prospect of such a programme. It would probably require a major security crisis to generate the political momentum needed for such a programme.

In these circumstances, the most important determinant of the programme is likely to be inertia, given that well-established projects and interests can mobilise great political support and the budget will be too tightly constrained to allow many new initiatives. Historical precedents suggest that change in direction is unlikely to result from a process of planned adjustment; instead it will be the product of reactive response to financial pressures and new security challenges. The major danger is that the projects which have the most powerful constituency will be the highly visible prestige projects: the campaign for EFA is an example. The danger is that these large projects will crowd out the smaller, less visible expenditures, whose contribution to military capability is crucial. This would repeat the mistake made so often in the past: maintaining the appearance at the expense of the substance. Platforms without the spares, facilities or weapon systems needed to make them effective and cuts in training, maintenance and munitions will all combine to produce a real military capability which is only a fraction of the nominal battle order.

Informed debate of the programme would be made much easier if more of the Long Term Costings were in the public domain, through an expansion of the Major Projects Statement. There are obvious problems: the MOD would need to emphasise the tentative nature of the plans; specific numbers for uncontracted projects would weaken their bargaining position with industry; and a few figures really are commercially sensitive. But even allowing for these problems, much more information could be provided. It is striking that most of the information on the possible cost of EFA has come from German rather than UK sources. The 1992 Statement on Defence Estimates contains an extensive shopping list of conventional and nuclear equipment for the 'smaller but better' forces planned, but there is little indication of how affordable the projects are. The affordability problem would get worse if a new objective, such as ballistic missile defence, were to be given high priority. Balancing the Long Term

Costings will be made even more difficult by cost escalation, which has certainly not been abolished despite the various initiatives in procurement, as shown by the NAO (1992a). The balancing act may be eased if the initiatives in reliability and maintainability and Technology Demonstrator Programmes bear fruit, but these are exactly the sort of initiatives which may well be cancelled to fit the prestige projects into the programme.

Implications for the Economy and Industry

The macro-economic implications of reductions in the defence budget of the size discussed above are very small and likely to be positive, as the money saved for defence is used elsewhere. This could reduce taxation, with a consequent boost to private spending; cut the deficit, reducing pressure on interest rates; or allow other forms of government expenditure, which would have positive multiplier effects. The balance of the evidence is that reduced military spending with appropriate compensating policies will reduce unemployment and increase GDP slightly.[3] Jobs will be lost in the arms industry and armed forces, but created elsewhere, employing those currently unemployed. Of course, the fact that the net effect on employment is positive is no consolation to those who lose their jobs at a time of generally high and rising unemployment. For while the macro-economic effects may be small and positive, the micro-economic effects on particular firms and localities are large and negative.

The defence industry is already suffering badly and there have been repeated calls for government action to help it. While there is a strong case for regional and industrial policies to help localities develop new employment opportunities and to make use of the skills released by the defence industry, it would be a mistake to target government policies on defence firms. In particular, governments should avoid the siren songs for two widely advocated measures: using government money to subsidise the conversion or diversification of the defence firms; and shaping procurement policy in the light of industrial consequences. Below, the state of the industry and the policy issues are examined in more detail.[4]

The defence industry's difficulties predate the fall of the Berlin Wall. Defence spending in the US and the UK peaked in the middle 1980s, as did world arms exports, though UK firms benefited from the Saudi Al Yamamah contract. The immediate response of most arms firms to the subsequent down-turn from the mid-1980s was to do nothing. At the time this was not self-evidently wrong. Defence is a volatile market and the optimal response to a transitory down-turn, such as the earlier period of detente, is to maintain capacity to provide an option on the next up-turn. However, over the next few years there was a belated recognition that the down-turn was permanent, and there was a surge of acquisitions and divestments in the late 1980s as the market was consolidated.

Some firms attempted to diversify, but in general they were not successful.[5] Diversification is inherently difficult; those other 'merchants of death', the tobacco firms, failed repeatedly despite their huge cash flows. The defence companies' closest markets, such as civil aerospace, shipbuilding and electronics, were suffering concurrent difficulties of their own, making expansion there unattractive. But above all, the strong defence culture of these firms was a major obstacle to commercial success.[6]

The main argument against the use of government finance to promote conversion by defence firms, such as the Defence Diversification Agency proposed by Labour and the Liberal Democrats, is the repeated failure of such attempts. As these companies recognise, their defence divisions have cultivated a culture which is optimised to the very specific demands of the military market and this culture inhibits adaptation to the very different demands of the commercial market. When you have put a lot of effort into learning how to do one thing really well, it is very difficult to switch to doing something completely different. Such a switch is hard enough for individuals; it is an order of magnitude more difficult for organisations, where procedures and social interactions reinforce the old attitudes, expectations and behaviour patterns. Individuals are much more likely to adjust if they move to a new, more commercial environment than if they stay with their old teams in their old plants. Subsidies for conversion can easily be an expensive way to preserve a culture that inhibits commercial success.

The slow response to the initial fall in demand, the failures of diversification, improvements in efficiency in response to government procurement initiatives and the end of the Cold War all left the industry with massive excess capacity. This excess capacity had to be rapidly reduced at a time of rising unemployment. The trade unions estimate that there were over 100,000 redundancies between 1990 and 1992 (MSF 1992), though the net loss of jobs is probably rather lower. However, current capacity is still substantially larger than can be justified by likely future demand for domestic procurement and arms exports. Furthermore, the economic forces to which the industry is subject are producing a new international division of labour. The industry is starting to be restructured on a global level by a series of cross-border mergers, acquisitions and joint ventures. What the industry will look like in the year 2000 is difficult to predict, but the global defence industrial structure will certainly shape British defence choices.

In these circumstances, it is natural to ask whether the MOD should try to shape the industry. Its current policy is not to have an industrial policy, but merely to choose the weapons that represent the best value for money for the armed forces. Although they have not always followed this policy, it seems to be the right one for a number of reasons. First, buying weapons is an inherently difficult task, involving complex scientific, military and commercial judgements. Further complicating it with an industrial policy dimension is like trying to hit two targets with a single missile – a recipe for disaster. It is noticeable that most of the disasters of British defence procurement (such as Torpedoes, Nimrod, the Harland and Wolff Auxiliary Oiler Replenishment vessel) were driven by concern for industrial consequences.

Secondly, the expertise of the MOD lies in military rather than economic planning, and there is no reason to expect it to have the experience and skills required to develop a coherent industrial policy.[7] At a minimum, effective industrial policies must work with, rather than against, the grain of market forces. It would require great skill on the part of the MOD to identify the current direction of market forces in the defence industry and design a policy that would reinforce them. Thirdly, an industrial policy is likely to involve a degree of protection, which will reduce the incentive for firms to improve efficiency and competition. Finally, accepting an industrial policy rôle is likely to leave the MOD vulnerable to lobbying by vested interests which, given the secrecy surrounding the decisions, could easily 'capture' the industrial policy. Thus an industrial policy risks turning the MOD into a mouthpiece for producer interests at the expense of the consumers, the armed forces, leaving it a military equivalent of the Ministry of Agriculture.

It is almost inevitable that, despite a declaratory policy of non-intervention, actual policy will continue to be shaped by industrial consequences, particularly in politically sensitive constituencies. Nonetheless, maintenance of the declaratory policy may keep the procurement process a little more honest in this respect than it would otherwise have been. There is one, not improbable, case where it would be extremely difficult to maintain a policy of non-intervention. Cases like Rolls Royce in the early 1970s and Westland in the late 1980s indicate that even non-interventionist governments find it difficult to maintain a hands-off attitude when a major defence contractor gets into severe financial difficulties. A private sector solution, if it were possible, would almost certainly require government support in the form of firm commitments to orders, financial guarantees, or subsidies to enable recapitalisation of the company prior to acquisition. One can imagine all sorts of potential political problems, particularly if the choice were between nationalisation and acquisition by a foreign (possibly state-owned) defence contractor.

There is a final way that the MOD can, and does, help industry; that is through export promotion. It does this by concern with export prospects in procurement (though not, it claims, at the expense of value for money for the armed forces); through the efforts of the Defence Export Sales Organisation; and through the support that ministers and the armed forces can provide in marketing. The MOD would argue that, subject to appropriate national and international controls, arms exports help industry and the British economy, support British foreign policy interests, and reduce the unit costs of weapons to the British armed forces. The political and security aspects of the international arms trade have always been highly-charged topics of much dispute, but the economic aspects seem often taken for granted.

While there is wide disagreement about the moral or military implications of exporting arms, there seems less disagreement about the economic implications: that it makes money for Britain. However, it is very difficult to know whether this is true. Certainly, the firms concerned expect to make money from it – they would not do it otherwise – but the position for the country as a whole is much less clear-cut.[8] The difficulty is that the complexity of arms sales and the potential for hidden government subsidies through various routes (development subsidies, export credit guarantees) make it impossible, from public sources, to judge the economic return to the country from arms exports. A serious Treasury or NAO analysis of the real economic return from arms exporting would be a valuable input into the debate.

Conclusion

Given the reputation of economics as the dismal science, it is worth starting with the good news. The threat to the UK is much less; the reductions in military spending should have positive effects on the rest of the economy; efficiency improvements in the MOD seem to be bearing fruit, in that defence prices are rising less quickly than other prices, and it is possible to project a budget and programme which are in balance by the end of the century. The bad news is that the projection is very sensitive to the assumptions and, in any event, defence faces a rather rough ride between now and the end of the century. The equipment budget will be badly squeezed even on official assumptions, and these may be over-optimistic. Given the strong commitment to a number of expensive prestige projects, there are likely to be damaging reductions in spending on items which are essential to the maintenance of military capability. The defence industry will continue to suffer real difficulties and will become increasingly international. The government could well face very difficult political choices in the event of a major contractor running into real financial difficulties.

The removal of the Soviet threat has created a range of new uncertainties and the decade ahead seems likely to be a time of turmoil in the budget, in the defence industry and in the security environment, as each adjust to the new international order or disorder. Defence planning to cope with such turmoil is likely to be incredibly difficult. The planning process may be improved, though probably not made easier, by a more informed discussion, and this Chapter has emphasised the ways in which the information available to outside commentators could be improved. These might include a breakdown of the projected budget by category, a more informative major project statement, and some information on the economic return on arms exports.

Appendix

Measuring the defence budget and technical notes for Table 1

Public expenditure figures can be somewhat confusing and defence budgets are no exception. The main figures are given in *Defence Statistics* (1992), which replaces Volume 2 of the *Statement on the Defence Estimates*. There are two main definitions, the 'Defence Budget', which is the relevant Public Expenditure category used throughout this Chapter, and 'Defence Expenditure', which is the definition used by NATO and the National Accounts. The difference is not large and Table 1.1 of *Defence Statistics* reconciles the two numbers. The Defence Budget figures in *Defence Statistics* are either 'Estimates', (what was voted by Parliament in advance), or 'Out-turns', (what was actually spent). In some years, Supplementary Estimates are presented to Parliament, as in 1991–92, to pay for the Gulf War. Some tables in *Defence Statistics* (1992) use the original Supply Estimates, others Supplementary Estimates.

In 1991–92, the contributions to the Gulf War from allies have also to be subtracted to give the Defence Budget as presented in the Autumn Statement. A further complication is that in 1992, the treatment of pensions was changed. Previously, the defence budget had included the actual value of pensions paid to retired members of the armed forces in any year. From 1993, the budget will be charged the accrued superannuation liabilities of existing employees, which is how pensions are normally treated by private firms. Since the pension contributions for existing employees, military and civilian, will be substantially less than the payments to retired members of the armed forces, this is a significant saving to the defence budget.

The defence budget can be measured at current prices (in nominal terms) or constant prices (in real terms, i.e. having removed the effect of inflation). Since there are a number of different price indices, there are a number of different ways that the correction for inflation can be made. All the calculations in this Chapter use the GDP deflator, which is the best indicator of the general level of costs in the whole economy, and is the index that the government uses in its public expenditure planning. *Defence Statistics* also includes a constant price measure of the defence budget calculated using a defence specific price index. The difference in the rates of inflation of the GDP deflator and the defence price index is known as the relative price effect. Traditionally, defence prices grew rather faster than other prices, but in the last couple of years they have grown slightly more slowly than other prices. This reduction of the relative price effect may reflect government efforts to increase efficiency.

In Table 1, the first line of figures gives the rate of growth of real GDP, calculated from the *Autumn Statement* up to 1995–96. Thereafter GDP is assumed to grow at 2.5 per cent, which is slightly more optimistic than the usual estimate of the underlying growth rate of 2.25 per cent. The second line gives the rate of inflation as measured by the GDP deflator from the *Autumn Statement*. The third line gives defence as a share of GDP.

The defence budget is measured in 1991–92 prices and is taken from the *Autumn Statement* until 1995–96 and calculated from my assumptions about GDP growth and the share thereafter. Personnel costs are obtained as the product of the numbers and the average costs (total payments divided by number employed). It is assumed that average real cost of a service or civilian employee grows at the same rate as the economy after 1992–93. Pensions are assumed to be 21 per cent of the armed forces pay-bill plus 12 per cent of the civil service pay-bill. This is rather lower than the figures in the *Autumn Statement*, p.45. My figures for spending on the armed forces seem to be very close to those assumed by MOD over the period, going by the implications of the assumed pensions payments over the 1992–95 period in the *Autumn Statement*, p.46. Other costs are assumed to be 21 per cent of the budget. Equipment spending is the budget less personnel and other costs.

Notes

1. This forecast for the share is broadly in line with the projections that would come from the econometric model described in Smith (1989).
2. 1991–92 was exceptional because of the cost of the Gulf War, which is included in the equipment spending but is offset in the defence budget by contributions of £1.5bn from other members of the coalition.
3. Smith (1992) discusses the economic effects in more detail; Dunne & Smith (1990) examines the association between military expenditure and unemployment using a century of UK and US data and post-war data for 14 OECD countries; and Barker, Dunne & Smith (1991) conducts econometric simulations of the effect of reduced military spending on the UK.
4. This discussion draws on Smith (1990) which examines the technical issues of procurement and market structure, Dunne & Smith (1992) which examines the industrial policy issues and Smith & Smith (1992) which considers the Corporate Strategies of the individual defence firms.
5. The general business lesson was drawn by William Anders, Chairman of the US defence contractor General Dynamics, who in 1991 dismissed the benefits of diversification as illusory, a waste of management time and shareholder funds because the failure rate was unacceptably high. US corporate strategies in the defence industry are reviewed in Lundquist (1992).
6. This is widely recognised by the companies themselves; Smith & Smith (1992) provide evidence. As a result, when these companies try to diversify by organic growth, they tend to do it by establishing commercial plants and divisions separate from the defence establishments. Racal's establishment of Vodaphone is an example. Cases where firms convert defence plants, such as Marconi's manufacture of satellite dishes, are much rarer.
7. Kuttner (1991) gives a number of examples of how the US Department of Defense misunderstood the dynamics of evolving technologies and markets.
8. The argument that the economic return to arms exporting may be negative is set out at more length in ORG (1992) which also includes a variety of responses.

References

Autumn Statement (1992), HM Treasury, Cm 2096, HMSO.
Barker T, J P Dunne & R Smith 'Measuring the Peace Dividend in the UK', *Journal of Peace Research* 28, (1991) pp.345–358.
Defence Statistics (1992) HMSO.
Dunne J Paul and Ron Smith 'Military expenditure and unemployment in the OECD', *Defence Economics* 1, (1990) pp.57–74.
Dunne, J Paul and Ron Smith 'Thatcherism and the UK defence industry', *The Economic Legacy 1979–1992*, ed. Jonathan Michie, (London: Academic Press, 1992), pp.91–111.
Fontanel, Jacques and Ron Smith (1991) 'A European Defence Union', *Economic Policy* 13, pp.393–424.
Kuttner, Robert 'How "National Security" hurts National Competitiveness', *Harvard Business Review* Jan–Feb 1991, pp.140–9.

Lundquist, Jerrold T 'Shrinking fast and smart in the defense industry', *Harvard Business Review* Nov–Dec, 1992 pp.74–85.
MSF (1992) *A strategy for aerospace*, Manufacturing Science Finance, Union, London.
NAO (1992a) *The 1991 Statement on Major Defence Projects*, National Audit Office, 121, HMSO.
NAO (1992b) *The Costs and Receipts arising from the Gulf Conflict*, National Audit Office, 299, HMSO.
ORG (1992) *International Control of the Arms Trade*, Current Decisions Report No 8, Oxford Research Group.
Smith, Dan and Ron Smith 'Corporate strategy, corporate culture and conversion: adjustment in the defence industry', *Business Strategy Review* Summer 1992, pp.45–58.
Smith, Ron 'Models of military expenditure', *Journal of Applied Econometrics*, 4, (1989) pp.57–74.
Smith, Ron 'Defence procurement and industrial structure in the UK', *International Journal of Industrial Organisation* 8, (1990) pp.185–205.
Smith, Ron 'The economic effects of the end of the Cold War', *Economic Outlook*, June, (1992) pp.36–41.
SDE (1992) *Statement on the Defence Estimates*, Cm 1981, HMSO.

6
Maintaining Balanced Forces

Philip Towle

If they are to have much influence on international affairs over the next decades, British governments need to build on the more successful aspects of national life. The armed forces together with certain other institutions, such as the BBC, the universities and the city of London, are of world standing. It makes sense for governments to foster these 'centres of excellence'. It also makes sense to foster institutions that can contribute to any reduction in the turmoil which is enveloping many parts of the world. The stability and tension of the Cold War years are being replaced by instability and anarchy. With wars in Bosnia, the Caucasus, Somalia, Angola and elsewhere, the 1990s are clearly not going to be the time to harbour illusions about 'peace dividends', let alone chiliastic notions of the end of history and the victory of democracy; the task of the government is rather to shape the armed forces so that they can make the best possible contribution to international order.

Many argue that these tasks cannot be fulfilled unless the armed forces become more highly specialised. They claim that, with an economy only two thirds the size of its German equivalent and one third the size of the Japanese, Britain must abandon its pretensions to great power status. It cannot maintain its current range of defence capabilities from amphibious warfare vessels to ballistic missile submarines and from Tornado bombers to armoured regiments. Such arguments are strengthened by the rise in the cost of defence equipment and trained manpower and by demographic changes in Britain itself. The counter-arguments set out below are that Britain has a vital interest in reducing international disorder and can afford to make a contribution towards doing so. Furthermore, while some reductions in defence spending may be justified, excessive defence specialisation would dramatically limit the number of circumstances in which the armed forces could be used effectively.

The International Scene

Within two years of the end of any great war the general factors which will dominate the international politics of the next decades are already evident. By 1920 it was already clear that the following years would be overshadowed by the tension between the French desire to maintain the status quo in Europe and the determination of the Germans to undo their defeat and humiliation. By 1947 it was apparent that, even if it did not lead to outright conflict, the Cold War confrontation between the United States and Britain on one side and the Soviet Union on the other would determine the politics of the next decades. So today, some years after the victory of the West in the Cold War, the general outline of the factors which will determine international relations over the next decades are visible.

Western Europe will be surrounded by two great arcs of instability. To the east, in the former Communist territories, weak governments, restless minorities and boundary disputes will lead to coups and to civil and inter-state wars. To the south, demographic and religious problems will have the same effect in the Middle East and North Africa. To the west, the United States will increasingly concentrate on dealing with problems within its own borders and in the North American Free Trade Area (NAFTA). The number of its troops based in Europe will be savagely reduced and many US bases in Britain and elsewhere will be shut down. On the other side of the world Japan, China and Korea will have to find a *modus vivendi* as their rapidly growing power increases the tensions between them.

The problems which dominated foreign policy and defence planning over the last 45 years have thus largely disappeared. Even if a successful fascist or military coup takes place in Russia, it would take some time for the new government to restore order and end the anarchy which has gradually been spreading in that unfortunate country. Indeed such a coup might not lead to order but to civil war on the lines of the conflict in Spain in the 1930s, with the rump of the legitimate government struggling against the majority of the armed forces. The part which chemical and nuclear weapons might play in such a struggle is difficult to discern, though the possibility of their use emphasises the importance of Russian developments for the rest of the world. Even if a right-wing coup were successful in Russia, a renewed military build-up there would only reduce outside investment and accentuate the country's economic problems. Destabilising and threatening as such a development would be, Western countries are more likely to be faced with problems arising from the collapse of states and the consequent civil wars or from the sort of border conflict which produced the Iran-Iraq War and the Iraqi attack on Kuwait.

Alliances and Crises

The crises which have already occurred in the post-Cold War world – in Kuwait, in Kurdistan, in Cambodia, in Bosnia – demonstrate that in each case the various Western countries will have very different views about the utility of sending their forces to the region. Furthermore it is often impossible to tell until the outbreak of a crisis how a nation may react. Before the Korean War powerful elements in both the American and British governments were against becoming involved in any war on the peninsula. Before the Argentinians captured the Falkland Islands in 1982 the Foreign Office had long been trying to find a way of meeting Argentine claims on the island whilst simultaneously satisfying the islanders. It was only when parliament debated the issue immediately after the invasion that the government realised it would have to take military action. If it is difficult to predict how the British public and parliament will react in a crisis, it is considerably more difficult to say how foreign peoples will behave.

Each coalition which deploys troops will thus be ad hoc. In other words the North Atlantic Treaty Organisation was united by a simple foreign policy – to oppose a Soviet attack – and defence policy followed from that. It will be very difficult to recreate such an agreed foreign policy over the next decades. Accordingly, if military arrangements, such as NATO, continue for some time it will be because of the advantages of commonality in equipment and training rather than because they have an agreed foreign policy and could automatically expect to operate together in actual crises. Nor is it likely that purely European security arrangements will be any more tightly drawn than NATO's. The prospect of a united Europe with a common foreign and defence policy remains remote.

It follows from this that on occasions when the British government and people believe that the use of force is appropriate to alleviate a crisis, they will not be able to assume that their actions will be supported by the military activities of another state even if such a state is closely tied to Britain by economic and other interests. Thus, in the Kuwaiti case, some Western states such as Italy, France, Britain and the United States joined in its liberation. Others were so hostile to military action that they refused to supply the ammunition which the British forces needed. In the case of Bosnia, the US administration under President Bush argued in 1991 and 1992 that the problem was one for the Europeans to solve; Germany maintained that its constitution prevented it from sending forces and Britain reluctantly moved towards deploying troops to help with the distribution of humanitarian aid for the Bosnian Moslems but was reluctant to use force against Serbia.

This fracturing of the Western Alliance greatly accentuates the problems of defence planners. So does the unpredictability of the new world order. Even during the Cold War, events outside Europe repeatedly caught British and other concerned governments by surprise and such problems are likely to increase. Not one of the major conventional military operations in which Britain has been involved since 1945 was predicted by the intelligence agencies. The Korean War of June 1950, the Argentine attack on the Falklands in April 1982 and the Iraqi attack on Kuwait in August 1990 were all equally unexpected. But, before these crises broke, the Ministry of Defence was generally able to argue its case against the Treasury's demands for economies by pointing to the magnitude of the Soviet threat. Then, when lesser crises suddenly occurred in Korea, the Falklands and Kuwait, the defence forces were large enough to cope with the threat. It is more difficult today to justify the size of the armed forces in terms of a specific threat but no less important for all that.

Defence Spending and the Economy

Arguments for maintaining a substantial defence capability are also often criticised on the erroneous grounds that Britain's lacklustre industrial performance since 1945 has been due to excess defence spending. According to this argument, Japan and Germany have been successful industrially because their defence spending was kept artificially low. However, Germany and Japan were equally successful industrially in the 1930s when their defence spending was taking a much greater share of their gross national product than was the case in Britain. According to Professor Paul Kennedy's figures, Germany spent the equivalent of US$3,298 million on defence in 1937, Britain 1,245 million and Japan 940 million.[1] This amounted to 5.7 per cent of the British GNP, 23.5 per cent of the German and 28.2 per cent of the Japanese. Similarly in the post-war world there is no correlation between defence spending and industrial growth.

PERCENTAGE OF GROSS NATIONAL PRODUCT SPEND ON DEFENCE

	1975	1978	1985	1991
Britain	4.9	4.7	5.2	4.2
France	3.9	3.3	4	2.8
Germany	3.7	3.4	3.2	1.9
S. Korea	5.1	5.6	5.1	3.8
Taiwan	9.3	7.7	6.6	5.4

(Source: IISS *Military Balance* 1979–1980, pp.94–5 and 1992–1993, pp.220–221).

Those who wish to distort the figures to argue the case for military reductions emphasise the comparison between British economic growth rates and German or French. A wider comparison with countries with far higher economic growth rates than either Germany or France, such as South Korea and Taiwan, shows the bogus nature of this sort of argument. Industrial growth is determined by much deeper cultural, political, educational and institutional factors than such superficial arguments allow. Yet we are in danger of allowing false analogies to push the government into making reductions in defence spending.

The other argument which is sometimes deployed against defence spending is that military force has been largely replaced by economic strength as an arm of international power. Recent history shows this is equally simplistic. Certainly there are severe legal and other restraints on the use of conventional military power. However, economic power is also limited, though in different ways. Economic sanctions failed to push the Soviets out of Afghanistan; they did not bring Saddam Hussein to heel and they did not discourage the Serbian people from voting for President Milosevic in the December 1992 elections. Although economic sanctions probably did encourage Ian Smith to bring the Rhodesian rebellion to an end and the South African government to negotiate with the African National Congress, in both cases they were reinforced by military threats. Moreover there are very few cases where overt economic sanctions have forced a dictatorial government to change its policy. Nor is this very surprising, since they fall on the poor and weak, not those in power. Economic warfare is often one of the most ineffective and indiscriminate types of power. In no sense can it be described as having fully replaced the use of armed force.

Defence Specialisation

If reductions in defence spending are, nevertheless, demanded, one solution would be for the United Kingdom to specialise in those areas for which its forces have for historic or other reasons shown particular aptitude – SAS operations against terrorists, amphibious operations by Royal Marines and the Parachute Regiment, anti-guerrilla operations etc. Those activities in which other Western armed forces have specialised or shown particular aptitude would then be abandoned. The Germans and other continental nations might be left to specialise in armoured warfare, the Americans in helicopter gunships, the French in nuclear forces and some of the smaller NATO nations in mine-hunting.

The advantages of such specialisation are clear and to some extent it has already taken place. The Americans alone can afford to maintain heavy bombers and large aircraft carriers. But further progress in this direction could, in theory, be made. For example Britain has not produced a competitive tank since the introduction of the Centurion at the end of the Second World War. Most of the other Western armies are equipped with German Leopards. It would make sense for Britain to leave Germany to specialise in that area. Similarly, the French have invested far more resources and effort into the *Force de Frappe* than the British have in their nuclear force. Again it would reduce duplication and save money in the long run if the French force became the only European nuclear capability.

But there are few economic advantages in the short run in specialisation of this sort. In some cases the British armed forces are already committed to certain lines of action by previous decisions. The decision to buy four Trident missile-carrying submarine boats was taken in the early 1980s when the Soviet military threat appeared to be growing. It would be difficult to justify today. Some potential enemies in the Middle East and Eastern Europe might develop nuclear weapons but Trident's destructive power is disproportionate to the likelihood and magnitude of the threat. However it is hard to see how much money would be saved by scrapping the Trident programme at this stage. Similarly the decision has already been taken to buy new tanks for the armoured regiments partly in order to keep a British tank manufacturing capability alive. Thus the opportunity for saving procurement costs by leaving the Germans to specialise in armoured warfare has already been lost.

In other cases certain equipment is so important that armed forces can hardly operate without it. After the wars in Vietnam and the Gulf the US armed forces have by far the greatest experience of employing attack helicopters in battle. They were also the only Western forces to have built up a large stock of chemical weapons. But attack helicopters are becoming so vital and can be employed in so many different environments that the army would be gravely handicapped without them. Corresponding difficulties could arise if the United States became the only country to specialise in protection against chemical and biological weapons. The spread of chemical weapons to ever more countries could leave British forces very exposed if they relied entirely on the United States for protective equipment. Similarly the Royal Navy would be severely limited in inshore operations if it abandoned all attempts to operate mine-hunters.

Moreover, as pointed out above, the British government cannot be at all confident that other nations will give support in crises where Britain has a major interest. Of course, some will argue that a degree of dependence on allies is inevitable given Britain's economic weakness, the inter-dependence of the Western economies and the difficulty of predicting the location and nature of the next major crisis. In the Falklands War Britain relied upon the United States' facilities on Ascension Island without which it would have been difficult, if not impossible, for British ships and aircraft to reach the South Atlantic. It relied on US intelligence for information about Argentine activities, and Britain also bought the latest Sidewinder air-to-air missiles for the Harrier aircraft from the United States. Without these it would have been hard for the small Harrier force to cope with the Argentine jets.

Helpful or even vital as some of these contributions were in 1982, British governments may severely circumscribe future actions if they increase the country's dependence on its allies. In particular, governments must expect the United States to concentrate more in the future on repairing its domestic and economic wounds. With 25,000 murders a year, many of them concentrated within the poorer ethnic communities, with the reappearance of race riots and with an increasing budget deficit, the Clinton administration must focus most of its energies on the domestic scene. Other countries are thus under pressure to undertake more of the burden of international policing, but some of the wealthier ones face particular difficulties in responding positively because of their past. Japan's defence effort is constrained by the history of the 1930s and it makes sense for it to concentrate its substantial efforts to enhance international stability on economic aid and support for the United Nations. Germany faces historic enmities in parts of Eastern Europe and will in any case be absorbed during the 1990s in reviving its eastern provinces.

British forces are by contrast welcomed in many parts of the world, partly because of their efficiency, partly because they are familiar and partly because Britain is seen as a declining and therefore unthreatening power. Their reputation for efficiency has been enhanced by numerous recent actions from the capture of the Iranian embassy in London by the SAS, through the Falklands and Gulf Wars to the actions of the Cheshires in Bosnia. Their behaviour towards the civilian population and local government is considered relatively predictable, whereas the behaviour of an army whose size has been suddenly increased may rightly or wrongly be considered more uncertain. Having granted independence to a large part of Africa and Asia, Third World governments consider it unlikely that London will suddenly start to reassert its dominance in such regions. It is logical, therefore, for Britain to respond to some of the requests for military assistance even if that response seems out of proportion to the size of Britain's population and economy.

It is also sensible for Britain to accept payment for some of its military actions. Public attitudes to such payments have long been unnecessarily ambiguous and the press has increased confusion by making references to mercenary actions. In the 19th Century much of the defence of the British Empire was paid for by taxes raised in India and elsewhere. Since 1945 the United States has constantly subsidised Europe's defences. Yet in neither of these cases were British forces described as mercenaries. Nor did the United States show any embarrassment in asking for funds from wealthy countries, such as Japan and Saudi Arabia, for its military actions in the Gulf. Wherever possible this should be the pattern in the future for a country such as Britain with a relatively weak industrial base. There should, for example, be no embarrassment or hesitation in asking for financial support if British forces are to be involved in policing the frontiers of Kuwait or those of other wealthy states. Money raised by the Falklands from fishing licences and, in the future, possibly from oil should be used to subsidise British forces on the islands. Where military support is politically acceptable, there is no difference between providing such assistance in return for payment and supplying educational, cultural or other services.

Interests and Commitments

Britain has an heterogeneous collection of interests and commitments, some formal, some emotional, but many of which are not shared with its European and American allies. European states have, so far, shown little sign of wanting to participate in the struggle against the IRA and Protestant paramilitary groups in Northern Ireland. Indeed many foreign publics harbour the vacuous notion that, if only the British would withdraw, Northern Ireland would be at peace. Recent experiences in Beirut and Bosnia, where sectarian violence led to genocide, may in time temper these views but so far there is little evidence of this. Nor do the European countries have emotional links with former members of the British Empire such as Australia and New Zealand or with smaller states such as Belize or Oman. Britain might well, therefore, find itself committed by the demands of its own public or by its particular economic interests to help friendly countries in the Caribbean, Pacific or the Gulf without assistance from Europe or the United States.

The Shape of the Armed Forces

It follows from all this that Britain needs to be able to retain flexible and efficient armed forces to meet a series of unpredictable contingencies. This will require gradual evolution away from forces equipped primarily to combat the Warsaw Pact towards lighter and more mobile ones. Air- and sea-lift are needed to bring force to bear over long distances. There is a temptation to reduce the Hercules, VC 10 and Tristar fleets and to rely in crises on hiring civil aircraft. But the Hercules can operate into airfields which are inaccessible to most civil aircraft. Air force crews can also take risks which would be unacceptable to civilians. Moreover, tanker aircraft flew some 730 sorties carrying 13,000 tonnes of fuel during the Gulf War, proving particularly valuable for extending the relatively short range of Tornado bombers. On the other hand, if economies have to be made, the four squadrons of Nimrod maritime patrol aircraft might not be replaced when they become obsolete, given the reduced threat from submarines.

The bomber force itself is larger than Britain is likely to require in most conceivable future wars. Only a fraction of the RAF's 228 Tornado GR1 aircraft were used in the Gulf War. However, accidents will gradually reduce the numbers available and it is difficult to see a replacement aircraft being bought until well into the 21st Century. Government figures suggest that the loss rate has been very much less than that for certain older aircraft, such as the Lightning, but six were lost or seriously damaged in 1990 and four were lost the following year, not including those destroyed in the Gulf War.[2] If five aircraft are lost on average each year, the force will be halved over two decades. To reduce losses in conflict, the Tornados will need updating with a stand-off missile so that they will not have to fly directly over well-defended targets such as airfields. If, on the other hand, some ground- or sea-based missile system is to be used for attacking fixed targets, the arguments against maintaining a Tornado bomber force of the current size will become much stronger.

Over the next decade the purchase of the Eurofighter 2000 aircraft will give the RAF a much greater ability to defend itself against the advanced fighters which are spreading across the world. On the other hand, large-scale purchases will add to the numbers of aircraft which the RAF has in store. The International Institute for Strategic Studies lists 323 of these. Some 76 are Tornados which will be used to replace those lost in service; but there are also 71 Jaguars, 60 Harriers and 28 Buccaneers. Procurement of the Eurofighter will add to the pressure to find buyers for these aircraft at the same time as competition for defence markets and the political sensitiveness of such sales is increasing.

The Royal Navy needs to prepare not for attacking large numbers of Soviet submarines under the North Sea and Atlantic but for amphibious operations in distant waters. Because of their mobility, the Royal Marines are particularly likely to be useful in future crises where the rapid deployment of a small force can obviate the need for much larger ones at a later stage. It is hard to believe that the Iraqis would have invaded Kuwait in 1990 if the Emirate had been reinforced beforehand by a Royal Marine Commando. Maintenance of an effective amphibious capability will mean replacing the two Fearless Class ships which were laid down in 1962. Compensatory cuts will be needed in other areas, one of them being the submarine force which was built up to combat the Soviet threat. Submarines may still present a problem as they spread to ever more countries which may want to interdict trade, but the size of the menace will be very much less than the Soviet threat in the 1980s. Given the speed and secrecy with which nuclear submarines can be deployed to distant waters, it would be sensible for Britain still to maintain a capability in this area, albeit a smaller one. It was the government's ability to deploy Conqueror to the South Atlantic which led to the destruction of the Argentine cruiser *Belgrano* in 1982 and thus greatly reduced the threat to the British task force.

Naval writers have long emphasised the stabilising effect which a small naval presence can exert in the Caribbean and elsewhere. Frigates or destroyers can assist in the interdiction of drug-running, the suppression of piracy and in humanitarian relief after hurricanes – all operations which have become more salient since the end of the Cold War. They can also help protect micro-states against mercenaries and terrorists, which such states have come increasingly to fear following attacks on the Maldives and the Seychelles. Against higher level threats the spread of anti-ship missiles to an increasing number of countries will make even highly-sophisticated warships vulnerable to attack. In such circumstances a larger task force including one of three aircraft carriers may be necessary, and even then the Falklands War showed how vulnerable such a task force had become to land-based aircraft and missiles. For Britain to maintain even an exiguous force in the Caribbean, the South Atlantic and the Gulf, as well as in home waters, a fleet not much below the current level of 11 destroyers and 32 frigates will be necessary. A steady flow of the newer Type 23 frigates is also required to compensate for the reduction in the numbers of seamen and officers (as the newer ships need smaller crews).

The Army is no longer planning single-mindedly to fight a massive tank battle in northern Germany and is increasingly being split into small contingents to assist friendly forces across the world. The government's Options for Change plans of July 1991 envisaged the strength of the Army being reduced from 156,000 men to 116,000.[3] It is already clear that these cuts were excessive. That is not to say that all cuts are mistaken; it would have been better to dissolve the 12 armoured regiments and to use the funds released to buy attack helicopters which can operate in a greater variety of terrain. But, as pointed out above, this option has already been foreclosed for the time being.

Finally, it is most unlikely that Britain will still have anything like 23,000 soldiers in Germany at the end of the 1990s. The hostility of the German public to military manoeuvres and to the occupation of many of its heaths by foreign armed forces has steadily increased. The foreign exchange costs are also considerable. The difficulty and cost involved in finding accommodation in Britain for troops withdrawn is obvious but unavoidable.

The fight against international terrorism will continue, and this is an area where Britain's SAS can play a major role. On the other hand, there is a danger that, because of its long experience of anti-guerrilla warfare, the Army may be sucked in to many of the guerrilla and civil wars which are so familiar a part of the international scene. Britain's willingness to take part in other operations in the Gulf, Kurdistan and elsewhere should strengthen its voice when it warns against the dangers of such a course of action. The United States economy never fully recovered from the Vietnam War; the war in Afghanistan helped to destabilise the Soviet Union; the Israeli military and political image has not recovered from the Lebanese imbroglio. Even the wealthiest countries with the strongest industries are strained by involvement in such conflicts. Not the least advantage of maintaining Britain's voice in the councils of the world is to warn against such dangers and the harm to the international community of excessive involvement in unconventional warfare.

That is not to say that Britain should avoid participating in all UN peacekeeping operations. On the contrary these are clearly going to be ever more important, even though the UN is facing increasing criticism for its failure to end the civil wars in Angola, Bosnia and Cambodia. But peacekeeping is only effective in certain limited circumstances, and particularly when the combatants are themselves willing to end the fighting. This needs to be reiterated constantly if the Army is not to be involved in a series of demoralising and futile campaigns.

Conclusion

Britain's defence forces should not be savagely reduced. There is little to be gained in financial terms from abandoning equipment, such as the Trident submarines, which have already largely been paid for. There is also little to be gained from excessive specialisation which will lead us to rely more heavily on allied assistance at a time when policy differences between allies are likely to prevent co-operation during crises. Certainly the training and orientation of the armed forces must change following the end of the Cold War. This means less emphasis on anti-submarine operations, on armoured warfare and on mass attacks by bombers. It means greater stress on amphibious warfare, on peacekeeping and operations outside Europe in general.

Future military operations will probably resemble the Falklands and Gulf Wars or the peacekeeping operations in Bosnia and Somalia, rather than a massive conflict in Central Europe. But the armed forces have repeatedly proved that they can take on 'out-of-area' operations of these types. Comparison between amphibious operations in the Falklands War with previous operations at the Dardanelles in 1915 and at Suez in 1956 suggests that British forces are now better trained and more professional than they have ever been. The government needs to emphasise such centres of excellence in British life in order to maximise our international influence.

It also needs to rebut more robustly the notion that defence spending has been responsible for the country's economic ills since 1945. There is no correlation between defence expenditure and economic growth. Britain's economic and industrial problems should certainly be addressed, but not at the expense of existing 'centres of excellence'.

Notes

1. Paul Kennedy, *The Rise and Fall of the Great Powers*, (London and Sydney: Unwin Hyman, 1988), pp.296 and 332.
2. Statement on Defence Estimates 1991, Volume 2, Cm 1559–II, pp.46–7 and Defence Statistics, 1992 Edition, p.57.
3. Statement on Defence Estimates 1991, Volume 1, Cm 1559–I, p.42.

7
Britain and Alliance Burden-Sharing

Malcolm Chalmers

Since World War Two, the defence provision of West European states has increasingly taken on the character of an international public good. With military conflict between members of the Western security community assumed to be unthinkable, defence effort has increasingly come to be seen as a contribution to NATO's collective defences. The run-down of European imperial possessions in the 1950s and 1960s has further reduced the uniquely national character of West European states' defence objectives.

A number of studies have suggested ways in which the costs of providing collective defence might be allocated in the absence of a central defence budget. It has been predicted, for example, that states' contributions will be proportional to both their total resources and their stakes in the provision of the collective defence. Yet, while such an approach helps explain the initial allocation of military tasks made in the 1950s, a full explanation also needs to take into account

TABLE 1 DEFENCE BURDEN SHARING IN NATO's
FIVE BIGGEST SPENDERS
(proportion of GNP devoted to defence in West Germany = 1.00)

	1965	1970	1975	1980	1985	1990	1991
Italy	0.77	0.82	0.69	0.73	0.81	0.75	0.75
W. Germany	1.00	1.00	1.00	1.00	1.00	1.00	1.00
France	1.21	1.27	1.06	1.21	1.28	1.29	1.25
UK	1.37	1.45	1.36	1.55	1.63	1.43	1.54
US	1.77	2.42	1.64	1.70	2.19	2.04	1.96

Sources: *NATO Review*, *SIPRI Yearbook*, various years.

the way in which NATO's burden-sharing regime imposed high costs on those seeking to alter this initial allocation.[1] Without such an analysis it is difficult fully to explain the remarkable degree of stability in the levels of defence burden in NATO's five largest members, relative to each other, for the last three decades. (*See Table 1*.)

An explanation of why the UK now spends 40–50 per cent more of its national income on defence than its European allies, therefore, is to be found more in the early 1950s than in the early 1990s. During this earlier period the UK was, albeit in retrospect only temporarily, Western Europe's leading power. Relatively less damaged from the war, its industries had yet to feel the full effects of German and Japanese reconstruction. Victory in war had been rewarded by a seat at the top table at Potsdam, in the United Nations, and in NATO. Britain was on track to become the world's third nuclear power. Defence spending was maintained at levels unprecedented for peacetime. Military withdrawal from empire was slow, and considerable financial and technological resources were devoted to the creation of Britain's strategic nuclear force.

Perhaps of greatest long-term significance, it was Britain's temporary strength that led Prime Minister Eden in 1954 to agree to the permanent stationing of four divisions and a tactical air force in Germany. This commitment, designed to provide a means of allowing German integration into NATO after the collapse of the European Defence Community project, came to consume an increasing proportion of UK defence resources. Yet, whenever the possibility of reducing the level of this commitment was discussed, the feared 'domino effect' on other countries' contributions was such that the UK had little alternative but to agree to maintain its commitment at then existing levels.

The legacy of the 1950s, therefore, was that Britain retained a broader range of military commitments than any other of its European allies. Most of the army's budget was devoted to supporting the deployment in Germany, as was a large part of the RAF's. The Royal Navy maintained Western Europe's largest conventional maritime force, as well as one of only two strategic submarine (SSBN) forces. And half of all government research and development spending was devoted to retaining a domestic capability to produce modern weapons systems for this wide range of rôles. In order to fund these commitments, the defence budget was consistently given a higher priority than in either France or Germany. By comparison, UK public spending in other areas – notably health and investment – tended to be relatively low by the standards of its neighbours. (*See Table 2*.)

TABLE 2   GOVERNMENT SPENDING AS % OF GDP

	Britain 1981–90	W Germany 1980–89	France 1983–89
Defence	4.7	2.8	3.3
Law and order	1.8	1.7	1.0
Education	5.1	4.6(6.5)	5.5(6.2)
Health	5.0	6.3	8.3
Investment	1.9	2.5	3.1
TOTAL	18.5	17.9(19.8)	21.2(21.9)

Source: The Economist, 28 November 1992, p.35. Figures in brackets include private spending on compulsory apprenticeship schemes.

By early 1990, however, it became clear that the Soviet Union was relinquishing control of Eastern Europe. In response, the UK government conducted an internal defence review, the results of which were announced to Parliament in July 1990 under the title Options for Change. Although often criticised as being either too cautious or too draconian, 'Options' was in fact a relatively coherent response to the circumstances of the time, and will in retrospect be seen as Britain's first post-Cold War defence review. As a direct consequence, the UK's commitment under the Brussels Treaty was amended, and the size of air and ground forces in Germany halved. The Navy was to lose one fifth of its frigates and destroyers, together with 40 per cent of its attack submarines. Overall, personnel numbers – military and civilian – were to be reduced by 20 per cent. Throughout the UK and Germany, a large-scale process of rationalisation and base closure got under way. And, as a direct consequence of these force reductions, the government planned to make an 11 per cent reduction in real defence expenditure (excluding Gulf War spending) between 1990–91 and 1995–6.[2] (*See Table 3.*) This will reduce defence spending as a proportion of GNP to around 3.2 per cent.[3]

By 1995, the savings made possible by the 'Options for Change' review will have been realised. Yet this is unlikely to prevent continuing Treasury demands for economies, given the government's commitment to reducing the proportion of national income consumed by the state. Pressure is therefore likely to build up for a fresh look at Britain's military commitments as a means of generating further savings after that date. As the House of Commons Defence Committee argued in late 1992:

The time has now indeed come to stand back and take stock of the totality of the proposals for British Armed Forces for the next decade, in the light of recent changes in the strategic environment, and of pressures on the defence budget.[4]

Most of all such a review is required because so much has changed since the Options for Change proposals were drawn up. In early 1990 it was already possible to assume that the threat of a short-warning attack on NATO in central Europe had disappeared. Yet, at least for the purposes of defence planning, it was still prudent to assume that the Soviet Union would continue to exist as a unified Communist state, and that it would continue to possess substantial forces capable of threatening the British Isles and surrounding waters.[5]

TABLE 3   ANNUAL UK DEFENCE BUDGETS 1990–2000

	Spending (£b, 1991/2 prices)	Change from previous year
Out-turn		
1989/90	24.0	
1990/91	23.3	−2.9%
1991/92	23.0	−1.3%
Estimated Out-turn		
1992/93	22.8	−0.9%
Plans		
1993/94	22.0	−3.5%
1994/95	21.5	−2.3%
1995/96	20.4	−5.1%

Source: *Autumn Statement 1992.*

Such planning assumptions appear increasingly inappropriate. The Soviet Union no longer exists, and one now has to stretch the borders of credibility very far to give much credence to the possibility of a Russian conventional attack on Western Europe. While Russia is in such political turmoil, NATO needs to maintain forces capable of deterring the threat a revival of militarism in Russia might conceivably pose. Given the deep cuts in Russian military budgets already announced, however, the NATO forces required for this rôle can be much smaller than before, and can be kept at lower average levels of readiness.

Given the remote possibility of a renewed Russian threat, the UK is now more secure from attack than at any time in its history. Since the origins of the modern state system, the central strategic concern of England's, and then Britain's, rulers has been to prevent the domination of continental Europe by a single hostile power or coalition. Whenever such a possibility arose – as it did from Spain, France, Germany and the Soviet Union successively – Britain sought to prevent it by allying itself with those who opposed hegemonic attempts. Most recently, British support for the Western Alliance was motivated by the fear that, without such an alliance, the Soviet Union might itself seek continental dominance.

Now that this threat has disappeared, however, the age of hegemonic ambitions in Europe is drawing to an end. The consolidation of democracy in France and Germany means that the UK can assume that no new military threat to the British Isles will come from Europe. More broadly, the creation of a global 'security community' between North America, Japan and Western Europe means that UK and West European forces are likely to be used only against states, like Iraq, with much more limited resources at their disposal.

As the impact of such assumptions sinks in, most Western powers are reducing their military forces. Soviet withdrawals from central Europe are being matched by sharp reductions in NATO force levels. Canada has announced that it will withdraw all its forces from Europe by 1994. Conscription has been abolished in Belgium, and is being reduced in length in most European countries. In addition to disbanding former NVA units, Germany is to reduce its army from 48 to 28 brigades, of which only seven will be at full strength, and continuing reductions in its defence budget are planned.[6] Italy is reducing army strength by 25 per cent, and its severe fiscal crisis seems likely to force further spending cuts. And France, perhaps Europe's most cautious disarmer, has already reduced its troop presence in Germany to half its previous level.

The United States, NATO's biggest military spender, is also planning comparable reductions. The level of US troops in Europe is now being drawn down at a rate of around 3,000 a month, and it is likely to fall below 150,000 by 1995 (half its previous level). Bush administration plans called for defence spending to fall from 5.5 per cent of national income in 1990 to 3.6 per cent in 1997. Under a Democratic administration, further savings appear likely, with one recent Congressional Budget Office study suggesting a reduction to 3.2 per cent of national income as a possibility.[7]

Defence plans will come under intense security in the years ahead in most Western countries, and the outcome of these processes cannot be predicted with accuracy. What is already clear, however, is that the force reductions planned under Options for Change are being more or less matched by Britain's European allies, and are therefore unlikely to be enough significantly to narrow the gap that now exists between British and European defence burdens. Even more strikingly, if further economies are not made the UK could find itself spending proportionately as much on defence as the US for the first time since the 1940s.

Stability in Burden-sharing

In order to narrow the gap between UK and continental European defence burdens, the government would have to make significant reductions in the *proportion* of capabilities for collective military operations which is provided by the UK. So far there is little indication that it is willing to accept the implications of making such reductions. In part this is because the government believes that it is only by making a substantial contribution to collective defence that it can justify the retention of the privileged positions it holds in NATO and the United Nations.

If Britain does not emerge from recession soon, it is possible that economic pressures will lead to further defence cutbacks, as indeed happened in the late 1960s. On the other hand, it cannot be confidently predicted that continued relative economic decline will lead to retrenchment in external commitments. There is a strong body of opinion that contends that diplomacy and war-fighting are two of the few activities which the UK, for historical reasons, still performs better than most other countries. Compared with other Western countries, the armed forces still enjoy a comparatively high level of popular esteem, and popular resistance to the inevitable casualties that result from military operations appears to have been blunted, at least in comparison with other rich countries, by the almost continuous involvement of British forces in conflict ever since 1945. Last but not least, the British arms industry, although currently undergoing a process of large-scale retrenchment, remains – as a result of the large domestic market – one of the few internationally competitive high-tech sectors in British manufacturing. The more difficult it appears to be for Britain to regain its competitive position in civil markets, therefore, the more some will argue that areas of British comparative advantage should be emphasised.

Moreover a series of specific undertakings made in the last three years demonstrate the government's commitment to maintain a major rôle for all three Services in European and global military arrangements. The Army has been given command of NATO's Rapid Reaction Corps (ARRC), a position likely to be of increasing importance compared with preparations for armoured warfare in central Europe, which are now organised through Main Defence Forces. The decision to accept this rôle has helped to protect a Service which might otherwise have found itself facing very steep reductions indeed in its capabilities for large-scale conventional warfare. Because of the ARRC commitment, the Army has been able to ensure that it maintains seven active brigades committed to NATO – equivalent to the total number of fully active German brigades. It has also secured agreement to a continuing modernisation programme which will increase the combat power of Britain's enhanced armoured division in Germany by one third. As a result, despite a reduction in British Army personnel in Germany from 56,000 to 23,000, the combat power of the Army in Germany will only be reduced by about 20 per cent.[8]

The other two Services are also proceeding with major modernisation programmes. Despite a 20 per cent reduction in the size of the frigate and destroyer fleet, the Royal Navy has continued to place orders for new Type 23 frigates and has begun exploratory work on introducing a new frigate, to replace the Type 42 around the end of the century. Plans are also under way to replace and modernise Britain's amphibious capability, despite the formidable cost involved. The Royal Air Force for its part is concentrating its greatest effort on securing agreement to proceed with production of the European Fighter Aircraft (EFA), the projected UK lifetime cost of which was recently estimated to be £20 billion.[9] As a result, this one programme is due to take a large share of the procurement budget throughout the next decade, further constraining the opportunities for significant budgetary cuts.

If the Ministry of Defence seeks to implement most of these programmes, it will be unable to make further cuts in the equipment budget. Together with the limited scope for further economies in personnel spending beyond those already budgeted for, therefore, current plans are likely to lead to a levelling off of defence spending at around £20 billion in 1991–92 prices, perhaps even turning into a gradual rise by the late 1990s.

Forces for Change

Whether such a trend will be politically acceptable remains to be seen. For it would imply a continuing willingness on the part of the British government to spend more on defence than any of its major

European Community partners at a time when the structure of incentives that ensured the stability of burden-sharing arrangements in the past has been significantly eroded. Over the last two years most NATO members, including the UK, have made a series of defence cuts with little if any prior consultation with allies. Previous frameworks for determining shares of common defences are weakening. And the pressure to find further defence economies in order to fund government priorities in other areas is likely to grow in the years ahead. The outcome of the 1992 spending round suggests that, while fear of possible employment consequences may slow the pace of defence budget cuts, it is unlikely to halt the process altogether.

Britain will still require some forces for both internal security rôles (i.e. Northern Ireland) and in defence of overseas dependencies (e.g. the Falklands). But requirements for these rôles are likely to remain relatively modest in scale compared with the costs of the UK forces provided as a contribution to a collective effort, whether that effort be organised by NATO, CSCE, the UN, or some other body, and whether that effort is intended for use in Europe or elsewhere.

The predominance of collective rôles is nothing new for British forces. Since withdrawal from East of Suez, most units of all three Services have had as their primary function their contribution to NATO. Yet during the Cold War the success of this collective effort was seen to be crucial for Britain's vital national interest, namely the deterrence of Soviet attack on Western Europe, and much of its contribution to collective defence was of forces designed to defend UK territory, and surrounding waters, from attack.

In the absence of a Soviet threat, by contrast, collective military efforts are unlikely to be related, even indirectly, to the defence of the British Isles. Moreover, whether such efforts involve peacekeeping and humanitarian missions (as in Cambodia and Bosnia), peace enforcement (as in Somalia) or full-scale war (as in Kuwait), the size of the UK contribution is likely to affect the viability of the collective effort only at the margins. For both these reasons, the size and nature of Britain's contribution to collective defence is likely to be much more a matter of choice than in the past.

This choice will be determined in part by inertia and in part by a continued desire to maintain national status. But fiscal pressures mean that loose burden-sharing criteria are already developing. The UK made the largest European military contribution to the UN military effort in the war against Iraq in 1991. Yet virtually the entire £2.4 billion cost of this operation was recouped from contributions from foreign governments, including £274 million from NATO ally Germany.[10] Britain's relatively large contribution to the UN force in Bosnia has been used to justify the relatively small size of the forces it is deploying as part of UN efforts elsewhere.

TABLE 4 OECD EXTERNAL SECURITY BUDGETS
Spending on Defence and Overseas Development Assistance (ODA): 1990

		Defence % GNP 1990	ODA % GNP 1990	Defence + ODA % GNP 1990
UK		4.0	0.3	4.3
France	*	3.6	0.8	4.4
Norway		3.3	1.2	4.5
Netherlands	*	2.7	0.9	3.6
W. Germany	*	2.9	0.4	3.3
Sweden		2.5	0.9	3.4
Belgium	*	2.5	0.4	2.9
Italy	*	2.3	0.3	2.6
Denmark	*	2.0	0.9	2.9
Switzerland		1.8	0.3	2.1
Finland		1.4	0.6	2.0
Ireland		1.1	0.2	1.3
Austria		1.0	0.2	1.3
Japan		1.0	0.3	1.3
Australia		2.4	0.3	2.7
New Zealand		1.9	0.2	2.1
Canada		2.0	0.4	2.4
US		5.5	0.2	5.7
WEU6 average	(excl. UK)	2.7	0.6	3.3
OECD average	(excl. UK)	2.4	0.5	2.9

* = WEU member.

Sources: World Bank, *World Development Report 1992*, 1992; *NATO Review*; International Institute for Strategic Studies, *Military Balance 1992–1993*, 1992.

Neither total size of defence effort nor per capita defence spending are satisfactory burden-sharing formulae, given that levels of national population and wealth vary so widely. A better guide to what might constitute an acceptable formula is likely to be found by looking at the formulae used in practice to determine how the budgets of international organisations (for example the EC, UN and NATO) are funded. With some exceptions at the margins – such as the hotly contested £2 bn UK rebate from the EC – the fundamental principle applied in all these organisations is that national contributions should be proportional to national income, perhaps with some special treatment for those on particularly low levels of average income.

Were such a formula to be used to compare UK defence spending with that of its allies, the question remains as to which countries should be used a basis for comparison. The more that the WEU or the EC are seen as the main institutions through which national contributions are channelled, the more that the defence budgets of other members of these bodies are the most relevant comparison. On this basis, the correct figure for comparison is the average 2.7 per cent of national income spent by the six other high income WEU states on defence in 1990.[11] A similar result (2.9 per cent) would be obtained if the comparison were restricted to the three other large WEU members (Italy, Germany and France).

Yet the focus of many future collective military operations in which the UK could be involved will be the UN, not the WEU. A wider burden-sharing comparison that takes into account the contributions of other members of the Western 'security community' may thus also be relevant. Such a comparison would have to include both the high level of US defence spending (currently 5.5 per cent of GNP, though due to fall to 3.6 per cent by 1997) and the lower level of defence spending in other OECD countries. (*See Table 4*). The average defence burden of 17 other high income OECD states[12] was 2.4 per cent of national income: rather lower than the WEU average.[13]

In the provision of an international public good, it is often considered legitimate to ask for greater contributions from those with a particular interest in meeting the requirement in question. On this criterion, however, the case for a reduction in the UK share of collective defence efforts would be even stronger. Of all the larger member states of the Community, Britain is furthest from the potential sources of conflict and instability to the East and South. It cannot entirely isolate itself from the effects of conflict in these areas, but it is, proportionately, less affected than Germany or Italy or France. On the basis of its relative stake in conflict resolution in the areas bordering Europe, therefore, a strong case could be made for the UK to make a below-average contribution to collective efforts.

Burden-sharing compensation?

As a result of the UK's perceived comparative advantage in providing the military element of international security, it could be argued that Britain should concentrate on what it does well, while other, more pacific, nations such as Germany and Japan, concentrate on financing other important elements of international order.

While such a division of labour might be acceptable in theory, however, many of the international organisations to which the UK belongs – such as the EC, UN and NATO – relate the contributions of member states to central funds closely to their shares of total income. The only large component of public spending comparable to defence, in which an international public good is mainly funded on a national basis, is overseas development aid.

It is, however, an important comparison. Aid budgets are often seen as a means of tackling the root causes of conflict, and thus complement – sometimes very directly as recent events in Somalia show – collective military provision. Aid and defence budgets are in this sense, therefore, the two biggest components of the 'external security budget' of most developed states. As Table 4 illustrates, the amount which Britain saves in underspending on overseas aid does not fully compensate for its disproportionate spending on defence. Adding the two categories of 'security spending' together, France and Norway are the only other European countries that match UK levels of spending. On average, the UK spent 4.3 per cent of GNP on 'security' in 1990, compared with an average of only 3.3 per cent for other high income WEU members and 2.9 per cent for 17 other OECD states.

The distribution of aid spending may have changed somewhat in the last two years. Germany has contributed by far the largest share of West European aid to Central and Eastern Europe, and this pattern seems likely to continue in years to come. Whether this increased aid can be seen as offsetting higher UK levels of military spending, however, is debatable. A large part of increased German aid to the Soviet Union is a result of commitments made in 1990 in order to secure the early withdrawal of Soviet troops from German soil. And German businesses are likely to be the main outside beneficiaries of the economic transformation taking place in Poland, the Czech Republic and Hungary. By contrast, the above-average UK contribution to collective defences cannot be justified by reference to any special or unique benefits which the UK derives from those defences.

As the genocide in Bosnia worsened in late 1992 and early 1993, the UK came under increasing criticism for its unwillingness to take a greater share of those seeking refuge from slaughter. Germany and Austria, and to a lesser extent Sweden and Italy, found themselves taking a disproportionate share of refugees while the Home Office seemed intent on devising ever more elaborate bureaucratic mechanisms to ensure that few if any refugees would get to Britain.

The government's policy on this question attracted widespread public criticism for its inhumanity and mean-mindedness, in response to which some modest concessions were made. Yet it is hard to argue that the UK's failure to take a higher proportion of refugees should be offset against the lower defence commitments of countries such as Austria and Germany. Even if the UK had adopted a more humane asylum policy, both geography and family ties mean that refugees from Central and Eastern Europe are more likely to go to some countries than to others. It is important for other states, such as the UK and Spain, to show solidarity with the countries most directly affected. Far from justifying the UK spending more on its armed forces than Germany, however, the likelihood that conflict in Eastern Europe will affect some Western states more than others could more logically be taken to suggest that these are precisely the states which should pay most towards the upkeep of the forces designed to help avoid such a failure.

Implications of a Common Security and Foreign Policy for Defence Burden-sharing

The growing crisis in Eastern Europe has reinforced the view of some EC governments, Germany amongst them, that a co-ordinated European response to security problems is required. With the end of the Cold War, there is a danger that states will place less emphasis on collective effort than in the past. If such a tendency is to be avoided, it is argued, the European Community must increasingly develop a common identity in the field of security policy. The first steps in this direction have already been taken in the Maastricht agreement on European Union, which envisages the development of a Common Foreign and Security Policy 'including the eventual framing of a common defence policy that might in time lead to a common defence'.

Central to the argument in favour of a common defence policy is the proposition that it is the logical result of the integration of policy in other areas, which is already taking place. EC members have already accepted the desirability of a common external policy in fora such as the GATT negotiations. The EC has had a leading rôle in organising aid programmes for the newly free states of Eastern Europe. And the crisis in Yugoslavia has demonstrated that the Community is now also seeking to acquire a rôle in crisis management, building on its considerable economic power and political attraction to carve out a distinctive foreign policy rôle. It is increasingly anomalous that EC countries co-operate on all these aspects of foreign policy yet leave defence – which in principle should be derived from foreign policy – to be dealt with elsewhere.

Moreover, the end of the Cold War has added other pressures for defence integration. The collapse of the Warsaw Pact has propelled the issue of Community enlargement to the top of the European agenda. Most Community leaders now accept that enlargement is inevitable, encompassing the EFTA states first but then also moving to the incorporation of the first ex-Communist states around the turn of the century. This prospect is in turn creating pressures for further increases in the Community's decision-making powers in order for it to be able to survive the incorporation of a more diverse, and larger, group of countries.[14] And the further this process of 'deepening' goes, the more difficult it will be for defence alone to be exempted from joint decision-making.

The unification of Germany as a result of the collapse of Communism provides a powerful additional argument for military integration as a means of assuaging fears of a resurgent German nationalism. Without an integrated foreign and defence policy for the Community, it is argued, Germany could increasingly pursue an independent policy of its own – as indeed it threatened to do over the issue of Croatian recognition at the beginning of 1992.

Finally, a profound change is taking shape in American foreign policy. The number of American military personnel in Europe is likely to dwindle to 50,000 or less by the end of the century. And with this is bound to come a reduction of the density of interaction between armed forces – in procurement, in training, in personal experiences – that is at the heart of NATO today. Moreover, the rôle of nuclear weapons in European defence is also set to diminish sharply, removing one of the main justifications for the United States retaining sole leadership in the Western Alliance. Even if US troops do stay in Europe, therefore, the pressure will grow for a cohesive 'European pillar' capable of becoming an equal partner in shaping joint security policies.

It is possible that we have now seen the high point of European integration. Economic and monetary union, if it takes place, seems increasingly likely to be confined to a small group of countries rather than encompassing the whole Community. The widening of the EC, rather than forcing the pace of deepening, could yet undermine it altogether. The deeply rooted differences that remain between national perspectives and traditions could still make further progress towards a common EC security policy impossible. And the trend towards US withdrawal could halt, allowing an American-dominated NATO to remain the most cohesive military structure in Europe.

Certainly the obstacles in the way of a common defence policy are considerable. NATO can operate on the basis of the consensus principle only because the US is able to use its material predominance to negotiate agreed policies from a position of strength. In the EC, by contrast, no single power has the ability to play a hegemonic rôle. As the Community has found in many other areas of potential controversy, therefore, the introduction of some form of qualified majority voting is probably an essential precondition for an effective common policy. Such a mechanism need not apply to all aspects of defence policy. If the potential gains from integration are to be achieved, however – for example in procurement policy or training – some form of centralised structure under majority control is necessary.

While the prospect of such a structure has receded in recent months, it is still an important element in the thinking of some of Britain's Community partners. Moreover, British commentators have often underestimated the dynamic of European integration in the past. They should therefore be wary of assuming too readily that common European defence is an idea whose time has passed. Its creation could have a profound effect on the rules for security burden-sharing. The allocation of defence effort between West European states reflects the distribution of power within NATO, created in the aftermath of the Second World War under Anglo-American hegemony. If a common European defence is created, even as part of a restructured NATO, however, past burden-sharing arrangements would need to be rethought.

In the first place, the UK would be likely to argue that a common policy would require all states (or at least all major states) to take an active part in collective military operations, even when this might involve loss of life. History dictates that this rule should be applied sensitively, particularly when the deployment of German troops might be seen to be counterproductive. While there are good reasons not to deploy Bundeswehr forces in Bosnia or Croatia, however, there is much that they could do in other parts of the world. Indeed, without the participation of the Community's largest member, a common policy would from the start suffer from an asymmetry of burden which even the most generous payments could not entirely offset.

Secondly, as in the case of other common EC policies, the UK would have a case for arguing that a common defence should be commonly funded on the basis of an equitable formula (perhaps based on national income). For if the states of the EC are each to have a say in a common policy, they should also have to share in the costs of carrying that policy out. The 1990s may offer a unique opportunity to share defence burdens more equitably because the total requirement for defence spending is falling sharply. A redistribution of burdens may lead those states who stand to lose most, such as Italy and Spain, to have second thoughts about their commitment to greater power-sharing on security policy. On the other hand, the UK and France would gain substantially, perhaps providing an important argument for both to support a move towards common defence.

The introduction of qualified majority voting on key aspects of common defence seems unlikely in the near future. There may, however, be a number of other areas in which some progress could be made in strengthening European security co-operation.[15] A measure that would be of particular relevance to the issue of burden-sharing would be an agreement that the voting members of the WEU create a common budget, funded in proportion to members' national income, which would be used to reimburse all the costs of members' contributions to collective military operations mandated or supported by the WEU. At present countries unable to make force contributions often make ad hoc financial contributions (as Germany did during the Gulf War). Yet the lack of a formula for calculating the size of these contributions makes their negotiation the subject of unnecessary and often humiliating wrangling. A concrete, yet limited, demonstration of the benefits of a common defence policy would be an agreement to put such payments on a regular and automatic basis.

British Force Requirements for the Year 2000

Whether or not any moves towards European defence integration take place, the end of Cold War requirements is likely to make the case for a further reappraisal of UK force levels difficult to resist. Even if some NATO provision still needs to be made against the possibility of future conflict with Russia, the withdrawal and reduction of its forces make the necessary level of such provision much less than before. The level of the Russian defence budget seems certain to fall to a fraction of the previous Soviet level. By the end of the 1990s, therefore, the size and quality of Russian forces will cease to be the most important yardstick against which to measure the adequacy of NATO forces.

Yet other potential yardsticks for Western forces are much less formidable in nature. Despite substantial oil revenues, large-scale arms imports, and recent battle experience, the Iraqi armed forces were no match for Western technological superiority. The allies could have won the 1991 war with far fewer forces than were actually employed.

Over the next decade at least, it is difficult to conceive of any other state that could mount a conventional military challenge to the UN greater than that posed by Iraq in 1991. The international community will need to preserve the ability to repeat an operation of this sort, as well as to conduct several smaller, simultaneous operations. And requirements for peacekeeping and peacemaking missions are likely to increase significantly, at least if recent involvements in Cambodia, Bosnia and Somalia are the start of a permanent, more interventionist trend. The type of forces required for these post-Cold War missions are, however, quite different from those required for fighting a large-scale conventional war against a technologically sophisticated opponent.

In deciding how UK forces should be structured in response to changing circumstances, the necessary starting point is to define what forces will be required for missions that relate specifically to British interests rather than those of any other state. Once these minimum requirements have been established, planners can decide what other forces are needed in order to fulfil perceived needs for UK contributions to international efforts.

Now that the UK is virtually free from the threat of attack from a hostile state, the most important of these requirements is internal: the need to maintain substantial forces to support the police in Northern Ireland. Ten Regular Army battalions are required at any one time in Northern Ireland, together with one regiment of Royal Engineers and one regiment of the Army Air Corps.[16] Given the need to ensure that the frequency of Northern Ireland tours is not too great, this requirement effectively sets a lower limit on the number of infantry battalions at around the currently planned level of 38.

Second, there are other civil or policing rôles in which the armed forces will continue to be required. Prominent amongst these is the need to combat the Provisional IRA on the mainland, for example through bomb disposal and protection of key installations. Other missions include search and rescue, and protection of civil shipping.

Third, as a result of its colonial past, the UK has responsibility for the defence of its few remaining overseas territories. The commitment to Hong Kong will lapse in 1997, and Spanish membership of the EC has encouraged hopes that the Gibraltar dispute can be resolved. But the commitment to the defence of the Falkland Islands will continue to have to be taken into account in shaping Britain's armed forces for many years. The construction of Mount Pleasant airfield means that, in the event of a crisis, reinforcements could be flown in quite rapidly, thus reducing the requirement for a naval task force capability. But the continuing stationing of some forces in place, both on the Islands and at sea, is likely to be prudent at least until a political settlement of the dispute with Argentina has been reached.

Fourth, there is now a cross-party consensus on the retention of a British strategic nuclear force. For reasons that have more to do with domestic electoral politics than military necessity, it is hard to imagine any circumstances, short of worldwide nuclear disarmament, in which the UK would be willing to give up its nuclear force entirely. This in turn means that budgetary provision will continue to have to be made for this force for the foreseeable future.

The political consensus behind the maintenance of some form of nuclear force does not extend, however, to all aspects of that force. Recent government statements suggest that it has begun to question whether previous plans for a massive expansion in warhead numbers are still appropriate. Moreover, a strong argument is developing for the RAF to abandon its separate nuclear rôle. Even if political reality seems certain to require the maintenance of some form of nuclear force, therefore, it could be much more like a 'minimum deterrent' than was envisaged only three or four years ago.

Beyond the forces neeeded to meet these four requirements, the government now has much greater latitude in determining force levels than in the past. Both in residual requirements for defence of Western Europe against Russia, and in the UK contribution to the UN's policing rôle (both within and outside Europe), the need to retain the ability to carry out independent military operations is limited. More important, from the British viewpoint, is that the UK be seen to be making a reasonable and fair contribution to collective military efforts.

What such a contribution should be is bound to be a subject of continuing debate in the coming years, as the major Western powers grapple to find a new burden-sharing formula to replace that in operation during the Cold War. Even if due allowance is made for the UK's continuing to spend less than others on overseas aid, however, a formula based on equalising levels of security spending within Western Europe suggests that the UK defence budget should be reduced to £14 bn (at 1991–92 prices) by the year 2000: £6 bn (or 31 per cent) lower than the level currently planned for 1995–96.[17]

Because few if any of Britain's contributions to collective defence are irreplaceable, the UK would have considerable scope in choosing how to meet this target. It would be constrained by the need to meet the specifically national requirements that have been outlined. Beyond this, much would depend on whether, and on what terms, a division of military labour could be developed with other major military powers. Tables 5–7 summarise one possible force structure which would be compatible with purely national defence needs as well as with the £14 bn target.

The Army is perhaps the Service for which national rôles impose the greatest limits on future cutbacks. It is difficult to see how the size of the infantry can be reduced much below its current level, given the continuing requirement to station 10 battalions in Northern Ireland. Moreover, the growth of UN peacekeeping and peacemaking missions relies disproportionately on the availability of well-equipped and professional infantry units from its leading members: a capability that is still in short supply internationally, and to which it will be important for the UK to be seen to be making a reasonable contribution. For both these reasons, it is assumed that a reappraisal of defence needs conducted now would lead to a greater demand for UK-based infantry battalions, as well as those based overseas under UN command, than was assumed to exist in Options for Change. (*See Table 5.*)

TABLE 5   THE ARMY 1990–2000

	1990 actual	1992 actual	1997 planned	2000 proposed
*Type of unit**				
Germany				
Infantry battalion	16	16	6	2
Armoured regiment	15	14	7	2
Artillery regiment	14	14	6	1
Engineer regiment	7	7	4	1
Army Air Corps regiment	3	3	3	1
UK				
Infantry battalion	32	32	31	32
Armoured regiment**	4	4	3	3
Artillery regiment**	6	6	10	8
Engineer regiment	5	5	6	6
Army Air Corps regiment***	1	3	3	3
Elsewhere				
Infantry battalion	7	7	3	5
Engineer regiment	1	1	–	–

Sources: Annual *Statements on the Defence Estimates*; own projections.

* Regular Army units only.
** Excluding training regiment.
*** Includes Northern Ireland deployment equivalent to an additional regiment, and RM squadron.

By contrast, current plans for the retention and modernisation of a substantial part of Britain's ground forces in Germany reflect an inability to come to terms with new strategic conditions. During the Cold War these forces played a vital rôle in fulfilling the UK's commitment to collective defence of NATO's front line. With the imminent withdrawal of Soviet forces from Central Europe, however, a UK force of divisional size is no longer necessary. The armoured forces of continental powers are much better placed than

Britain's to provide any capability that is still thought necessary to counter the remote possibility of a long-warning Russian attack, in part because such a capability will continue to be seen as a necessary part of their national defence. In order to symbolise the UK's commitment to collective defence, there may be a case for the retention of a brigade-sized force in Germany. Most of the rôles currently planned for 1st Armoured Division could, however, be more appropriately fulfilled by others.

The retention of a large British force in Germany is often justified by the fact that it has enabled the Army to be given the command of NATO's Rapid Reaction Corps. While the decision to grant Britain this command was widely greeted as a diplomatic triumph, however, it may not be enough in itself to justify the retention of such large forces on the continent. Indeed Britain's eagerness to take on this commitment is all too reminiscent of the 1954 decision to maintain large ground forces in Germany, tying the UK to an expensive long-term commitment because of the temporary inability of continental powers to cover this commitment adequately themselves.

Yet there was at least a clear military logic underpinning the forward basing of UK troops in the 1950s. The presence of large Soviet offensive forces in East Germany left Western Europe vulnerable to blitzkrieg attack. Without the peacetime deployment of substantial numbers of Allied troops on the continent to deter such an attack, NATO's defence posture would not have been credible. Even if the UK's contribution to that posture was too great, the need to base substantial forces on NATO's front line was not in question.

Once Soviet troops leave Central Europe in 1994, however, Germany will be free from the threat of short-warning attack, and it will be increasingly hard to construct a credible military rationale for the forward basing of a UK armoured division on its territory. Provided that it does not become an issue of dissension in German domestic politics, there may be a political case for some token presence to symbolise the continuing commitment of the two states to collective defence, and to provide a hedge against the unlikely possibility of revived Russian expansionism. For this purpose, however, a brigade-size force, parts of which might be corps support units, should be more than sufficient.

In order to make a continuing contribution to international military efforts, including UN peacekeeping efforts, the UK should retain substantial ground forces at home, focusing on areas of national excellence such as heliborne light infantry, commando intervention forces (Army and Marines), and combat engineers. The ability to make a major contribution to large-scale armoured warfare, comparable to that made in the Gulf War, should however be given up. Since it is difficult to conceive of any situation in which

Britain's relatively small armoured forces would be decisive, an increased reliance on other states to provide this capability should be acceptable.

Whether such a change would mean that the UK was deprived of the command of the ARRC is far from clear. As long as France is outside NATO's military structure, and Germany is unable to send forces outside NATO territory, it would be difficult for either to take the UK's place. Yet, given the important rôle which France plays in international security, its absence from the ARRC reduces the Corps' credibility as the central structure for detailed planning and co-ordination. It should be an important goal of UK policy to overcome the institutional confusion that surrounds the organisation of collective defence. The UK's pride in gaining leadership of the ARRC should not be allowed to become an obstacle to the creation of more inclusive defence structures in which, inevitably, it would not be able to maintain such a dominant rôle.

The size of the Royal Air Force could also be reduced substantially in the light of recent international changes. Air forces will be of continued importance in warfare, and it will be important that the UK, along with its Western European allies, maintains access to related technological developments in both military and civil research. Given the end of the Soviet threat, however, significant savings can be made in major front line rôles.

First, the need to maintain a capability for defending the UK against bomber attack is likely to come under intense scrutiny. In the wake of the 1957 defence review, UK air defences – like those of the US – were cut sharply because of the belief that no defence could stop at least some nuclear bombers getting through. As the possibility of a protracted conventional war gained credence, however, the need to protect the UK against Soviet long-range bombers was increasingly recognised, and a major investment programme in air defences was initiated. One hundred and seventy Tornado F3 aircraft were purchased, tasked with intercepting incoming Soviet bombers over the Atlantic; seven Boeing early-warning aircraft (AWACS) were ordered at a cost of more than £1 bn; and a massive programme has been undertaken to improve the quality of UK ground-based radar through the Improved UK Air Defence Ground Environment Programme (IUKADGE). In contrast to the proposals for steep cuts in continental forces which it contained, Options for Change made only a token reduction in UK air defence capabilities, reflecting the assumption that the Soviet threat from the north remained unchanged even as the threat in Central Europe was being drawn down.

With the disintegration of the Soviet Union, however, the threat of attack on the UK by aircraft is no longer plausible. Given the West's

TABLE 6 THE RAF 1990–2000

Front-line combat aircraft squadrons

	April 1992 actual	April 1995 planned	April 2000 proposed
RAF Germany			
Strike/attack	6 Tornado GR1	4 Tornado GR1	–
Offensive support	2 Harrier	2 Harrier	–
Air defence	2 Phantom FGR2	–	–
SUBTOTAL	10	6	–
UK			
Strike/attack	1 Tornado GR1	2 Tornado GR1	2 Tornado GR1
	2 Buccaneer		
Offensive support	1 Harrier	1 Harrier	2 Harrier
	2 Jaguar	2 Jaguar	2 Jaguar
Maritime Patrol	4 Nimrod MR	3 Nimrod MR	3 Nimrod MR
Reconnaissance	2 Tornado GR1a	2 Tornado GR1a	1 Tornado GR1a
	1 Jaguar	1 Jaguar	
	1 Nimrod R		
Air defence	7 Tornado F3	6 Tornado F3	4 Tornado F3 (and/or EFA)
	2 Phantom FGR2		
SUBTOTAL	23	17	14
TOTAL	33	23	14

Sources: Statement on the Defence Estimates 1992, Vol.1, Annex D; Statement on the Defence Estimates 1993; Statement to the House of Commons by Rt. Hon. Tom King, 25 July 1990, p.8; own projections.

limited success in preventing the spread of missile technology, a threat to the UK from ballistic missiles could well emerge in the medium term. There is thus a case for some precautionary investment in researching anti-missile defences, perhaps in co-operation with countries such as France and Italy which are nearer the potential sources of such threats. In the light of competing demands on the defence budget, however, it will be increasingly hard to justify the large active forces that continue to be dedicated to the air defence of the UK.

It will be hard for the government to mothball systems that have been the result of so much recent investment. Ministers may also be cautious about making highly visible reductions in forces for UK defence, given both the current mood of Euro-scepticism in the Conservative party and the crucial rôle which Fighter Command played in preserving the country's freedom in 1940. On the other hand, the refusal to fund a mid-life update for Tornado F3 suggests a shift in priorities may already be beginning to take place.

A reduction in the size of the forces devoted to UK air defence would have the added attraction of having relatively little impact on Britain's ability to contribute to collective military efforts, and would therefore be less likely to attract adverse comment from Britain's NATO allies. Since a central motive for maintaining the defence effort is to protect and enhance Britain's international status, this may provide an additional reason for preferring cuts in this capability rather than in others.

For the same reason, the Royal Air Force's nuclear rôle appears increasingly vulnerable. The Army's Lance missile and nuclear artillery capabilities have been disbanded. Royal Navy ships and aircraft, and Royal Air Force maritime patrol aircraft, no longer carry tactical nuclear weapons. From 1994, Britain's sole remaining sub-strategic nuclear capability will be eight Tornado GR1 squadrons able to drop free fall WE177 nuclear bombs.[18]

It is likely to be particularly difficult for the UK to continue with its plans to base four of these squadrons in Germany, where opposition to any form of foreign basing is in any case likely to grow after Soviet withdrawal is completed in 1994. Further weight will be added to the case for abandonment of the RAF's nuclear rôle by the fact that the programme to upgrade existing capability by the purchase of tactical air-to-surface missiles (TASM) is at that especially vulnerable stage in the procurement cycle where it is still possible to make large savings through cancellation.

Nor would the cancellation of TASM, followed in due course by an abandonment of the RAF's WE 177 free fall bombs, require that the UK give up its ability to use nuclear weapons in a 'warning shot' before unleashing an attack against enemy cities or command centres. It is very difficult to imagine situations in which a national capability of this sort would be necessary. For those nuclear planners who still believe a sub-strategic capability is needed, however, the deployment of Trident in 1994 or 1995 should provide some degree of reassurance. In the Cold War, the possible use of strategic submarines in a pre-strategic rôle was limited because of the danger that the Soviet Union might be able rapidly to locate missile launch-points, thus endangering the survival of the submarines in question. As the extent of such concerns lessens, however, the current requirement for Britain to maintain two separate nuclear forces – based on submarines and aircraft – may be dropped.

The direct savings from TASM cancellation would be a useful contribution to an MOD economy drive. More significant in the long term, however, it would also allow further savings to be made in the hidden costs of the nuclear arsenal: secure command and control systems, maintenance and security of the nuclear stockpile, and research and development of new systems.

Finally, the RAF's strike/attack and offensive support capability is a source of large potential savings. Given the expense involved in maintaining and re-equipping modern air forces, current plans to retain 14 such squadrons (six of them in Germany) could be curtailed sharply. There is little national requirement for a force of this size and, given reduced total requirements, other European states – notably Germany, which has recently assumed command of NATO's Rapid Reaction Force (Air) – should be able to take a greater share of providing forces for collective defence. With the imminent withdrawal of Russian forces from Central Europe, the military need for basing six squadrons of combat aircraft in Germany is particularly problematic.[19]

The reduction in the RAF proposed in Table 6 would leave it with 14 well-equipped squadrons of combat aircraft. This is a substantial reduction from the 23 currently planned for the mid-1990s, and would generate substantial savings in the RAF's budget. Given planned reductions by other states, however, a force of this size would still allow the UK to make a significant contribution to collective defence efforts in Europe and elsewhere. If it were thought prudent, some of the surplus aircraft could be stored, rather than scrapped, as a hedge against the long-term possibility of a revived major war threat.

One of the largest sources of savings from such a reduction would be in the required buy of the EFA in the late 1990s. Under strong UK pressure, and in return for a programme of significant cost reductions, the German government agreed in late 1992 to the continuation of the programme. In order to reduce EFA's impact on its own defence budget, however, Germany now plans to buy only 150 aircraft, and to delay a final production decision until 1995. Italy and Spain have also announced reductions in their planned purchases to 130 and 70 respectively.[20] By contrast, apparently unaffected by the end of the Cold War, the RAF remains committed to buying 250 aircraft, more than 40 per cent of the total programme. The slimmed-down RAF suggested here should make it possible to reduce the UK purchase to around 100, saving more than £3 bn on aircraft production alone.[21]

Finally, significant economies are possible in the Royal Navy. The

TABLE 7   THE ROYAL NAVY 1990–2000

	1990 actual	1992 actual	1997 planned (est)	2000 proposed
Type				
Frigates and destroyers				
Type 42	12	12	12	6
Type 22	14	14	10	4
Type 23	1	4	15	15
Type 21	6	6	–	–
Leander	14	4	–	–
Type 82	1	–	–	–
TOTAL	48	40	37*	25
ASW Carriers	3	3	3	2
Helicopter Carriers	0	0	1	1
Assault Ships	2	2	2	2
Ballistic missile submarines				
Polaris	4	3	–	–
Trident	–	–	2	4
Attack submarines				
Oberon	10	3	–	–
Upholder	–	3	0	0
Trafalgar	5	7	7	7
Swiftsure	6	5	5	3
Valiant	2	1	–	–
Churchill	3	–	–	–
TOTAL	26	19	12	10

Sources: Statement on the Defence Estimates 1992, Vol.1, Annex B; Statement to the House of Commons by Rt. Hon. Tom King, 25 July 1990, p.8; own projections.
* Current government plans are for 'about 35' frigates and destroyers by the mid-1990s.

primary rôle of UK naval forces in the last two decades has been to contribute to NATO forces in the North Atlantic. As the size and overall capability of the ex-Soviet Navy continues to decline, therefore, naval forces provide a further area where the UK could seek to achieve a reduction in the size of its contribution to collective defence. Maritime capability will still be needed in order to contribute to Falklands defence. Moreover, as one of Europe's largest naval powers, the UK is well placed to continue to be a major contributor to UN/WEU missions, including blockade, protection of civil shipping, and projection of power ashore. Given the capabilities of Allied navies, however, these commitments do not require a force of the size projected in Options for Change.[22] Provided that the capabilities of the Russian navy continue to decline, therefore, a reduction in Royal Navy strength is possible. Table 7 assumes that a Navy of 10 attack submarines and 30 major surface combatants (perhaps with a number of other vessels in storage) will be adequate for these tasks.

A planned programme of force reductions, along the lines suggested here, would allow the UK to reduce its defence budget by around 40 per cent over the decade while still making an important contribution to collective defences. There are clearly many different ways of achieving the same level of overall budgetary reduction, but all of them would require choices to be made about the extent to which the UK was willing to rely on others for the success of its military actions. I have assumed that the UK would be least willing to reduce its freedom of action in this regard in circumstances of direct national interest – such as fighting the Provisional IRA – and most willing in regard to operations (such as a major land war in the Gulf) to which it would only contribute as a junior partner to other powers. Yet I also assume that, as long as Britain maintains a national defence policy, specialisation will not be taken to the point of totally giving up any single capability. Some armoured regiments and strike aircraft would be maintained, for example, despite a decision to allow others to provide most of the forces in these two areas. Until Western European defence integration has advanced much further, considerable duplication of capabilities – both in the front line and in support services – is probably inevitable.

Where governments choose to strike the balance between specialisation and self-reliance will depend most of all on how far countries feel they can rely on others in a crisis. Yet it is also true that a trend towards specialisation in force provision may itself generate pressures for greater integration and mutual obligation. When France moved most of its fleet to the Mediterranean in 1914 under a rôle specialisation agreement with Britain, leaving its Channel coast defenceless against Germany, it provided an additional reason why the British government found it difficult to avoid war. In the same way in the 1990s, the more that other West European states need German capabilities, for example, the more they are likely to seek means of integrating Germany into a collective structure which ensures that its forces will be used when agreed.

Conclusion

During the Cold War, some states paid more towards the costs of providing collective defence than others. A combination of US leadership and common fear of Soviet military power, however, meant that attempts by both the US and the UK to redress these inequalities proved unsuccessful. The risks involved in upsetting long-standing burden-sharing arrangements were so great that no one country felt it to be in its interests to make a significant change in the relative size of its contribution.

With the end of the Cold War, however, these arrangements have become much looser. Most Western states have announced dramatic reductions in force sizes, and further unilateral cuts seem likely to follow in years to come. States now have more choice as to what military capabilities to maintain than in the past.

In considering its choices, the central question for the UK will be how to relate its own level of contribution to those of its major European allies. If the commitments made at Maastricht do lead to the evolution of formal mechanisms for reaching common views on security issues, then the increased influence which states such as France and the UK derive from high levels of military spending may be substantially diluted. They may, as a consequence, make more equitable defence burden-sharing a condition for more equitable power-sharing within the Community.

Even if the obstacles to creating a common European policy prove insurmountable, however, war between the major states of the Community will remain unthinkable. The UK will remain free from any significant military threat to its own territory, and domestic pressure for further reductions in its contribution to collective security operations is likely to grow. The UK will compare the level of its contribution with its European neighbours, many of them also members of NATO and the EC. Whether a Common Defence Policy develops or not, therefore, the levels of spending in continental Europe are likely to remain important yardsticks against which to measure the size of the UK defence effort.

A policy of reducing UK defence spending to European levels would reduce British weight in military decision-making. Yet it is far from clear how damaging this loss might be. If its high level of military investment only enhances Britain's influence on specifically military matters (for example conduct of the war in the Gulf or the shape of arms control regimes), and if those matters are rarely ones of direct British interest in other respects, it is unlikely that the expenditure of an additional £6 billion a year can be justified. Only if military commitments produce non-military benefits – for example by allowing the UK to win arguments in the EC on other issues of national concern – can a stronger case be made.

Part of the reason for the continuing commitment to high defence spending is habitual. Just as German attitudes to defence are still in large measure a reaction to their country's disgrace in 1945, so too British attitudes are dominated by the nation's survival in 1940 and 1941, and by the subsequent rôle of the Anglo-American alliance in liberating Europe from Hitler and then securing it against a new threat.

The world still requires the US to be an active participant in the global security system, supporting UN humanitarian efforts, helping to enforce arms embargoes, providing a deterrent against the rise of 'rogue' regimes. In contrast to the 1940s and 1950s, however, the British rôle in these US efforts is likely to be marginal. Despite the commitment of a large part of the UK's armed forces to the US-led effort in the Gulf, the key US ally in that conflict was not the UK, but Saudi Arabia. Britain is no longer a world power, and there are few reasons – other than nostalgia – why it should behave as if it were.

The breakdown of the Cold War burden-sharing regime thus provides an opportunity for Britain to rethink the national purposes which justify the expenditure of a considerable part of the government budget. Where no clear national purpose can be demonstrated, the case for a new, and more equitable, burden-sharing regime should be supported. The UK has taken a disproportionate share of the costs of collective security for the last half a century, despite its continuous relative economic decline during this period. Others should now take their turn on watch while Britain rebuilds its strength at home.

Notes

1. John Duffield, 'International regimes and alliance behaviour: explaining NATO conventional force levels', *International Organisation*, 46/4, Autumn 1992, pp.819–856.
2. *Autumn Statement 1992*, p.19.
3. *Ibid.*, p.19. This calculation relies on the rather optimistic assumption of 3% annual real growth in GDP between 1992–93 and 1995–96.
4. HCDC report on the Statement on the Defence Estimates 1992, HC 218 (1992–93), November 1992, p.viii.
5. One attempt to set out these assumptions explicitly, which relates UK force planning to developments in Soviet capability, is contained in Malcolm Chalmers, *UK Defence Requirements 1990–2000*, Safer World Foundation, July 1990.

6. Geoffrey Van Orden, 'The Bundeswehr in transition', *Survival*, XXXIII, July/August 1991, p.366.
7. Congressional Budget Office, *The Economic Effects of Reduced Defense Spending*, February 1992, p.10.
8. Statement on the Defence Estimates 1992, Cm 1981, p.32.
9. HCDC report on the *European Fighter Aircraft*, HC 299, March 1992, p.22. The cost of £20 billion at 1991 economic conditions assumes a UK buy of 250 aircraft and includes the UK share of development (£2.7bn), production (between £7bn and £8bn), and operation and support (around £10bn).
10. David Hencke, 'Gulf War left UK £650 million in profit', *The Guardian*, 2 December 1992.
11. Portugal, Greece and Spain are excluded from the calculation on the assumption that lower income countries might not be expected to contribute as much proportionately as higher income countries.
12. Excluding Spain, Portugal, Greece and Turkey.
13. If weighted by national income, the average is 3.5%.
14. Commission President Jacques Delors has spoken of the need to 'work out a new political and institutional programme for a structure comprising 24 or 30 countries'. ('Delors proposes a Greater Europe', *The Guardian*, 14 October 1991.)
15. Such measures might include: (a) agreement by France and the UK to subordinate their UN Security Council votes to the decision of the European Community; (b) the adoption of a common EC policy on arms transfers; (c) a reform of NATO, based on an equal partnership between WEU and the US and with a European military commander. For further discussion, see Malcolm Chalmers, *Biting the Bullet: A European Defence Option for Britain*, Institute for Public Policy Research, 1992.
16. HCDC report on *Options for Change: Army – Review of the White Paper, Britain's Army for the 90s, Cm 1595*, HC 45, February 1992, pp.xvii-xxi.
17. This assumes: (a) the UK reduces its external security budget (defence + ODA) to the average of other high income WEU members by 2000; (b) defence budgets in other high income WEU members fall by 25% over the decade; (c) economic growth averages 2% per annum in all countries; (d) WEU ODA budgets rise from 0.6% to 0.7% of GNP over the decade, while the UK ODA budget rises from 0.3% to 0.4%.
18. Statement on the Defence Estimates 1992, p.28.
19. HC 218, 1992, p.xii argues that the case for basing Harrier squadrons in Germany needs to be re-examined 'in view of the changes in the geo-political situation in Central Europe, the increased range of the Harrier and air-to-air refuelling, and the German restrictions on low flying training'.
20. David Fairhall, 'Reprieved fighter flies off course again', *The Guardian*, 6 January 1993.
21. This assumes that marginal savings from cancellation are £20 million per aircraft at 1991–92 prices, less than the average aircraft cost of £25 million. Further savings would be possible in spending on weapons systems, maintenance and repair.
22. This assumes that the UK would only be required to take part in large-scale naval operations against a major power (such as Russia) when the United States navy was also involved.

8
The Implications of Broader Security Challenges

George Ashmore

Security tends to be an overworked word these days; we hear of social security, global security, operational security, and many other versions. It is clearly important, but it is ill-defined; indeed it is not clear that the word always has the same underlying sense. More importantly, it is changing. In most analysis related to nation-states, security, unqualified by any other term, has generally referred to the ability to cope with military threats. That is still an important factor, but in the developed world it is becoming relatively less important; and for all countries other, non-military, threats are now arising which pose problems of at least equal severity.

Military Security

As regards the military dimension, despite the many points of conflict now manifest both in Europe and beyond, the last few years have seen fundamental changes for the better in the factors affecting British security. The most serious of the old threats, the Soviet Empire, has gone. While some new issues have arisen, Europe as a whole, and Britain in particular, should be able to enjoy a very high degree of security in the traditional sense of that word. This country, like most of northern and western Europe, is subject to very few military threats of any substance. The military threat to the homeland as understood for perhaps five centuries has disappeared. Quasi-terrorist attack by a small number of foreign governments cannot be ruled out, but a major assault, whether or not to be followed by invasion, is not remotely in prospect. Some states in eastern Europe are unstable, and old rivalries in the Balkans have emerged in forms which give rise to military conflict. There may also be problems with refugees or economic migrants which affect the stability of some western and northern European states and so are of some concern to Britain. However, they do not threaten this country directly, and will not require the same sort of military response as that which NATO prepared against the Soviet threat.

It is often said, of course, that one must look at capabilities as well as intentions; that is, the current absence of ill intentions does not remove the need to be ready to deal with changed designs. That has, however, always been applied selectively. One must apply a degree of judgement about intentions; for example, we have not, for many decades, prepared to deal with a hostile US. It could be argued that, because of its internal flux, there will be a need to deter the main Soviet successor state; however, that is by no means demonstrated and, to the extent that it exists, it can be done collectively with far fewer forces than allowed under the CFE Treaty. Looking around the world now it is difficult to see any state which is likely to have, in the medium term, both the will and the means to make significant military threats against Britain. A similarly optimistic judgement applies to the problems of internal subversion and of threats to overseas possessions or trade.

Most of our trade is with areas (Europe, USA) where the threat from state military action is minimal. Sending a gun-boat because French farmers are being difficult is no solution; indeed it did not help in the more directly relevant issue of the dispute with Iceland over fishing rights. The Royal Navy's ability to give comprehensive protection in distant waters is very limited and that could not be changed by action on any actual foreseeable scale. In any case, it is difficult to see the circumstances in which Britain's trade and shipping would be at risk from a hostile power intent on waging a military campaign against the UK alone, except possibly as regards a threat to oil supplies.

The threat of internal subversion is not great in Britain, though Northern Ireland will continue to be a problem, with some spill-over to the mainland. In addition, rising nationalism in Scotland and Wales could have some impact but in the foreseeable future that is much more likely to involve political rather than military responses. As regards overseas territories, the UK has all but completed its withdrawal from empire, though certain small residual dependencies may require police or coastguard protection against piracy or drug barons. The only two territories which could involve weightier action (in the light of the scale of the potential threat to them) are the Falkland Islands and Belize. Neither could be described as a vital national interest and, for a variety of reasons, a re-run of the South Atlantic campaign is unlikely.

Nor is the nuclear threat what it was. Preventing proliferation, not nuclear aggression, is now the first priority. The pace and ultimate degree of nuclear disarmament of the Soviet successor states, over and above the disposal of obsolete short-range systems, cannot yet be judged. Whether Russia (the only state which could be a major threat to Western Europe) would go so far as zero must be doubted. START II, when implemented, will make very significant reductions, but its implementation will take some time, and the Treaty seems likely to be a resting place for at least a few years. Meanwhile the doctrine of flexible response is not now much spoken of as the appropriate formula to deter Russia.

As regards proliferation, a number of other (non-Western, non-former USSR) states are already possessors of nuclear weapons, and more are endeavouring to become so. There is reasonably widespread collaboration to try to limit proliferation, whether as a consequence of the break-up of the USSR or as indigenous development. However, proliferation is likely to be fuelled by the increasing number of reactors, civil as well as military, and by the continuing spread of plutonium, as well as of the skills and perhaps materials and devices from the former USSR. A major factor in some areas is fear of a neighbour, rather than a desire for conquest. The solution in those instances lies by way of a proper political settlement. No military action, or nuclear provision, by Britain is likely to contribute to that.

UK Military Requirements

In July 1990 the government published proposals for a new approach to Britain's defence entitled Options for Change. The reasoning behind Options for Change was that the world was still in a very uncertain state, and the government, therefore, had to proceed with caution. No current capability should be dispensed with; if necessary the UK should be able to rebuild its forces of any particular sort. Thus the reductions in heavy armour took the Royal Armoured Corps to the minimum level from which reconstitution could be made. A further significant factor was the need for internal security provision for Northern Ireland; coverage of that was important for determining the number of infantry battalions. The proposals nevertheless left forces of sufficient size for the UK to seek and obtain a significant rôle in the NATO Rapid Reaction Corps (ARRC), including the provision of a heavy armoured division.

The process was carried further in the 1992 Statement on the Defence Estimates (SDE 92). The government has looked again at the country's underlying defence needs, and defined new defence rôles.

SDE 92 noted that in future the country's armed forces would be more mobile, flexible, and better-equipped. That is clearly movement in the right direction, though no fundamental departure from the philosophy of Options for Change was indicated, for SDE 92 also made clear that the retention of heavy armour in the form of Challenger I and II was still the intention. However, the utility of heavy armoured forces in Europe would seem to be very limited, as is their suitability for rapid redeployment elsewhere. If such forces were required in significant numbers for the purposes of European security, whether within or without Europe, then rôle specialisation would, in any case, have to be given serious consideration. There would seem to be no need for the UK to seek to take on this rôle.

Since publication of SDE 92 the political climate has moved, in some degree, towards peace enforcement (as opposed to traditional peacekeeping). The forces mainly required for both, as well as for internal security duties, are well-trained and mobile infantry, with good supporting logistics. Such forces would be appropriate to deal with the limited threat of subversion within the UK, as well as to provide elements for dealing with threats of instability on Europe's borders and for international peacekeeping (or enforcement) duties. Dealing with internal subversion will also require modest numbers of special forces, and some units of troops not trained for all-out war, but specifically for internal duties. Even if substantial investment in peace enforcement is envisaged, the requirement will still be very largely for infantry, with a relatively small amount of sophisticated weaponry (e.g. combat helicopters). The Serbian army may be able to threaten Bosnia or Croatia with its tanks and artillery, but dealing with those assets would not be a major task for modern Western forces with a modest amount of up-to-date equipment. When they had been dealt with, the task would then require well-trained infantry on the ground.

By 1995 British armoured forces will be reduced to 11 regiments; there are clearly going to be problems in their training in Europe (and especially in Britain). Reductions of a further six armoured/armoured reconnaissance regiments and four more self-propelled artillery regiments would produce worthwhile savings. However, such a reduction in tank regiments would mean that the retention of this arm would not be viable in the long term. Even without such further reductions the size of the armed forces will be so small as to provide no strong basis for an indigenous tank manufacturing capacity. However, if the security situation deteriorated, it would take perhaps five years or more for Russia, the only potential source of a major direct threat, to reconstitute itself. European allies, and the US if need be, would thus have time to consider the response, which could sensibly be based on German armoured forces, with UK air and infantry contributions. That would, of course, require a much greater degree of rôle specialisation than has hitherto been judged prudent, and consequently a much greater degree of multinational integration than has been seen between Britain and even its closest European allies. Meanwhile, sufficient assets would be left to enable support to be given to peace enforcement in, say, Bosnia.

Despite their commitment to the ARRC, the British armoured forces are not readily transportable a long way from their place of deployment, at any rate with the lift which the UK has. Even allowing for a real need for UK contributions to Out-of-Area (OOA) activities in high-intensity operations, little would be lost if heavy armour were not available. Infantry with air support might not be suitable for every conceivable contingency, but a medium-sized European power, with a weak economy, can hardly be expected to make provision for all possible types of warfare, especially where its own vital interests may not be directly involved. The inability to produce an armoured division for OOA intervention could be a negative factor in relations with the US, but in the perspective of relatively few calls for one, and the ability to provide other teeth arms, it is hardly a conclusive argument for retention of an expensive capability of limited utility. It would be even less of one if an ability to defeat enemy armour by other means were available.

A move out of armour would enable some armoured infantry to be replaced by mechanised formations, with further savings. The calculation of the overall infantry needs should, in any case, be revisited, though no mathematical precision is possible. Ultimately the number of battalions required will be largely determined by how far one may prudently assume that Northern Ireland and other areas of prime importance to Britain will not make critical demands at the same time. A further significant factor, however, is the need to reduce turbulence for the personnel involved, which frequent postings, emergency or otherwise, would entail. Without under-estimating the Northern Ireland problem, the fact is that only 6–8 battalions are there on long tours and a further four on roulement. Allowing for the possibility of some measure of support for the Army's infantry from the Royal Marines, the RAF Regiment, and from a few other formations, a calculated need of 39 battalions would seem at the top end of the range to provide what is necessary for Britain's overall defence requirements.

The question of what air capability should be retained is more complex. There is a need to control (i.e. police) European air space, and to protect ground forces policing unstable parts of Europe from relatively small and unsophisticated air forces. Air defence of the UK, however, is no longer a major problem. Operations out-of-area could be more difficult without advanced air assets but, again, a judgement is required as to what the UK could most sensibly contribute. So long as theatre nuclear forces (TNF) are retained there will be a need for a delivery vehicle. There will also be a need for maritime reconnaissance; less clear is the need for maritime strike but, since the same platforms may serve for that as for TNF delivery, the capacity can be retained relatively cheaply.

The arguments for TNF have, of course, been affected by the collapse of the USSR. Formerly, a system was needed as part of flexible response, and an air-delivered weapon has some important advantages of flexibility over a submarine-launched ballistic misisle (SLBM). An OOA nuclear rôle would again make air-delivered TNF a priority, but there are very strong arguments against Britain's assuming such a rôle. It is not necessary to debate those here; for present purposes the facts are that the UK *has* air-delivered nuclear weapons, and that the platforms for delivering these are capable of performing other demanding rôles.

The key issue is on the form of air support to be given directly to ground forces. The scale of that will be determined by the nature of the hostilities and, to a degree, by the size of the ground forces engaged. For any engagement in the Middle East there will be a need to destroy armour and to break-up formations beyond artillery range, and also to keep hostile battlefield support aircraft away. Leaving aside the scale, there is a significant need for rotary wing aircraft with good survivability. As regards fixed-wing aircraft, a tentative suggestion would be to reduce the Tornado GR force by a further two squadrons, and air defence by three. The case for continuing with the Jaguar is not made out – though it does provide a relatively cheap capacity for ground attack out-of-area.

The rôle of navies in war is to secure the use of the seas for one's own side, and to deny it to the enemy. In peace and war they can also be used to project power ashore. Britain will need general-purpose maritime assets on a scale to deal with relatively modest threats in the surrounding seas. Vessels maintained for other purposes may be employed to protect shipping in distant seas from harassment, but no large-scale investment could be justified for this on its own. Likewise, general purpose assets may enable Britain to earn political credit of various sorts by, for example, allowing deployments to the Persian Gulf or other troubled areas. However, the possibility of such benefits is not sufficient on its own to justify substantial investment in a blue water fleet.

The one sea in which there could be serious threats to European interests is the Mediterranean, which is an area of potential conflict of interest with many non-European nations. Its security at once raises the issue of the US rôle there, and also of European relations with Turkey. Britain's direct concern is very limited. Given the political will, Europe, however defined, could muster the necessary resources to deal with any Mediterranean threat; it could not, however, launch significant military action elsewhere out of the continent.

In the light of the above analysis, the case for the UK's small aircraft carriers is not made out. They were designed as anti-submarine assets. Whilst submarine proliferation has been a factor in recent years, with some nations seeking to acquire nuclear submarine capabilities, no potential adversary requires the retention of this asset. Three carriers were our contribution to dealing with the full-blown Soviet threat; with the great reduction in that threat, retention of a modest number of nuclear submarines (SSNs) together with land-based air assets, should provide adequate insurance against the comparatively small numbers of hostile submarines likely to threaten British interests in any future conflict.

The numbers of SSNs required could be less than is currently envisaged; a smaller number should be sufficient to deal with any Third World threat. Moreover, some further scaling down of the Options for Change provision for destroyers and frigates also seems possible. Whilst no definitive proposals can be made, a reduction of SSNs from 12 to 6, of destroyers/frigates from 40 to 20, and the scrapping of amphibious capability would all seem to be feasible without hazarding UK security (even allowing for the problems of keeping a capability to build SSNs). Together with the disposal of the aircraft carriers, that would enable a substantial proportion of the resources provided for general naval forces to be saved, perhaps as much as £1,000 million.

Final choices on the scale of British military provision depend, of course, not only on a judgement about the threats but also about how the country can best meet them, in collaboration with allies and partners. The two possible options are in a European framework, and with the US. The latter is likely to be reappraising its commitments to Europe, with the change of administration. Meanwhile the apparent clarification of European defence co-operation which followed the Maastricht agreement has been clouded, at least temporarily.

Both political pressures and economic factors will point towards more and more collaboration and rôle-sharing with European partners for the defence of Europe. Rôle-sharing does expose a country to difficulty when an ally on whom it depends is not prepared to play its allocated rôle. However, the assets which the UK retains should enable it to meet any threat to vital interests which is not shared by at least one significant ally, whilst we should be able to rely on support from allies in matters where they have an interest at least as great as Britain's. Thus the threat to Britain from an armoured blitzkrieg from a resurgent Russia is much less than would be the threat to Germany, or even France. Reliance on those allies to play a significant rôle in resisting it is therefore not imprudent.

Obviously, any government would prefer to be able to do everything itself, but that is not possible for a medium-sized power. We need to get the best return from what we can afford to invest in military assets and, at the same time, to keep that investment as low as reasonably possible. That becomes the more important as other calls upon national resources, to meet other, non-military, threats, increase. Even if there are (as there may well be) compelling reasons for Britain to play a rôle out-of-area, and to have appropriate assets and doctrine to participate in major operations, it should not plan on fighting a campaign alone.

Broader Security Challenges

It is becoming ever clearer that a definition of security in purely military terms is not sufficient. Britain will need armed forces, properly trained and equipped, but that does not dispose of the nation's security needs. The British people do not feel themselves altogether secure; the question is whether their doubts about health, or employment, or environment reflect in any real sense security threats to the country or its people. Retaining a major emphasis on military threats would entail considerable disadvantages, which could, in fact, undermine security as a whole. Even without the present improvements in the West's military situation, recent developments demonstrate the need to consider resource, environmental, and demographic issues as relevant aspects of security. These issues, which involve very significant non-military threats to all, or almost all, nations, give rise to some profound problems for British security.

The debt and ecological crises pose threats of international proportions – the former to the domestic stability of poor states, the latter to all, but perhaps especially to the industrialised North. The Earth's capacity as both sink and reservoir is limited. The demands and burdens are a function of population numbers and standards of living, and there is increasing evidence that the limits are being neared. The two most important issues, in terms of impact in the course of the next century, are world population growth and global warming. These are connected, inasmuch as population growth, particularly through energy consumption, has had and will have a significant impact on global warming. Each of them, moreover, is a complex issue in its own right, and each will bring in its train other environmental, economic, and ultimately security, issues.

Such issues are, it is true, a long way from the forefront of most people's view of Britain's most pressing concerns; they are global rather than national questions. However, if one looks at what is likely to happen to the world as a whole over the medium term, the case for national concern becomes clear. A tolerable standard of life for most of the world's inhabitants will not be possible unless certain difficult, and sometimes obscure, issues are tackled. Without a tolerable way of life for the masses of humanity, the affluent minority can have no assurance that it will continue to hold and enjoy its present benefits, even if it is prepared to close its mind to the moral issues involved. Failure to deal with these security issues would produce very unpleasant direct results for the affluent North. In due course they would produce even direr indirect problems, probably reintroducing a military threat to the developed world.

For poor nations with burgeoning populations, often directly exposed to sea flooding and environmental degradation, the future, in the absence of effective moves to tackle the problems, would be much worse. They would for the most part be unable to mitigate their sufferings by technical means. They would lack both skills and resources; if they wished to command additional resources, they would have to take them by force. In the first instance, the attention of such states would be towards their neighbours, poor like themselves, and competing directly for the same energy, water or foodstuffs. However, in due course their attention could be expected to turn to the developed nations, enjoying much greater resources. Those very resources would preserve the advanced nations for a long while, especially where geography was favourable as in the case of the US. Over time, however, numbers would tell, not only in the sense of physical pressure (and the US cannot even at this stage keep out poor Mexicans) but also in various political fora where the poor would predominate both in numbers of states and in population, if weight were given to that. In such a Hobbesian world, one would expect the proliferation of weapons of mass destruction to be given a substantial boost, and some would come into the hands of ruling élites not subject to the restraints and calculations which bore on both sides in the Cold War.

The world which we should then be considering would be one in which the seas and the air were increasingly polluted; in which renewable resources were over-exploited so that some at least became exhausted; in which genetic diversity was lost, along with important parts of the earth's regulatory mechanisms; in which there would be increasingly bitter clashes. In that world, which may very well be the one which comes about, one could certainly not say that there was no military threat; it would be one in which there was a very real need to be able to respond to military assault.

The underlying problem in the stress on the Earth is world population. That is estimated as likely to increase from 5,300 million in 1990 to 7,500 million at the lowest by 2100. The mid-20th Century figure was under 3,000 million, and the 1900 one about 1,500 million. Not only are the figures for the next century large, well beyond the current capacity of the environment to absorb the impact, but also there are and will be increasing pressures for those living in the Third World. Energy consumption per head in the US is tens of times that in Africa; there would seem no realistic prospect of extending the US levels even to the present world population, much less to a considerably larger one. Since First World patterns of consumption are even now not sustainable, we are already faced with a major problem.

Even if the demand for food and other organic resources could be met, there would still be a major problem in terms of energy consumption and waste products. This applies even if Third World populations remain very poor – there is no way in which the planet could absorb the effects of those populations consuming at anything like First World levels. One is led back to the second major aspect of the problem, namely global warming.

The clear balance of judgement of the scientific community is that if nothing radical is done about greenhouse gas emissions, unprecedented global warming will occur. The full effects are still unknown and some could be counter-intuitive. Nevertheless, we could expect a rise in sea levels which would inundate some small island nations and cause severe flooding in coastal cities, developed or undeveloped. There would also be major and erratic climate changes. As well as an increase in sea levels, the direct results would include a reduction in rainfall in the productive parts of the northern hemisphere, and an increase in drought in Africa. Adverse effects on health would occur in all populations against a background of increasing world population. However, whilst both Europe and North America would suffer substantially from a half-metre rise in sea levels, that would not be a disaster for them. They would be rich enough to take some precautionary measures, for example by way of sea defences; they could also afford some resettlement. The diversion of resources would not be welcome, but it would be possible. That would not be the case in the Third World.

More difficult to deal with for the rich nations would be the loss of fertility in northern food-producing areas. Whilst there might be some gainers from global warming, the net impact on the northern hemisphere could be expected to be adverse. There would be a major problem in feeding the developed nations with foodstuffs from temperate zones. Because of the pressures in the rest of the world, ocean fisheries could be expected to be seriously over-fished, even assuming that there were no adverse effects on stocks from climatic change. The last assumption may itself be too optimistic.

Possible Responses

The measures needed to deal with the new security issues involve the limiting of population growth, especially in the Third World, and the lessening of energy consumption, especially in the developed countries, and above all in the US. Since both of these could readily involve substantial resource transfers from North to South they will require an open-minded and far-sighted approach to policy formation in all developed countries. However that, and the political will to take the necessary measures, may well not be forthcoming.

The difficulties in the way of ameliorating the population problem are manifest. Many governments in the Third World continue to be very resistant to imposed programmes of birth control, and there is comparatively little that Britain alone can do to change that. However the issue most certainly needs tackling, and the UK should argue in the EC, the UN and elsewhere for the adoption of appropriate policies, and above all the targeting of the right sort of aid. The latter might include not only the obvious birth control programmes, but also other kinds of development which could reduce the desire or need for large families. To do that, many problems which presently threaten, or are felt to threaten, personal, economic and social security would have to be tackled. Research might be usefully focused on such work as a main priority of development expenditure. In addition, Western aid should certainly focus on helping the Third World to develop along sustainable lines which do not degrade the environment.

As to global warming, there are some encouraging signs that the UK is now keeping up tolerably well with other concerned nations, as in the early limitation of carbofluoro carbons (CFCs), and in the (conditional) willingness to limit CO_2 emissions. However, there is still very much more to do, and most of that is not yet on the British political agenda. More radical thought will have to be given to subjects which at present seem politically difficult, such as taxes on CO_2 emissions, and transfer payments from polluting nations to those which can offer a sink. The last means payments from the rich North to the poor South, which will certainly not commend themselves to Western electorates. However, without such payments, it is difficult to see how energy use may be sufficiently restrained, or the benefits of advanced technology transferred, or tropical rainforest (a splendid sink) preserved.

The fact that much of the above, particularly, on birth control, will not commend itself to the Third World is no reason for not pressing it hard. If the richer countries do not, by persuasion and application of resources, bring about a change, then there will be very little hope of establishing a sustainable global economic or ecological system. The application of resources will be crucial; to persuade Third World countries to go along with appropriate measures the West will also have to face up not only to debt relief (perhaps now generally recognised) but also to reviewing terms of trade, access to markets, and the like. All that implies something other than a simple application of the existing systems.

Linkages and Practicalities

We are thus in a position where there are arguments for substantial changes in our armed forces, and for a substantial refocusing of attention on non-military threats. However, before concluding that that is the way to go, there are some difficult questions to be answered. These include consideration of whether it is, in fact, prudent to diminish our military effort, given at least some very grim possibilities for the future; whether, if we were to reduce our armed forces, the resources released could in fact bolster British security in the wider sense; and whether, even if in principle they could do so, the analytic and decision-taking machinery could cope with the necessary changes and redeploy resources to good effect.

Some parts of the world will certainly still see armed conflict, even if the worst, Hobbesian, outcomes of the global security problems are avoided (and we may not, of course, be so fortunate as to avoid them). The countries concerned do not, for the most part, bear directly on British security but this country will still need armed forces, and a sensible military policy will be a necessary (though not sufficient) condition for security, even on the most optimistic prognosis. The nation will need to think hard about what its armed forces are likely to be used for, but I believe that significant reductions would be feasible, even allowing for the possibility of the bleaker outcomes.

Firstly, the reductions may enable Britain to do something to prevent that deterioration, both directly and by example. Secondly, what it is suggested we give up is unlikely to be relevant to the military issues which would face Britain in the event of the bleakest eventuality. If we are to have to fight, it is unlikely to be against massed armour sweeping across Europe, like a 21st Century revisitation by Attila; nor are hundreds of submarines likely to be the threat; nor is there likely to be a need to penetrate sophisticated air defences not very far from our own shores.

Warfare in the 21st Century, in so far as it poses a vital threat to Britain, may be as different from that in the 20th Century as 1915 was from 1815, but not necessarily in the sense of more industrialised or more technical. We should not expect to have to fight in the manner in which we have come to expect major military operations to be conducted at the end of the 20th Century. Military provision made now, with today's systems, would be no counter to the threat. Britain and other affluent nations would have to respond to novel military threats at a time when their own societies and economies were under great strain, so strengthening for the long haul is more important than immediate provision. Finally, high technology might well fail to provide effective counters to low intensity warfare, or to weapons of mass destruction. Now is the time to think about how to counter the threats of the Hobbesian world, not simply to try more of the same militarily as well as environmentally.

The proposed changes in our armed forces would, in principle, release substantial resources. However, the extent to which these would be available for redeployment to deal with other security threats is limited. In the first place, the defence budget is already under severe strain; the reductions in the 1992 Autumn Statement, the fall-off in receipts from the sale of surplus property, and the effect of past pay settlements, all mean that there is scarcely enough money to go around. Even allowing for that, though, it should be possible to release some resources, if sufficiently radical options were chosen. The question is whether they could be made available to meet the threats to Britain's security in a more cost-effective way. In short, would (say) £1,000 million provide more security if spent on armed forces, or in other ways; *would* it be so spent, and if so, how?

Since the military threat has so diminished, redeployment of resources to other needs would, prima facie, be cost-effective. The need for a shift in resources is made manifest by consideration of future generations' requirements. If, for example, consumption of non-renewable resources is not restrained, and global warming abated, future UK citizens will face not only a diminished life style, but one diminished in an unpleasant and irrational way. The issues go wider, however, than between different UK generations. Unless appropriate development is fostered in the Third World, global problems will pose serious threats to Britain itself in due course. Those will be direct threats, not just the further indirect ones following from the breakdown of order in the Third World. There are issues of morality here, but also of prudence. Reducing carbon emissions in the West, and paying (say) India and China to install the most modern technology will benefit both future British citizens and the rest of the world's population. Similar arguments apply to investment in controlling world population growth.

However, it will certainly not be instantly clear to Western publics, ministers, or parliaments why, desirable as it may be to moderate population growth in the Third World, or slow down global warming, the security of UK citizens would suffer if these were not done; or, at any rate, would suffer more than if the money were spent on British armed forces, or even domestic social benefits. To make a switch in domestic spending priorities on a scale going much beyond the modest one of the 1992 Autumn Statement – some more for housing (most for a very limited aspect), some less for defence, for example – is probably not to be expected. A significant shift of resources to overseas aid is even less likely, and tackling the global agenda will be much more difficult even than a shift in domestic priorities. Moreover, most Third World countries are not yet at a stage where they are prepared to change their priorities radically.

Nevertheless, it is necessary for developed nations to review, radically, policies on defence, environment, and energy, and to factor the results into both domestic and foreign policy. They must consider the balance between domestic needs and wider world needs, guided not by altruism but by a concern for the sort of world which UK citizens will face two generations hence. To achieve a shift will be far from easy. The policy-generating machinery needs to address the fundamental changes in provision that would enable major issues of efficiency and equity to be attacked.

Major decisions are required, of an unprecedented sort, and tackling them is the more difficult in as much as there is no generally agreed new security agenda, much less any ranking of the issues involved. Moreover, all the global issues are of great technical complexity. However, the main problem is that the political will may be lacking, a lack unlikely to be remedied by the institutional arrangements in Britain. The ascertainment of the way forward through our future security needs requires a clear-sighted analysis of the problems which the nation faces.

The current machinery of government is not good at providing such an analysis, nor at devising balanced measures to counter the problems involved. This makes effective responses to such complex issues less than easy. In part that is the inevitable result of the concern with immediate pressing issues; in part it is the consequence of the weak economic performance of the country, which distracts attention from other issues. A useful start would be the establishment of free-thinking policy machinery in Whitehall to consider the areas involved. A highly desirable next step would be an economic review of sustainability in which those who argue that growth will solve all would be faced with the questions of growth in what, drawing upon what inputs, and over how long a time.

Conclusion

To sum up, there has been a step change for the better in the country's military security situation; there has, however, also come upon us over the years a major change for the worse in other security-threatening matters. This has taken place against a background of Britain's relative economic decline, with its political weight in the world now much less than it was in 1945, and, of course, even further below its 1914 position. It is no longer able to project military power worldwide – the glories of the Grand Fleet and of the Indian Army are no more, and no endeavour to secure significant influence by purely military means could be successful.

Meanwhile the country faces pressing problems in health and education. As a proportion of GNP, UK spending on health per head is relatively modest for a developed country, and GNP per head is lower than in many Western European nations. There is also a major need to improve education and training where, not only against other Western economies but even against (say) Singapore, the UK performance is not impressive. A switch in domestic priorities, not only financial but also in terms of perceived gravity and urgency, would enable these issues to be the more readily addressed.

The global security issues affect almost all countries; in their train they may bring renewed military problems of a high order. Even before that happens, however, we are faced with the need for urgent decisions. The problems are by any standards difficult; not only is there a major conceptual and presentational step in moving from security as it has been seen for centuries to a concern with the wider issues, especially if that involves some trenching on sovereignty, but the social sciences are not so far advanced as to be able to give very good guidance as to how societies and economies work.

When one adds to that the facts that the issues to be tackled are global in scale, and involve widely differing societies and the conflicting chemistries of different political regimes, early progress in changing security expenditure priorities seems unlikely. That said, we are now more aware, and that is the first step towards establishing security on a new basis. The road will be long, and we may not reach the end in good order, but we have no real alternative to setting off along it. Standing on present priorities and expenditure patterns, is not a viable option.

Morever, Britain does have some significant strengths; it has political gravitas, and its armed forces command respect for their professionalism. The reductions discussed in this Chapter would not remove that; they would, however, if the resources were applied appropriately, enable Britain to add to its existing authority by tackling, and being seen to tackle, the new security agenda. They would, in particular, bear fruit in the European Community, and to a lesser extent in the Security Council. Britain will not again be a world power, but the correct choice of policies, focused not on past glories (however real they were) but on present realities, will enable it to have a significant influence in places and affairs which matter.

DEFENCE FORCE STRUCTURES

9

The Shifting Trade-offs in UK Defence Planning

Philip A.G. Sabin

Whatever proportion of its national resources Britain decides to devote to defence in the future, there remains the question of how those resources should be spent to obtain the most cost-effective defence forces. Issues of resource allocation *within* the defence field were central to the British defence debate during the Cold War, as is evident from the heated debates a decade ago over the relative priority to be accorded to continental and maritime, or conventional and nuclear, forces.[1] Such issues of resource allocation are no less relevant today, and new priorities must be applied to cater for the radically changed strategic circumstances of the post-Cold War world.

The problem of defence priorities is in fact much more complex and far-reaching than was reflected in the 1980s debates over whether spending on Trident should be diverted to conventional forces, or whether John Nott was right to focus cuts on the surface fleet in his 1981 defence review. Such debates took place in the context of relatively stable and consensual assumptions about the Soviet threat, the NATO alliance and the basic rôle of British defence forces. The end of the Cold War has overturned this fundamental stability, and appropriate defence priorities in 1993 may be as different from those in 1983 as the UK's Cold War defence priorities were from those in the inter-war period or in the decades before the First World War.

The choices involved are not simply a matter of striking the right balance between army, navy and air force, or between nuclear and conventional forces. Instead, they involve complex multidimensional trade-offs in resource allocation, as is very evident from the writings of defence planners such as Richard Mottram and Sir Michael Quinlan in recent years.[2] Britain's 1992 Defence White Paper contains a heartfelt essay on the problems of 'Defence Planning in a Changing World', which points out the imperative of choice between versatility and front-line size, between quality and quantity, between readiness and reconstitution, and between independence and reliance on allies. It goes on to argue that:

> Every one of these issues has resource implications, and every choice therefore carries opportunity costs. Few of them, moreover, are black-and-white either/or choices: they mostly require the striking of balance.[3]

As Michael Clarke discusses in the Introduction to this volume, the government has already responded to such choices within the context of its Options for Change defence review, and has promised a shift to more mobile and flexible forces to fit in with the demands of the new strategic situation. However, much has changed since the preliminary conclusions of this review were first outlined in July 1990.[4] In November 1992, the House of Commons Defence Committee described as 'barely credible' the idea that 'the "key choices" made in 1990 have, by hook or by crook, proved to have been the right ones, and have produced solutions robust and flexible enough to cope with unforeseen changes'.[5]

The government has resisted such criticisms, but has also proved willing to modify its defence plans at the margins to take account of changing strategic circumstances. In February 1993, the Ministry of Defence announced that it would leave the army with 40 infantry battalions rather than the planned 38, in response to widespread fears of infantry 'overstretch', especially in light of the new deployment in Bosnia.[6] By contrast, even deeper cuts were announced in other areas, as the prospect of a conventional attack on Western Europe receded still further and as the squeeze on defence funding became acute.[7] The 1992 White Paper sought to justify this pattern of rolling incremental adjustment:

> Practical defence planning can never start from scratch; it is shaped by existing assets, undertakings and expectations, and by the long timescales of any extensive change. In a business as complex, dynamic, interdependent and concrete as a complete defence programme the imperative of choice is continuous.[8]

The trouble with this incremental response to change is that it may be inappropriate to cope with a strategic transformation as radical as that which has occurred over the past five years. If Britain really is faced with defence requirements as different from those during the Cold War as those in turn were from defence requirements in the 1920s and 1930s, then tinkering at the margins with defence plans developed before the full scope of the transformation became apparent may not be an adequate response. To see whether this is in fact the case, an assessment will be made of how closely the balances struck under Options for Change match the new strategic situation in terms of five fundamental resource trade-offs:

- Readiness vs Reconstitution
- Independence vs Integration
- Flexibility vs Specialisation
- Mobility vs Punch
- Quality vs Quantity

Readiness vs Reconstitution

The first trade-off concerns how much prior warning of any military commitment Britain can count on, and hence how far it can economise in areas such as forward deployment and instant readiness for war, so as to invest instead in mobilisation capability to tackle a longer-term threat. British defence planners have adopted a wide range of stances on this issue during the 20th Century, from counting on only a few days warning of a Warsaw Pact conventional attack (and even less warning of a nuclear attack) during the Cold War, to the '10-year rule' which was in force from 1919 to 1932, and which enshrined the planning assumption that no great war was to be anticipated within the next decade.[9]

The problem facing defence planners today is that the amount of warning which may be expected varies greatly depending on the scenario involved. On the one hand, warning time of a ground offensive against Europe from the East was already considered to be shifting from two days to two years as Soviet forces withdrew from Eastern Europe in 1991, and must now be closer to 10 years after the collapse of the USSR.[10] On the other hand, experience in recent years has shown that other contingencies may arise with virtually no notice, but may still require the use of large proportions of the British armed forces, as did the Falklands and Gulf Wars.

To resolve this dilemma, Britain needs a more sophisticated planning approach, which categorises potential threats not only in terms of warning time, but also in terms of gravity and credibility. The big difference between potential short-notice contingencies today and those during the Cold War is that now there is much less likelihood of a sudden threat to Britain's own survival. The UK's involvement is therefore much more discretionary, and if necessary it can wait to mobilise its forces before responding, without fear that this mobilisation process will be hindered by direct attack. Although there are obvious penalties in a delayed response, as in 1956 when world opinion turned against Britain's bid to recapture the Suez Canal, or as more recently in Bosnia when an earlier intervention might arguably have had more chance of success, the UK has been able to weather the frustration and humiliation involved far more readily than it would have been able to shrug off a successful surprise attack against Britain itself by a state such as Nazi Germany or the USSR.[11]

When assessing the potential for a more direct threat to Britain or its European allies in the future, it is important for the UK to adopt a more sophisticated approach than the straightforward '10-year rule' of the inter-war years. Different potential threat scenarios must be considered, and a distinction drawn between political, technical and economic obstacles to their realisation. Only thus can a holistic view of the gravity, credibility and warning time associated with these potential threats be attained, allowing balanced decisions on the readiness needed in various elements of Britain's defence forces.

Where the theoretical capability for an attack already exists, and the only obstacle to its employment is political, the key variable is not warning time but credibility. On the one hand, the former Soviet nuclear forces now constitute perhaps the greatest remaining threat to the UK itself, and Britain would be foolish to count on years of warning of a crisis, given the pace of political turmoil in the former USSR. On the other hand, political factors make some theoretical threats utterly incredible within even the longest planning horizon. Where the UK once planned for possible future wars with France, the USA or Germany even in the absence of immediate political tensions, this has now become unnecessary thanks to the development of stable democracy and European integration.

In other cases, the obstacles to potential threat are more technical, in that the requisite capability does not yet exist. This applies particularly to the development by North African or Middle Eastern states such as Iran or Libya of long-range missiles and of nuclear, chemical or biological warheads capable of threatening Western Europe, including the UK. The gradual acquisition of sophsticated sea denial capabilities such as submarines and advanced mines by regional states which might have an interest in interdicting Western maritime commerce falls into a smaller category. In these cases, there is an argument for Britain to invest more in long term than in immediate preparedness, and to sacrifice readiness now in favour of developing an increased capacity to respond, if necessary at short notice, in the early 21st Century.

Finally, defence planners must consider threats which do not currently exist but which could arise through a conventional military build-up on the part of the state concerned. Here, the prime variable is the economic strength of the potential aggressor. The fastest arms build-ups in the world today are taking place among the booming economies of East Asia, and it is fortunate that these states are too far from Britain to pose direct security concerns. A more immediate potential threat is that the oil wealth of the Middle East might be converted into military power, as happened in Iraq before the Gulf War. However, the states of the region are already heavily militarised, and it is hard to see them developing a much greater conventional military challenge to Europe itself, given the geographic and logistic obstacles involved.

It is the former Soviet Union which British defence planners have continued to highlight as holding the greatest potential for a revived conventional military threat to the West in the long term. However, the political disintegration and economic collapse in the former USSR in fact provide a fairly sound guarantee that it will *not* be able to revive its erstwhile military threat, whatever leaders might come to power. Defence Secretary Malcolm Rifkind even went so far as to claim in April 1993 that Britain's own conventional forces were now effectively more powerful than those of Russia![12] Like the states of Eastern Europe and North Africa, the Soviet successor states currently threaten British security more because their economic and political *weakness* may prompt a flood of migrants or of destabilising exports such as arms or drugs than because their economic strength contains the foundations for a potential future military challenge.

What all this suggests is that the UK must now balance short-warning threats which are in themselves insufficiently grave to warrant the costs of instant readiness, against longer-warning threats which are insufficiently credible to warrant shifting to a stance of long-term mobilisation. Britain's response to this dilemma as part of Options for Change has been to relax its readiness in some areas, but to continue to emphasise preparedness for short-notice contingencies, and to assume the leadership of NATO's new Rapid Reaction Corps (ARRC), designed to reach trouble spots quickly while less ready forces from other NATO nations are mobilised if required.[13]

This division of labour makes sense in that the UK's all-volunteer forces are more suitable for swift and politically controversial deployment than the conscript forces of other European allies. However, the risk is that Britain may be left bearing an undue defence burden if the mobilisation rôle which it has left largely to others comes to seem less important now that the USSR has collapsed. Although some have argued that the UK *should* play a disproportionate rôle in future European defence (in return for greater allied efforts in other fields) because its military professionalism is uniquely suited to tackling the new security agenda, this does not make it any easier for Britain to afford the forces required.[14]

NATO Secretary General Manfred Wörner has already complained that not enough contributions are being offered by Alliance nations to the Main Defence Forces intended to back up the ARRC.[15] Although many states are instead eager to contribute forces to the high-profile ARRC itself, the forces involved are often of dubious readiness, and none even approach the scale of Britain's contribution of over two divisions. There is thus a risk that, by concentrating from the start on the rapid reaction mission for which its professional forces are so evidently suitable, Britain has left itself with an unsustainably high share of the European defence burden now that the collapse of the USSR has reduced the pressure on other allies to prepare for major remobilisation.

One possible solution would be for the UK to relax the readiness of the bulk of its own forces, and to save money by mothballing military equipment and relying more heavily on cheaper reserve personnel. Such a policy has much to recommend it at the moment, when there is a surplus of equipment and redundant manpower due to the run-down of forces maintained during the Cold War. However, the long-term sustainability of such a posture is doubtful, as equipment ages and skills become out of date. Hence, not only would this approach clash head-on with Britain's rapid reaction commitments in NATO, but it would also leave the UK with decreasing military capability in the medium- and long-term, just as the potential threat from new technology in the Middle East and elsewhere might be becoming more acute.

Britain's volunteer reserve forces would have great difficulty finding the recruits to bear an increased burden, and such part-timers could not be trained as easily for the wide range of contingencies with which they might now be faced as they were during the Cold War for specific missions such as rear area security in Germany. Although recent initiatives to ease the call-up of volunteer reservists for limited contingencies should help Britain to cope with one-off crises like the invasion of Kuwait, the problem facing the Regular Army today is more one of routine and continuing overstretch, thanks to protracted and indefinite commitments in areas like Ulster and Bosnia.[16]

Not all the UK's defence capabilities are required on a day-to-day basis now that there is no imminent threat to be deterred, so an alternative response to resource constraints might be for the UK to slim its regular forces down even further, but to retain their diversity in order to facilitate subsequent expansion if required. This 'cadre' approach would have the advantage of maintaining a core of military experience and technical expertise on which larger forces could be rebuilt, as happened in the 1930s.

As argued earlier, however, there seems little prospect of a clear new threat gradually arising as did Nazi Germany before the Second World War, and hence little chance of the kind of sustained expansion in defence spending that would allow Britain's forces to be filled out once more. The result could all too easily be the maintenance on an indefinite basis of vestigial defence forces, lacking in cost-effectiveness, and inadequate to cope with *any* specific challenge which might unexpectedly arise at some point in the future, especially if (as seems more than likely) it takes a very different form from the massed armoured and submarine threat against which British forces have hitherto been structured.

A better way for the UK to avoid bearing an undue share of the NATO defence burden, while fitting in with the unique strengths and limitations of its all-volunteer forces, might be for it to continue to emphasise fairly rapid reaction capability, but to reduce the range of rôles which it tries to cover. Which rôles it might concentrate on will be discussed at length in later sections. Here, it remains only to highlight the vital rôle of intelligence efforts in sifting through the complex mix of political, technical and economic factors discussed earlier, to give as clear and timely a warning of potential threats as possible so that appropriate defence responses may be set in train. Whatever balance is struck between readiness and reconstitution, wide-ranging intelligence efforts deserve even higher priority today than during the clearer confrontation of the Cold War.

Independence vs Integration

Before 1945, Britain tried to enlist the support of allies where possible in its struggle against continental adversaries such as Napoleon and Hitler, but it eschewed permanent alliances and maintained its own independent military forces to ensure its freedom of action in colonial operations and in circumstances like 1940 when allied support failed. During the Cold War, on the other hand, the UK accepted an unprecedented degree of peacetime military integration in the collective defence arrangements of NATO, even stationing a significant proportion of its forces forward in Germany. However, like most other NATO members, it kept its forces under national command and reserved the right to use them independently in conflicts like the Falklands War.

The biggest problem facing Britain in deciding how this arrangement should be shifted to fit in with the new strategic circumstances of the post-Cold War world is uncertainty over which allies to rely on. On the one hand, there is general agreement that purely national contingencies such as Northern Ireland or the Falklands will in future be very much the exception, and that all major operations will be conducted in conjunction with allies. On the other hand, the 1992 Defence White Paper makes clear that military operations in support of the UK's wider security interests 'could be conducted by NATO, WEU, the UN or ad hoc coalitions under UN or CSCE auspices'.[17] Recent experience in the Persian Gulf and in the former Yugoslavia illustrates that the dependability of individual allies may vary widely from what used to be expected in the context of a united NATO defence against the Warsaw Pact.

As with all of the trade-offs discussed in this Chapter, the trade-off between independence and integration takes the form not of an either/or choice but of a spectrum of possibilities. At one extreme is a position similar to that of France, whose defence forces have tried to field a comprehensive mix of nationally-produced equipment, even at the expense of production economies. The spectrum then proceeds through reliance on cheaper foreign suppliers or multinational production for the supply of certain equipment, and through rôle specialisation whereby the country relies on allies to provide certain defence capabilities. This leads on to the other extreme of complete integration, whereby capabilities are actually possessed as a joint alliance asset, as is the case with NATO's AWACS force.

Britain currently stands nearer to the independence than the integration end of the spectrum, deploying a wide range of nuclear and conventional forces, the bulk of which are furnished with nationally-produced equipment. This is not due to alter much under Options for Change, with no individual capability being abandoned altogether, and with national or co-operative equipment programmes continuing to dwarf overseas purchases. The proportion of British forces deployed forward in Europe will fall, and the UK will retain corps level command facilities (albeit of a multinational formation) through its leadership of the ARRC. Is the UK right to maintain roughly this same position on the spectrum between independence and integration, in view of the conflicting pressures of diminishing defence resources on the one hand and uncertain reliability of individual allies on the other?

As regards defence production, there are strong arguments for shifting further towards multinational co-operation and overseas purchasing, as shrinking force structures make purely national arms production even more uneconomic. It is hard to see dependence on other Western nations for arms supplies proving a strategic liability, and the oft-quoted experience of Belgian intransigence over ammunition supplies during the Gulf War must be set against the benefits of commonality as seen in US supplies of advanced missiles during the Falklands War. However, multinational co-operation remains preferable to simple off-the-shelf purchases from overseas, because of the ability of a domestic defence industry to modify equipment at short notice in a crisis, and because the fewer British jobs that depend on the defence effort, the less of a constituency there will be for maintaining defence spending in the absence of a clear external threat.

Turning to force ownership, it might be suggested that the decreased willingness of the United States to intervene in crises like that in Bosnia means that European nations including Britain need to *widen* their range of force capabilities, to include elements like surveillance satellites and strategic lift, for which they currently depend heavily on the USA.[18] However, if experience in the Falklands, Chad and Bosnia over the past decade is anything to go by, American reluctance to intervene in global conflicts is more likely to make itself felt through unwillingness to place US servicemen in the firing line than through a refusal to provide logistic or intelligence support to European operations. It is thus doubtful whether Britain should divert scarce defence funds to the duplication of US combat support capabilities, when the real challenge may be to provide actual combat forces in sufficient strength to make up for a lack of direct American participation.

Inability to take active US involvement in a conflict for granted diminishes the case for the UK to leave the provision of capabilities such as amphibious forces, aircraft carriers or air superiority fighters entirely to the Americans, however better equipped they may be. There are also strong arguments for Britain to maintain existing capabilities which involve close collaboration with the USA (such as Trident, nuclear attack submarines and global intelligence gathering) so as to retain as much bilateral contact and influence as possible as a counter to American retrenchment. The UK's armoured forces in Germany have often been claimed to play a similar part in cementing US force deployments in Europe, but this now seems rather more dubious given the lack of a clear American rôle in the ARRC.

There have been many suggestions recently for Britain to integrate its defence forces even more with those of its European allies, as part of the move towards a common European foreign and security policy.[19] However, it is far from clear that EC integration will offset the fact that Europe's defence problems in the post-Cold War era no longer revolve round the unifying scenario of a threatened armed invasion from the East. The Gulf War vividly illustrated the disunity this could create among European nations, even when faced with such a clear-cut challenge as the invasion of Kuwait.

The Maastricht process, which many hoped might remedy the lack of European co-ordination evident in the Gulf, has lost its momentum, and the prospect of EC expansion to include new states in central and eastern Europe poses obvious problems for the practicality of an integrated European defence.[20] There are particular problems in counting on German military co-operation in a crisis, not only because of that state's sensitivity about military force but also because the sensitivity of other states may make the direct involvement of German forces inappropriate, as in the former Yugoslavia.

All this having been said, it would be senseless for Britain with its increasingly strained defence resources to give up on alliance arrangements and to maintain a range of capabilities approximating those of a miniature superpower, merely because no single ally can be counted on to be present in every circumstance. Instead, the UK should strive to maintain the existing NATO integrated military framework, since this facilitates co-operation with a wide range of allies, at least some of whom will be involved alongside Britain in any given contingency. Within this framework, the UK should retain those capabilities essential to protecting its narrow national interests, but be prepared to forgo capabilities which are needed only to defend wider Western interests and which are fielded by several allies besides the UK.

The dilemma for Britain is that the single most like-minded major power, and the one which on recent experience can be best counted on to join the UK in military action (namely France), is outside NATO's integrated military framework and favours a more European approach to future defence. However, France faces even graver problems than Britain in maintaining its present wide range of defence capabilities now that resources are so scarce.[21] The logic of the situation thus points towards increasing bilateral co-operation and rôle specialisation, so that the two powers together may maintain a defence capability unavailable to either in isolation.[22]

The key requirement is for Britain to co-ordinate its force planning more closely with its allies, so that the various shifts of emphasis complement one another rather than leaving duplication in some areas of overall defence capability and yawning gaps elsewhere. A multinational framework for such co-ordination exists within NATO, but its utility is limited by France's continuing semi-detached status and by the political sensitivity of rôle-shedding in the context of the burden-sharing debate. Hence, the UK might find it easier to pursue bilateral co-ordination with nations such as France and Germany, and then come to NATO and WEU with a joint plan for force restructuring which minimises the adverse strategic impact of the changes and is less politically embarrassing than if either nation had proposed defence cuts independently. Which capabilities Britain might agree to de-emphasise will be discussed at the end of the following section.

Flexibility vs Specialisation

Despite the wide range of capabilities which British forces currently possess, individual capabilities have tended to become fairly specialised due to the UK's growing preoccupation during the Cold War with specific missions associated with a potential conflict with the Warsaw Pact. Hence, the Army focused on defending its assigned corps sector on the Central Front in a high-intensity armoured battle, the RAF concentrated on intercepting Soviet bomber attacks on the UK and on bombing Soviet airfields in Eastern Europe, and the Royal Navy emphasised anti-submarine warfare (ASW) in the Eastern Atlantic. The penalties of such specialisation were illustrated during the Falklands War, when British forces suffered high casualities due to their lack of integral airborne early-warning, and would have been hard-pressed to conduct the operation at all had John Nott's plans to focus the UK's maritime force structure even more heavily on anti-submarine operations already been implemented.[23]

The Falklands experience, as well as other naval deployments such as the Armilla Patrol in the Persian Gulf, led to a reprieve for the Royal Navy's amphibious forces and aircraft carriers, and encouraged the upgrading of the new Type 23 frigate from an austere ASW platform into a more general-purpose vessel.[24] This reversal of the trend towards specialisation gathered momentum as the Cold War came to an end. A central principle of Options for Change has been to increase the flexibility of British forces to cope with the more diverse challenges of the post-Cold War world. The priorities contained in John Nott's review a decade earlier are reversed rather than reinforced, with no single type of military capability to be abandoned altogether, and with the heaviest cuts being made in those specialist forces such as tanks and submarines to which Nott gave highest priority.

The trouble with this new emphasis on flexibility is that it flies directly in the face of diminishing resources. Flexibility is expensive, so to have *more* flexible forces than during the Cold War at a time when considerably *less* money is available is a challenge indeed. For one thing, funds may have to be invested to widen the capabilities of previously specialised forces, a case in point being the current plan to phase out Britain's relatively new Tornado F3 interceptors without a mid-life update, and to replace them with the more manoeuvrable and flexible European Fighter Aircraft (EFA). Moreover, the more diverse the UK's military capabilities are, the lower the economies of scale in such areas as training and the development of new equipment. As the 1992 Defence White Paper points out, 'a highly flexible force structure, with at least a little of something for almost every contingency, will have high overhead costs to support its specialisms'.[25]

One obvious way of attaining flexibility despite such resource pressures is by reducing the overall size of Britain's defence forces. Sir Michael Quinlan sees the trade-off very much in terms of 'versatility as against mass', and he argues that, 'historically, Britain has conducted the huge contraction of its force structure these past 40 years mostly by reducing scale rather than narrowing coverage'.[26] This is certainly the way that Options for Change has tried to achieve increased flexibility in the face of diminishing resources, and it looks like being a key means of squaring the circle in the future, to judge by Malcolm Rifkind's statement in April 1993 that:

> The prospect of a conventional attack by Moscow in Europe has decreased even further and this, quite rightly, has implications for the number of aircraft, ships or army units required to meet that particular threat.[27]

There are very strong arguments for this approach of simply slimming down British forces in order to retain diversity. The old mass threat from the Warsaw Pact has now gone, and the UK faces a much more unpredictable array of contingencies in which the *appropriateness* of British contributions to a multinational military effort is likely to matter more than their sheer size. However, there are limits to how far this logic can be taken, and it would be dangerous simply to shrink the scale of UK forces much beyond that planned under Options for Change while trying to retain the same diversity of capabilities.

For one thing, such continued shrinkage would exacerbate the problem of diminished economies of scale, making the maintenance of a wide array of very small capabilities highly inefficient and uneconomic. Moreover, many current or potential commitments involve long-term rather than one-off deployments, and hence require considerably more forces to service because of the requirements of troop rotation. This applies to the maintenance of Trident submarines on patrol or naval or air detachments in areas like the Falklands or the Middle East, and can be seen most clearly in the overstretch faced by the infantry in meeting commitments in Ulster, Bosnia and elsewhere.[28]

Furthermore, US force cuts and the growing shakiness of the American commitment to take the lead in defending European interests make it less feasible for Britain and other European nations to let the United States bear the bulk of the military burden. Where the USA eschews direct intervention, Europe will need forces large enough to do the job on its own. Even where the US is willing to commit combat forces, it is likely to demand a serious European contribution to sharing the burden and the casualties, rather than just a token military commitment to demonstrate political solidarity.[29] For all these reasons, a policy of maintaining smaller and smaller capabilities in every area could all too easily lead to Britain's armed forces becoming 'Jack of all trades, master of none'.

An alternative solution to the trade-off would be to back off from the ideal of all-round flexibility, and to focus Britain's defence preparations on a smaller range of potential contingencies. There are many ways in which this might be done, but two diametrically opposite approaches would be either to focus on the narrow territorial defence of British interests at the expense of wider overseas intervention, or to emphasise the UK's strengths in low-intensity operations while running down capabilities for high-intensity warfare now that the Warsaw Pact threat has so completely collapsed.

The trouble with both of these approaches is that it is not so easy in practice to draw a sharp line between defence and intervention, or between low- and high-intensity warfare. The best and most cost-effective way of defending Europe against challenges such as a flood of refugees, a maverick nuclear threat or interference with shipping or citizens overseas may well be judicious armed intervention rather than a preclusive defence of Europe's borders and airspace. Even nations such as Germany and Japan, whose armed forces have recently been focused very much on self-defence, are now being expected to take a more active and interventionist stance, and this is all the more true for Britain with its self-image as a world power and its desire to defend its permanent membership of the UN Security Council.[30]

Similarly, it would be difficult for the UK to move to the other extreme of focusing its whole defence effort on such intervention operations, because it is precisely the active employment of force in such circumstances which may trigger the kind of escalation from which the need for high-intensity defence capabilities could arise. This is illustrated by recent experience in the Gulf and in Bosnia, with the UN attack to liberate Kuwait prompting ballistic missile retaliation by Iraq, and with the threat to UN peacekeepers in Bosnia requiring heavier ground, sea and air back-up to protect or extricate the forces involved. Hence, there are severe limits to how far Britain can reduce the need for flexibility by emphasising just one end of the spectrum of capabilities.[31]

This leaves just one way of addressing the trade-off concerned, namely by focusing on capabilities which are *in themselves* flexible and multi-rôle, at the expense of others which are suitable only for specific missions and which hence may prove of little use in other types of contingencies. Options for Change already moves some way in this direction, by cutting armoured forces and submarines more than infantry and surface naval vessels respectively, and by leaving intact capabilities such as air transport which are likely to be stretched to the limit whatever contingency is involved. The RAF's planned purchase of large numbers of EFA also fits into this pattern, since EFA is intended to be capable of ground attack as well as air superiority operations, hence allowing standardisation on one multi-rôle platform with consequent benefits in economies of scale.[32]

More radical progress along these lines would involve even deeper cuts in more specialised capabilities, perhaps leading to their complete elimination. However, the trouble with such an approach is that multi-rôle capabilities tend to be more expensive than specialised ones (as with the Type 23), and that specialised forces do have an often crucial edge in the type of conflict for which they were designed. Submarines are now arguably the dominant weapons in combat between navies, and give Britain a particular edge over Third World fleets, as the Falklands conflict showed. The Gulf War demonstrated that tanks, too, are of great importance in land warfare even in contexts other than the erstwhile East–West confrontation, though their dominance is much less secure given the profusion of anti-tank capabilities being developed.

The key is to ensure, through the kind of co-ordination with allies discussed in the previous section, that at least some allies retain any given kind of specialised capability, rather than all opting for flexible, multi-rôle forces which cannot adequately perform some critical task. The UK can then take the calculated risk of relying more on its allies for certain specialist capabilities not vital to its own national defence. Despite sweeping defence cuts, the American military establishment will probably remain large enough to maintain almost the entire range of such specialised capabilities, but, for the reasons stated earlier, it seems unwise for the UK to rely on US capabilities alone, except in the case of costly combat support facilities such as satellites. Hence, the question becomes which capabilities can Britain afford to leave to a combination of the USA and other European allies?

The obvious answer is heavy armoured forces. These are unnecessary for the direct defence of the UK, and their deployment in Germany for lack of training areas at home involves substantial additional costs and local political objections. It seems to make much more sense for continental nations like Germany and Turkey to emphasise these capabilities, especially since the most important rôle of such forces is the kind of residual European self-defence task with which Germany remains most politically comfortable. In return for those nations' agreement to continue to stress heavy armour, Britain could promise to retain specialist capabilities such as submarines and maritime patrol aircraft, in case a serious naval challenge should arise.

Candidates for specialist rôle-sharing between Britain and France are less obvious, because the two nations occupy similar strategic positions and currently possess a similar wide range of defence capabilities. However, there is a good case for the UK to leave to France the congenial rôle of providing independent European capabilities in such fields as space and tactical nuclear forces, in case the American alliance should come under even greater strain. In return, Britain might agree to bear more of the burden in hunter-killer submarines, or to maintain the capability for long-range air bombardment currently embodied in the Tornado GR1 force. One can also envisage more fundamental rôle-sharing in which Britain concentrates on providing land-based tactical air power through a large EFA force, while leaving to France the provision of carrier-based maritime air power, but this would involve spreading rôle-specialisation to more flexible capabilities in a way which might not prove possible unless Anglo–French defence co-operation becomes much better established.

The more obvious expedient of deep reductions in heavy armour is, of course, just as radical a policy, given Britain's heavy investment in this capability during the Cold War. There are strong counter-arguments to such a shift, in particular that it could jeopardise British leadership of the ARRC and perhaps even weaken NATO by increasing the relative prominence of the ill-defined 'Franco–German corps'.[33] The combination of France's lack of appropriate capabilities and Germany's political reluctance to use force during the Gulf War illustrates the potential drawbacks for Britain of relying too much on its allies to provide heavy armoured forces. Hence, attention will now be turned to other trade-offs in British defence planning, to see whether they weaken or strengthen the case for this particular solution to pressures on the defence budget.

Mobility vs Punch

British forces did not need great intrinsic mobility to fulfil their primary Cold War rôles. The Army deployed its heavy equipment and a third of its regular manpower forward in its assigned defence area in northern Germany, and planned to reinforce this in time of crisis with large numbers of regular and reserve personnel, using civilian transport such as cross-Channel ferries. The Royal Navy and RAF relied on operating from established bases in the UK and Germany. Only certain specialist forces such as the Royal Marines and the UK contributions to the small NATO mobile forces of the time required greater mobility. Hence, the tendency during defence reviews was for mobility assets to be cut back in an effort to boost the 'tooth to tail' ratio, and for as much reliance as possible to be placed on civilian assets, as with the privatisation of the Belfast heavy cargo planes.[34]

John Nott's 1981 Defence Review did emphasise the need for air transport to tackle out-of-area contingencies, and the Falklands War the following year prompted a number of moves to increase the 'reach' of British forces, most notably a much wider provision for aerial refuelling. Mobility, like flexibility, became a key guiding principle of the Options for Change review, and associated capabilities such as air transport, Army helicopters, amphibious forces and the fleet train were spared the cuts which were imposed in other areas of defence capability. The question is whether this approach of simply maintaining the previous level of mobility provision while the force as a whole shrinks is enough to address the much increased mobility demands of the post-Cold War world.

Now that the Eastern threat has collapsed so completely, there seems very little likelihood of British forces actually having to fight in the areas and from the bases at which they are now deployed (with the obvious exception of Ulster). Even should a direct threat to NATO territory arise, this is more likely to involve southern flank nations such as Greece or Turkey than to take the form of a renewed threat on the Central Front. More probably, British forces will be called upon to deploy outside current NATO territory, for the kind of operations conducted recently in the Gulf, northern Iraq, Cambodia and Bosnia.

The UK's deployment and support of an armoured division plus associated air and maritime capabilities in the Persian Gulf for the war against Iraq was by far the most demanding of these tasks, and might suggest that existing mobility capabilities are adequate to meet the mobility demands of the post-Cold War world. However, there were several favourable circumstances which eased this particular mission, notably the leeway of several months for a gradual build-up, the lack of a naval threat which allowed the use of foreign-flagged commercial shipping, and the availability of port facilities, extensive airfields and indigenous fuel supplies. The logistic challenges faced in Bosnia and northern Iraq, despite the much smaller scale of the operations and the greater proximity to NATO territory, illustrate the problems which may ensue when time is shorter, terrain and climate harsher, lines of communication less secure, and infrastructure inadequate.

What Britain must do is to strike a new balance between mobility and combat potential, so that on the one hand it does not have to leave part of its forces sitting idly at home in a crisis for lack of logistic capability to deploy and sustain them, while on the other hand it does not make its forces so light in the name of mobility that they are incapable of performing the required task in the face of serious opposition. Striking the right balance is very difficult because, as discussed above, logistic requirements vary enormously between different scenarios, making it impossible to agree a single ideal 'mix' that will cover every case.[35]

The foremost need is for a more integrated consideration of mobility requirements in force planning as a whole. At one level, this is necessary to prevent high-profile 'teeth' programmes like EFA crowding out vital mobility enhancements as resources become increasingly squeezed. More fundamentally, it is needed to ensure that mobility becomes a prime consideration when planning combat capabilities themselves, since whether such capabilities can be employed in distant and unforeseen theatres is now just as important a criterion of their military utility in the post-Cold War world as is their flexibility in performing different missions.

The mobility of a given type of force is a compound of many factors – its speed, range and endurance when moving under its own steam, its capacity to traverse different types of terrain and to operate in harsh climatic conditions, the weight and volume of logistic capacity needed to transport it and to keep it supplied, its ease of maintainability once deployed, and its dependence on established bases. Different types of forces have different strengths and weaknesses across these various parameters: for example, aircraft are fast and unlimited by terrain, but ships have greater range and endurance and so are less dependent on local bases. However, it is possible to identify several overall conclusions which British force planners may draw from the increased importance of mobility in the new strategic situation.

For one thing, the reach and/or short-field capability of aircraft become even more vital, to enable operations at some distance from established bases. This suggests that Britain needs to place even more emphasis on air-to-air refuelling and on the provision of tanker capabilities, and that Harriers and combat helicopters, which do not depend on established runways, are now even more important for the provision of responsive air support.

Second, limits on base loading and logistic capacity suggest that high quality combat forces and equipment will tend to be more cost-effective, as long as this does not mean fragile high technology which is insufficiently rugged for operations in field conditions. Hence, the UK should emphasise quality over quantity to get the maximum punch from a given size of force, especially through greater reliance on precision-guided munitions (PGMs).

Third, heavy land forces are the most problematic in terms of mobility, because of their dependence on large, surface-bound logistic capabilities to deploy them and to keep them supplied, and because of their limitations in difficult terrain such as the hills of Bosnia. Experience in Bosnia has shown that mechanised infantry may nevertheless have an important rôle to play in such contingencies, but it is much less clear whether the UK's heavy Challenger tanks, with their even greater mobility limitations, offer a cost-effective security investment in the new strategic situation.

Given all the other arguments for Britain to de-emphasise this specialist capability, the added constraints of lack of mobility suggest that there is a very strong case for making deep reductions in heavy tanks and moving to a mix of mechanised infantry and combat helicopters. Such a force could use other means such as PGMs to tackle enemy armour, and could be deployed more rapidly in order to meet the strategic requirements of the ARRC. Indeed, the UK could argue that such a reorientation of its forces gives it a more appropriate package of capabilities for its ARRC commitment, while also helping it to fulfil its national needs in Ulster and its global responsibilities as a permanent member of the UN Security Council.

As regards the provision of logistic capabilities themselves, the cheapest approach is simply to rely on chartered or requisitioned commercial shipping. There has been concern for many years about the inexorable shrinkage of the British merchant fleet, as operators find it cheaper to use foreign manpower and 'flags of convenience'. The government has so far resisted offering subsidies to the UK shipping industry in order to halt this decline, though it has identified a need to do something to preserve adequate numbers of British crewmen.[36] Although the problem is not as grave in the context of multinational, often UN-sponsored, operations as it was when considering Britain-alone scenarios like the Falklands War, it seems unwise for the UK to rely on foreign charters as much as it did during the Gulf War (when only five of the 162 vessels used were British) now that regional naval and air capabilities are placing maritime logistics at increasing risk.[37]

Air transport is much more expensive than surface-bound logistics, and so Britain cannot hope to rely on it for any but the smallest and lightest deployment. However, air transport capabilities do have the enormous advantages of speed and the ability to cross all types of terrain – land or sea, mountains or forests, even enemy-held terrain if the anti-aircraft threat is limited. Given the flexibility which these twin attributes provide, Britain's small air transport forces are likely to be used to the limit in future crises just as they have been in the past, whether the mission be providing humanitarian aid to beleaguered communities, backing up a crisis deployment of air assets, or providing logistic flexibility and tactical mobility for surface forces.

There are strong arguments for *increasing* Britain's fixed and rotary wing air transport capabilities to cope with the much greater mobility demands of the new strategic situation, and it is vital that defence planners take a holistic view of UK force requirements so that the RAF is not forced (or allowed) to make cutbacks in this area as a 'sacrifice' to pay for EFA procurement. Although there is no point in trying to duplicate the much larger airlift resources of the USA, there is enough chance that those resources may be held back or may be fully occupied moving American forces themselves to justify some degree of enhanced European provision in this area, as has been suggested by the WEU. Otherwise, Britain and its European allies may have enough combat capabilities to tackle a particular mission but be prevented from doing so by a lack of strategic mobility.

Quality vs Quantity

The final trade-off to be considered is the perennial tension between sophisticated but expensive capabilities and cheaper but less capable forces. Britain has traditionally preferred to rely on small but high quality professional armed forces, except when an overwhelming threat necessitated a resort to conscription as happened during the two World Wars. However, it has tended to economise by cutting corners on equipment spending, leading to the jibe that Britain's forces were 'the best trained and worst equipped in NATO'.

Although this criticism is seen to be wildly overdrawn when one compares British defence equipment with that of France and of most southern flank members of the Alliance, it is true that at times of particularly strained defence resources such as the mid-1970s and late 1980s, the UK has tended to make damaging economies in spares, ammunition stocks and the like in order to avoid cutting front line strength. As one defence official admitted in retrospect:

> What you actually had in the shop window as part of your deterrent posture was of paramount importance. You did not actually expect to have to use it.[38]

A key justification which the government has employed for the force cuts under Options for Change is that they will enable the remaining forces to be 'smaller but better'. In the face of understandable suspicion that this meant 'smaller now, better later (if ever)', the 1992 Defence White Paper included a special section detailing the re-equipment programmes in train. It claimed, for example, that 'the implementation of our plans for new and better equipment will mean that the capability of the Army's contribution to the defence of mainland Europe will reduce by only some 20 per cent, despite reducing the number of divisions committed to this rôle from four to two'.[39]

However, as Ron Smith points out elsewhere in this volume, the planned reductions in Britain's defence budget mean that there will have to be further deep cuts in manpower beyond those planned under Options for Change to have any chance of raising the proportion of the budget spent on equipment above the low level to which it had been reduced by 1990.[40] The UK thus faces exactly the same hard choices in the mid-1990s as it faced in the late 1980s, over whether to make further cuts in force structure or to economise instead by delaying the procurement of new equipment and compromising readiness and sustainability through progressive underfunding.

The first priority must surely be to maintain the unparalled quality of the *personnel* in Britain's armed services. It is this which has given the UK a unique advantage in recent conflicts, compared with states which have sometimes been able to spend more lavishly on military equipment, but which have not been able to man it with the same calibre of personnel. Good people, at all levels down to that of the individual serviceman, are at a particular premium in the new strategic situation, given the need for sensitive handling of tangled missions like those in Bosnia and Somalia. The professionalism of Britain's military personnel, honed by long service and by the demands of Ulster, represents a more distinctive contribution to multinational military efforts than any specialisation which the UK might seek to cultivate in a particular aspect of military hardware.

The reduction in manpower requirements under Options for Change should help Britain overcome the demographic trough which otherwise threatened even greater undermanning of the previous force structure.[41] However, it will remain necessary to avoid parsimony on pay and conditions of service, so as to attract and retain skilled personnel in the face of increasing competition from other employers as the economy improves. It is also important to reduce commitments in line with the manpower available so as to minimise demoralising overstretch, and to maintain the realistic training which is a key ingredient in the quality of British service personnel.

Turning to equipment, it has been argued by some that there is less need for Britain to field the most advanced weapons now that the previous high technology threat posed by the USSR has crumbled. This may be true in certain limited respects, such as the diminished need for an air-launched nuclear stand-off missile now that there is little or no requirement to be able to penetrate deep air defences to threaten limited nuclear retaliation for an overwhelming conventional attack. However, sophisticated Eastern and Western military equipment continues to be exported throughout the world and, judging by the asymmetric outcomes of the Gulf War and of recent Arab–Israeli battles, the most cost-effective response for Britain is not simply to *match* the sophistication of such hardware but to seek a qualitative edge which will yield disproportionate advantages in combat.

There are many other characteristics of the new strategic situation which also point to a need for high quality defence equipment. As was pointed out in the previous section, limits on base loading and logistic sustainability in distant operations suggest that individual weapons and platforms should be as effective as possible. Furthermore, the increased sensitivity to casualties and 'collateral damage' which was apparent during the Gulf War means that British personnel must be given as much protection as possible from the appalling potential effects of modern weapons, and that intelligence and precision-targeting capabilities must be improved to minimise the risk of harming innocent civilians.

The high financial cost of maintaining professional rather than conscript forces is a major reason why the UK's spending on defence equipment has been squeezed, but in fact this reliance on professionals rather than conscripts is in itself a major reason to emphasise high quality equipment. Not only does it make no sense to dilute the effectiveness of expensive personnel by giving them sub-standard weapons, but it is also vital to introduce new equipment which is less manpower-intensive than older models, in order to allow personnel levels to be reduced as is currently planned.

US armed forces have tended to respond to the trade-off between quality and quantity by fielding a 'hi-lo mix' of systems, ranging from ultra-sophisticated weapons such as the F-117 to cheaper platforms such as the F-16 for use in less demanding threat environments. The trouble with this compromise as far as Britain is concerned is that the UK force structure is too small to field different types of equipment for the same task without crippling loss of economies of scale, and that the high quality element would probably be too small to allow force rotation through a long-term commitment like the Armilla Patrol in the Persian Gulf. Hence, Britain should probably settle for a single high standard of equipment somewhere between the most sophisticated components of the US arsenal and the less capable export models found in Third World arsenals, and should rely for diversity on the 'old-new mix' which will continue to exist as equipment is progressively replaced or modernised.

There is even less room for economies on spares and ammunition stocks than on equipment itself now that British forces are for use rather than ostentation. During the Gulf War, the UK managed to deploy one armoured division to Saudi Arabia only by ruthless cannibalisation of the ammunition, spares and equipment of the other two divisions left behind in Germany. After Options for Change, there will be no more slack capability to cannabalise in this way, and so Britain must make a significantly greater proportional investment in sustainability if its forces are to cope with the insatiable logistic demands of modern warfare.

What all this means is that the UK would be very ill-advised to respond to budgetary pressures over the next few years by postponing re-equipment programmes, cutting back on training, reducing stocks and spares, and other classic ways of underfunding the armed forces. Instead, it must be prepared to make further reductions in the size of the Services, in order to maintain forces of the quality and fighting capability needed to tackle the real military challenges of the 21st Century. Since across-the-board force cuts would exacerbate inefficiencies and compound existing overstretch, it seems preferable to focus the cuts on particular specialist capabilities, of which the leading candidate on several grounds appears to be heavy armoured forces.

Conclusion

British defence policy over the past 40 years has involved a series of incremental responses to immediate budgetary crises, the aim throughout being to minimise the impact of the financial crunch on defence capability. Quite reasonably, this has meant that planners have been reluctant to make radical shifts in force structure, because the resultant disruption and waste of previous investment would necessitate even deeper force cuts in order to balance the books. Defence provision has thus displayed considerable inertia, with change occurring only at the margins, in line with the fairly gradual shifts in the strategic context itself during the Cold War.[42]

The formative phase of the Options for Change reductions occurred at a time when it was still possible to see the strategic transformation in incremental rather than revolutionary terms. The USSR remained the major potential threat, albeit with its capabilities reduced in some areas by arms control and the break-up of the Warsaw Pact. The dramatic revival of Britain's rôle as a 'world policeman' during the Gulf crisis had yet to occur. It is hardly surprising in view of the prevailing uncertainty about future developments that planners took the time-honoured course of simply phasing out older systems in those areas now thought to be of diminished priority, rather than trying to design a new force structure from the bottom up.[43]

By analysing the shifting trade-offs in UK defence planning, this

Chapter has tried to assess whether the force structure outlined under Options for Change is sufficiently out of tune with the fundamentally different strategic situation which Britain now faces that a radical reappraisal of this kind is required. The analysis has highlighted a number of imperatives for British defence planners in the post-Cold War world, among which are the following:

- The need for good intelligence, to build up as accurate a picture as possible of the gravity, credibility and imminence of potential contingencies;
- The need to co-ordinate force planning more closely with allies, in particular France which may become Britain's most likely single partner in military operations;
- The need for a more integrated consideration of mobility requirements in force planning, taking into account base availability as well as deployability and logistics;
- The need for forces which exploit the unique strengths of British military skill and professionalism, and which are well-equipped and sustainable enough for use rather than ostentation.

As regards the central issues of flexibility and force balance, a key determinant is the level of resources which the UK is willing to devote to defence. The Options for Change force structure still makes considerable sense *at that level of force provision*, but if further defence cuts are required (as seems inevitable), it does not make sense either to resort to the progressive underfunding which occurred in the late 1980s or simply to slim the force structure down even further across the board. Instead, certain capabilities must be at least maintained at existing levels and preferably enhanced to meet the demands of the post-Cold War world, while others suggest themselves for deep reductions in order to compensate.

In the former category fall infantry and air transport capabilities, which have played a major rôle in every post-Cold War commitment from the Gulf War and northern Iraq to Bosnia, Cambodia and Ulster. They embody the mobility and flexibility which have rightly been identified as key requirements for British forces in the new situation, and the infantry also offer British professionalism in its most distinctive form as a contribution to multinational operations in tangled crisis areas.

In the latter category fall heavy armoured forces, and especially tanks. They are specialised capabilities, lacking in mobility, and of doubtful long-term viability given current developments in anti-tank weaponry. They are unnecessary for direct defence of the UK, and cannot even be based there for lack of suitable exercise areas. Many of the UK's allies have their own armoured capability, often much larger or much closer to potential battle zones. Although Britain's tanks proved useful during the Gulf War and form a key part of its current contribution to the ARRC, there are strong arguments that a different use of the resources involved could prove much more useful in many potential contingencies without fatally compromising Britain's response in any.

The trouble is that the UK has already committed itself to expensive re-equipment of its armoured forces with Challenger II tanks, Warrior troop carriers, MLRS rocket-launchers and AS90 self-propelled guns.[44] However, only two of the eight remaining armoured regiments are as yet due to be equipped with Challenger II, and there is still scope to save money by phasing out some or all of the rest without upgrading their Challenger Is. Although incremental adjustments such as phasing out a fighter squadron here, a few frigates there, may seem preferable in the short term because they allow the maintenance of more balanced forces, the repeated need for such economies over a period of years could in the long run emasculate Britain's forces across the board.

The danger is that the unexpected dissolution of the direct threat to the UK and its NATO allies will prompt continued downward pressure on the defence budget, but that the response of force planners to the repeated funding crises which will result will be belated and incremental. From a short term perspective, it always seems wasteful and dangerous to sacrifice a well-established defence capability, however little use there may seem for it at present. Maintaining balanced forces so as to keep one's options open invariably seems like the lesser evil. It is only when viewed over the longer term that repeated 'salami-slicing' of this kind is seen to have caused even greater cumulative damage than would have resulted from a bold decision at the outset to concentrate on providing a narrower range of capabilities.

Hence, the key imperative which emerges from this analysis is that defence planners need to take a more realistic long-term view of the financial sustainability of the defence programme into the 21st Century, in the light of the level of resources which it is politically practical to expect. They will then have more of a chance to co-ordinate their defence cuts with allies, rather than reacting at the last minute to immediate budgetary crises. This may seem a counsel of perfection in the light of previous experience, but the alternative is for Britain to continue pretending it can play the leading rôle in European defence in land, sea, air and nuclear capabilities alike until its contributions in each area become so underfunded and lacking in cost-effectiveness that it finds itself with only the shadow and not the substance of military power.

Notes

1. See John Baylis (ed.), *Alternative Approaches to British Defence Policy* (London: Macmillan, 1983).
2. See Richard Mottram, 'Options for Change: Process and Prospects', *RUSI Journal*, 136/1, Spring 1991, pp.22–6, and Sir Michael Quinlan, 'British Defence Planning in a Changing World', *The World Today*, 48/8–9, Aug/Sep. 1992, pp.161–2.
3. Statement on the Defence Estimates, 1992, Cm 1981, (London: HMSO, July 1992), pp.13–14.
4. See *Hansard.*, 25 July 1990, cols.470–73.
5. HCDC report on the Statement on the Defence Estimates, 1992, HC 218, (London: HMSO, November 1992), pp.vii–viii.
6. See 'Frontline champagne toast', *The Times*, 4 February 1993, and the HCDC report on *Britain's Army for the 90s: Commitments and Resources*, HC 306, (London: HMSO, January 1993).
7. Statement on the Defence Estimates, 1993. Cm 2270, (London: HMSO, July 1993), pp. 9-11.
8. Cm 1981, p.14.
9. See David French, *The British Way in Warfare, 1688–2000* (London: Unwin Hyman, 1990), pp.181–87.
10. See Tom King's remarks in the House of Commons Defence Committee report on *Options for Change: Army – Review of the White Paper, Britain's Army for the 90s, CM 1595*, HC 45, (London: HMSO, February 1992), p.2.
11. On the damaging mobilisation delay during the Suez crisis, see Hugh Thomas, *The Suez Affair* (London: Weidenfeld & Nicolson, 1967).
12. In his words, 'The British armed forces will remain the most professional in the world, and one of the most highly respected and most successful. After the United States, they are also, probably, the most powerful, leaving aside Russia's nuclear forces. If this seems a strong claim, one has only to ask where one would find another country with such military weight in the international community? Not in Africa, the Americas or Asia. And, with the possible exception of France, not elsewhere in Europe.' See *The Sunday Times*, 18 April 1993.
13. See Lt.Gen. Sir Jeremy Mackenzie, 'Allied Command Europe's Rapid Reaction Corps', *RUSI Journal*, 138/1, February 1993.
14. See Christopher Coker, 'The Audit of War: An Interpretation of Options for Change', *European Security Analyst*, April 1992, and Christopher Bellamy, 'Soldier of Fortune: Britain's New Military Role', *International Affairs*, 68/3, July 1992.
15. See 'NATO chief favours action on Bosnia', *The Independent*, 22 April 1993.
16. See 'TA soldiers set for front line role'. *The Independent*, 18 June 1993, and the HCDC report on *Options for Change: Reserve Forces*, HC 163, (London: HMSO, February 1992).
17. Cm 1981, p.9.
18. On recent hints of a less prominent US world rôle, see 'White House in foreign policy row', *The Independent*, 27 May 1993.
19. See, for example, Calum Macdonald MP, *A new model army: towards a European defence community* (London: Fabian Society, October 1991), and

Malcolm Chalmers, *Biting the bullet: European defence options for Britain* (London: IPPR, June 1992).
20. See 'Community opts for expansion in two stages', *The Independent*, 23 June 1993.
21. See Diego Ruiz Palmer, *French Strategic Options in the 1990s*, Adelphi Paper 260, (London: Brassey's for IISS, 1991).
22. On existing measures of co-operation, see the HCDC report on *Anglo/French Defence Cooperation*, HC 91. (London: HMSO, November 1991).
23. See Eric Grove, *Vanguard to Trident* (Annapolis: Naval Institute Press, 1987), Ch.10.
24. See the HCDC report on *The Future Size and Rôle of the Royal Navy's Surface Fleet*, HC 309, (London: HMSO, June 1988).
25. Cm 1981, p.13.
26. Quinlan, 'British defence planning', p.161.
27. *The Sunday Times*, 18 April 1993.
28. HC 306 (1993). John Keegan highlights the way in which the Ulster commitment reduces the deployability of the Army as a whole in his article, 'Bogged down at home while the whole world beckons', *The Daily Telegraph*, 26 January 1993.
29. On US force cuts, see 'Clinton defies military over defence rethink', *The Independent*, 23 June 1993.
30. See 'US backs expansion of Security Council', *The Independent*, 11 June 1993.
31. For a fuller discussion of these options, see my article on 'British defence choices beyond "Options for Change"', *International Affairs*, 69/2, April 1993, pp.280–3.
32. See the HCDC report on the *European Fighter Aircraft*, HC 299, (London: HMSO, March 1992).
33. See Edward Foster, 'The Franco–German Corps: A "Theological" Debate?', *RUSI Journal*, 137/4, August 1992.
34. See Michael Carver, *Tightrope Walking: British Defence Policy since 1945* (London: Hutchinson, 1992).
35. On the differing logistic challenges of earlier British operations, see Julian Thompson, *The Lifeblood of War: Logistics in Armed Conflict*, (London: Brassey's, 1991).
36. See HC 218 (1992), pp.xxxvi–xxxvii.
37. See 'Gulf war equipment may have ended up in Bosnia', *The Independent*, 22 June 1993.
38. HC 218 (1992), p.xvi.
39. Cm 1981, pp.32–3. See also HC 45 (1992), pp.xxxvii–xxxviii, and HC 218 (1992), pp.xv–xxviii.
40. See also my own arguments to this effect in 'British Defence Choices', pp.273–7.
41. See the HCDC report on the Statement on the Defence Estimates, 1991, HC 394, (London: HMSO, July 1991), p.xviii.
42. See John Baylis, *British Defence Policy: Striking the Right Balance* (London: Macmillan, 1989).
43. I myself took a very cautious view at the time of the advisability of deeper cuts, especially in the Army in Germany, while the possibility of a revived Soviet threat remained. See my study on *British Strategic Priorities in the 1990s*, Adelphi Paper 254, (London: IISS, Winter 1990).
44. See Cm 1981 (1992), p.64–5.

10
Concentration of Effort and Complementarity

David Greenwood

The recent history of British defence policy-making and planning is well known. Having resisted calls for a full-scale defence review throughout the later 1980s, the Ministry of Defence (MOD) examined Options for Change in the national defence effort in the first six months of 1990. The results came out in July of that year.[1] A full prescription for the country's future defences appeared later, in the 1991 Defence White Paper, sub-titled *Britain's Defence for the 90s*. This confirmed a reduction of around 20 per cent in service manpower, with the largest cuts falling on the Army and Air Force; and a real reduction in the budget of approximately five per cent over the five-year period 1990/91–1994/95. The (then) Secretary of State for Defence, Tom King, said Britain's armed forces would be 'smaller, but better'.[2]

The force structure choices summarised in *Britain's Defence for the 90s* left the country's strategic nuclear capability intact and meant only marginal change in provision for the direct protection of the United Kingdom itself. But they entailed big reductions both in ground and tactical air forces for the European theatre (including a halving of army numbers in Germany) and in naval and maritime-air forces for the Atlantic and the Channel (with the surface fleet trimmed to three carriers plus 'around 40' escorts and the submarine fleet to 'about 16' boats). Stationed forces further afield were to be maintained for as long as necessary.[3]

In the first Defence White Paper of the second Major government, published in July 1992, ministers finally produced a formal statement of the purpose of post-Cold War defence policy and a fresh categorisation of the tasks of the Services. The statement of purpose was a blinding glimpse of the obvious.[4] The rôle definitions had a 'defence for all reasons' ring about them. They provided a portmanteau rationale for the contribution that Britain had already decided to make to revised NATO defences plus any future contribution to forces for the Western European Union (WEU); and declaratory policy cover for participation in military operations conducted by NATO, WEU, the United Nations or ad hoc coalitions acting under the authority of either the UN or the regional Conference on Security and Co-operation in Europe (CSCE). NATO would 'continue to be the focus ... of peacetime planning and training', the White Paper said.[5]

Pressures for Change

In mid-1992 the planners who had laboured to produce the post-'Options' programme, and the weasel wordsmiths who had applied the policy gloss, had reason to feel well satisfied with their work. Sensible structural adjustments had been made. All conformed to the guidelines that had emerged from the NATO-wide strategy and force structure review endorsed by Alliance ministers at their Rome meeting in November 1991. Indeed the United Kingdom had undertaken to lead a key new formation in the remodelled peacetime order of battle for Allied Command Europe (ACE), namely the ACE Rapid Reaction Corps (ARRC). On the face of it, therefore, what had been delivered was an *appropriate* programme for the new strategic circumstances. Moreover, the defence effort had been trimmed to fit, fully-funded, into the Treasury's budgetary straitjacket for the early 1990s. There was some hope, therefore, that it might also be a *sustainable* programme: no 'funding gaps' as in the 1980s, no impossibly constricting cash limits putting a permanent 'volume squeeze' on the programme, no perennial panic to make ends meet.

Hence, perhaps, the whiff of smugness about the personal introduction which the new Secretary of State for Defence, Malcolm Rifkind, wrote for the 1992 White Paper. 'The major restructuring of the armed forces ... will match them to our changing defence needs', he claimed, 'enabling them to face the future with confidence'. In a paragraph on NATO, he referred to the 'vigour and vitality' that had found expression in 'a new Strategic Concept which sets a new direction for the Alliance' and noted that the organisation had 'overhauled its military strategy and force structures to meet the changing strategic environment'.[6] However, most of Mr Rifkind's top advisers must have known that the post-'Options' programme might not be sustainable after all — so much for facing the future with confidence — and a few realised that it might not be appropriate

Concentration of Effort and Complementarity 177

either, because of further evolution in the security environment. By mid-1992 there was a feeling around that fresh, tougher force structure choices might shortly have to be made.

Such premonitions were confirmed in the second half of 1992; and the need for further, and far-reaching, reappraisal of the defence effort has been getting steadily more apparent since. The MOD is plainly not going to receive sufficient resources to finance the post-'Options' programme properly. Furthermore, NATO is not going to stick by (nor indeed should it stick by) the 'overhauled' arrangements with which the United Kingdom took pains to conform.

These are the pressures for change. In what follows I analyse each of them and their implications for future defence choices. Three principal conclusions emerge. The first is that, domestically, concentration of effort is the only satisfactory answer to inadequacy of resources. The second is that, for NATO, an important post-Cold War rôle beckons, as a 'coalition-in-waiting' for contingency operations in and around Europe. The third is that British force structure decisions should be taken with an eye to what the country can best contribute to the Alliance's assumption and fulfilment of this rôle.

The Domestic Predicament: Underfunding

Downward revision of the budgetary projections underlying the post-'Options' programme began in the 1992 Public Expenditure Survey round. The MOD had been looking forward to slightly more cash each year through the mid-1990s, which implied only a modest shrinkage in the real value of the budget. Thus the 1992 Defence White Paper recorded allocations as follows:

	1992–93	1993–94	1994–95	1995–96
£ billion (cash)	24.2	24.5	24.8	?25.0

What emerged from that summer's scrutiny of all public spending plans, however, was a very different profile: a bit less money than had been budgeted for the current year and a lot less than previously planned for in the next three. As given in the Chancellor of the Exchequer's Autumn Statement (November 1992), the exact figures were:

	1992–93	1993–94	1994–95	1995–96
£ billion (cash)	24.0	23.5	23.8	23.2

TABLE 1 PROSPECTIVE UNDERFUNDING TO 1998–99

(a) *Cash*

Financial Year	Resources required £bn	Resources allocated £bn	Difference (underfunding) £bn
1992–93	24.2	24.0	0.2
1993–94	24.5	23.5	1.0
1994–95	24.8	23.5	1.3
1995–96	25.0	23.0	2.0
1996–97	25.2	22.5	2.7
1997–98	25.4	22.0	3.5
1998–99	25.5	21.5	4.0

(b) *Constant prices (1990–91)*

Financial Year	Resources required £bn	Resources allocated £bn	Difference (underfunding) £bn
1992–93	21.3	21.2	0.1
1993–94	21.0	20.1	0.9
1994–95	20.2	19.1	1.1
1995–96	19.3	17.8	1.5
1996–97	18.5	16.5	2.0
1997–98	17.7	15.4	2.3
1998–99	16.9	14.3	2.6

Source: See text.

Moreover, the 'buzz' from Whitehall in the first half of 1993 was that the later planning totals were most unlikely to survive the 1993 Survey 'round'. The MOD just might, with luck, get (say) £23.5 billion for 1994–95, £23.0 billion or thereabouts for 1995–96, and maybe £22.5 billion for 1996–97. In other words, the outlook was *less* cash each year, implying a fall in the value of the defence budget after inflation fully commensurate with the envisaged contraction in the national force structure; and hence a return to the under-funding that had characterised the 1980s.[7]

The effects have been seen already. The word has gone out to restrict military activity levels – ship-days at sea, track mileage/live firing, flying hours – conveniently 'rationed' by line managers' tight fuel budgets in some instances. Selected procurement programmes have been trimmed, stretched-out or postponed (and some outright cancellations must be in the offing). Also, the force structure is being hollowed-out in places. The surface fleet is a case in point: those 'about 40' destroyers and frigates will reportedly consist of a couple of dozen ships that will do their full operational stint year-in-year-out while the remaining escorts work to a less demanding schedule. There has been downward adjustment of manpower targets as well. Mid-1990s Service strengths will not be what they were going to be.[8]

A new 'funding gap'
Despite these clear distress signals, the scale of the prospective 'volume squeeze' on the post-'Options' defence programme is not widely appreciated. Yet it is straightforward enough to portray the MOD's predicament, using a simple 'funding gap' analysis to highlight the difference between the *resources allocated* (or likely to be allocated) in the budget, as estimated earlier, and the *resources required* to sustain the original programme, as reflected in the financial projections initially associated with it. Such an analysis is shown in Table 1, which is divided into (a) figures in cash and (b) figures at constant 1990–91 prices, the latter to emphasise that it is the extent and pace of contraction that is at issue here.

It will bear repeating that, from 1994–95 on, the sums in the resources allocated columns of Table 1 are *estimates* of how much money the MOD will get in the second half of the 1990s. But they are plausible values, given the state of Britain's public finances; and, if they are right, the post-'Options' programme is going to be massively underfunded by the closing years of the decade.[9]

We have been here before, of course, most recently in the early and middle 1980s. Moreover, that not-too-distant experience is one from which there are lessons to be learned. 'How did the MOD cope with underfunding?' is an obvious first question. There are interesting supplementaries as well: were things done then which, with hindsight, ought not to have been done? And is there anything that might have been done at that time, was not done, but ought to get more serious attention in present circumstances?

Lessons from the 1980s
So far as 'coping' is concerned, the defence minister who had to grapple with the prospect of insufficient funds, Michael Heseltine, regarded the imminent 'funding gap' not as a warning that it might be wise to review military dispositions (to get resources allocated and commitments back in equilibrium) but as a challenge calling for

improved management of the defence business (to reduce the resources required for the forward programme). Hence his reorganisation of the MOD itself, the effort put into pruning manpower in support functions, various contractorisation and privatisation initiatives, and his campaign to get better value for money spent on procurement. In fact, when he took over at the MOD, Heseltine probably believed that by such means he might cover the entire financial shortfall. By the time he was ready to – or, rather, driven to – relinquish his portfolio, however, even the supremely self-confident champion of rigorous resources management had to admit defeat on this count. The last Defence White Paper that he presented, in 1985, contained the admission that it would be necessary over the next several years to 'plan flexibly to match the forward programme to the available cash'.[10] While that is what the MOD has always had to do, in the 1985 White Paper the words had a special resonance.

Moreover, the prognosis was correct. The tight 'volume squeeze' on the defence programme led to reduced military activity levels (training included) and modified procurement plans (down-graded equipment specifications, stretched acquisition timetables). It even impinged on force levels (early decommissioning of older warships, deliberate undermanning of many army units). Indeed with the exception of the strategic nuclear capability (Polaris/Trident) it was a case of lean cuisine, and undernourishment, for the Services in the later 1980s.

Since no forces had to be sent in harm's way during the period, except in Northern Ireland, it did not really matter that some units were not up to strength, that much equipment was neither up to date nor up to scratch, and that combat effectiveness was probably not up to standard. The consequence of prolonged undernourishment became starkly apparent, however, in the Gulf crisis and conflict of 1990–91. In the case of the Army, it took weeks of local training to get formations battle-ready; it was necessary to scour Germany for just two armoured brigades' worth of serviceable Challenger tanks (plus spares) and to go cap in hand to allies for ammunition and other stores; and several infantry battalions had to be brought up to fighting strength by the introduction of soldiers from other regiments (at who knows what cost in unit cohesion). In the case of the Air Force, the lack of a stand-off airfield-attack weapon proved costly in planes (and crews) during the early air campaign; and when the emphasis shifted to precision interdiction, the RAF's fresh-from-the-factory Tornadoes could do the job only with the help of target illumination from long-in-the-tooth, ex-Fleet Air Arm Buccaneers – until, that is, a new thermal imaging and laser designation (TIALD) system could be rushed directly from the test bench to the front line.

Thus, as I have observed elsewhere, 'the forces sent to liberate Kuwait ... distinguished themselves despite, and not because of, the way in which the defence programme had been managed in the preceding decade'.[11]

We should note the corollaries. The RAF would not have been able to do precision interdiction – with minimum collateral damage – if there had been no Buccaneers available and no TIALD system in the procurement pipeline. It could not have mounted a sustained counter-air effort, had that been necessary, because of the high attrition associated with use of munitions requiring direct overflight of well-defended bases. As for the Army, it is clear that what was accomplished could not have been accomplished – or only at a much higher cost in casualties – if Operation Granby had been a 'come as you are' engagement with an astute and resolute opponent. Many units would have had to fight with unserviceable vehicles, few spares, inadequate stocks of ordnance and empty personnel spaces.

The conclusion is obvious. Maintaining an inflated nominal order of battle, but leaving it seriously underfunded, may be acceptable if the only thing that matters is keeping up appearances, for the benefit of adversaries and allies (or, indeed, one's own self-esteem). But it is a risky strategy if there is any chance that forces might have to be committed to combat, especially if it could be necessary to despatch them at short notice. What is more, so far as air-land battle is concerned, the real risks are borne by the men in the cockpits and the armoured personnel carriers. It is therefore unwise – irresponsible even – to manage the nation's defences in this way, and we should not do so in the 1990s as we did in the 1980s, particularly since whatever case there might have been for 'keeping up appearances' when the arithmetic of the NATO–Warsaw Pact military balance was all-important has now collapsed, while there is an increased likelihood that British forces will be called upon not only to take part in future coalition actions of various kinds but often to provide the spearhead for such operations.

So much for what *was* done in the 1980s which, with hindsight, ought not to have been done (or at least ought not to be repeated). What, now, of what *might have been* done at that time, was not done, but should perhaps receive more careful consideration as another 'funding gap' looms?

Trident
First, short-term financial headroom could have been created by a mid-1980s decision to leave the strategic nuclear business by phasing-out the four-boat Polaris force and cancelling the follow-on Trident programme. This was never considered seriously by any Thatcher-led administration, however; and when, after a third

successive defeat at the polls in 1987, the Labour Party concluded that its nuclear allergy was an electoral liability, effective opposition to retention of a strategic nuclear capability ceased.

The stirrings of a revival are discernible, though, based partly on strategic assessment (who now is supposed to be deterring whom, from doing what?) and partly on economic considerations. The 'peace dividend' thesis is now invoked against completion of the Trident acquisition where earlier the military 'opportunity cost' argument – in terms of undernourished conventional forces – was used against starting the procurement. It is most unlikely, however, that there will be a fresh 'great debate' on Trident. The ability to hold would-be adversaries at risk of awesome retaliation still counts for something, so the strategic rationale for the capability has not evaporated altogether. What is more significant for the present argument is that the boats and missiles are built (or under construction), so abandoning the project now would yield only modest savings.

Thus it is odds-on that the Trident procurement will take its course; and, since no transformation of the budgetary situation would result, there would be no merit in abandonment at this juncture. In time, however, the question of a Trident successor system will have to be addressed. That will be the time for thorough examination of a range of options: from continuing independent provision, through Franco–British collaborative endeavour, to straightforward non-replacement.

Clues to current official thinking are few and far between, and there is a hint of ambivalence about recent formal pronouncements. The 1992 Defence White Paper contains a discursive piece entitled 'British Nuclear Forces: Underpinning our Defence'. This asserts that 'the United Kingdom's independent nuclear force will remain the bedrock of our security'. The main text of the White Paper, however, commits the government to 'keeping under review the level of the capability which will need to be deployed to maintain an effective deterrent into the next century'.[12] It might have been more candid to have said that for so long as other European states have strategic nuclear arms– France, Russia and the Ukraine, for instance – the United Kingdom will have them; but exactly how many submarines should be kept in commission, and how many missiles with how many warheads should be sent on any given patrol, and whether a next-generation seaborne system should be acquired in due course are matters that ministers will think about while they can, and decide upon only when they must.

Specialisation
There is a second way in which the MOD might have sought escape from its funding dilemma of the 1980s, but chose to ignore. It could have planned for concentration of the defence effort on a narrower

spectrum of conventional capabilities. These could then have received proper sustenance.

This course had its advocates throughout the decade. Its principal supporters were analysts – including the present writer – who were sceptical about the national preoccupation with preserving all-round competence, and enthusiastic about the notion of systematic task-sharing among the European members of NATO (to ensure effective and efficient use of Alliance resources in the event of a real decline in member nations' expenditures, to finesse the transatlantic burden-sharing issue, and much else). In other words, the case for greater 'concentration' in the British defence programme was developed as part of a wider argument about NATO's force structure and about how, with all countries strapped for cash, national contributions might nevertheless be elicited which would enable that structure to amount to more than the sum of its parts. Thus in one of my own contributions to this debate, written in early 1987, I argued that the domestic issue was 'what should be the form of the nation's contribution to NATO in the 1990s: an all round contribution as now, accepting that in trying to do a bit of everything some things may not be done – almost certainly will not be done – particularly well; or a specialised contribution ... aimed at concentration ... on selected tasks'. Favouring the latter option, I argued further that 'it is in the context of Alliance-wide exploration of task specialisation' that the relevant selection should be made.[13] Rôle specialisation could be the answer to Britain's predicament and NATO's too.

People began to recognise this, persuaded (one would like to think) by research on how functional specialisation might work and how rôles and responsibilities might be redistributed to produce a coherent Alliance division of labour.[14] Indeed, at the end of 1988 NATO's Defence Planning Committee (DPC) formally called for an examination of opportunities for 'rationalisation and division of labour ... with a view to ... optimal use of the unique capabilities and strengths of individual allies'; and General Jack Galvin, then Supreme Allied Commander Europe (SACEUR), endorsed the initiative and asked countries to 'consider urgently a collective plan' for task specialisation.[15]

Nothing came of that appeal. By mid-1989 Eastern Europe was monopolising attention. At NATO's headquarters work on reallocating rôles and responsibilities gave way to work on redefining them (the strategy and force structure review). In national capitals interest in a general rearrangement of country contributions waned, pending the outcome of that exercise.[16]

So far as the United Kingdom is concerned, however, the basic 'concentration' argument has lost none of its cogency. As shrinking budgets make defence programme adjustments necessary yet again, I would still favour less emphasis on preserving all-round competence and more on sustaining unique capabilities and strengths (to ensure that Britain does well what it does do, even if it cannot do everything). One alternative is another spell of undernourishment, with potentially disastrous consequences in a security environment where combat readiness and combat effectiveness are going to count for more than nominal strength. The other is retention of a supposedly balanced force structure but at steadily diminishing force levels. This not only becomes increasingly inefficient as contraction proceeds but also leads, sooner or later, to a situation where in principle one's forces can take on any task but in practice it is a case of not here, or not there, or not yet, or not for long – and maybe not at all. Neither alternative appeals.[17]

I believe also that specialisation is a matter that should be addressed with allies and partners. As noted earlier, the government sees NATO as the medium through which the country will 'insure against any major external threat' and 'the focus of ... our peacetime planning and training'.[18] It has also subscribed to the Maastricht Treaty which foreshadows a common foreign and security policy 'which may in time lead to a common defence policy' for Community Europe, nominating the WEU as the vehicle for intra-European co-operation *ad interim*.[19] It has further stated that it envisages any military action necessary for 'maintenance of international peace and stability' being undertaken 'by NATO, the WEU, the UN or ad hoc coalitions under UN or CSCE auspices'.[20] Thus in the future it is most unlikely that British forces will have to operate independently. In almost every imaginable scenario they will act, if called upon to act at all, only with allies.[21]

We ought, therefore, now to be picking up where NATO left off in the late 1980s and looking at how best to share rôles and responsibilities, but in relation to the requirements of transformed strategic circumstances. That is probably what we *would* now be doing, using a SACEUR-sponsored task specialisation plan, if the Alliance had remodelled itself in the light of such requirements. Unfortunately it has not done that. Policy and posture were examined in 1990–91; and a 'new model' force structure was devised. In framing this, some attention was paid to aptitudes (as in inviting the United Kingdom to be lead nation in the ARRC). However, neither the strategic precepts that emerged from the review nor the derived concepts of operations provide a sound basis for planning for the later 1990s and beyond. Nor therefore does the related force structure blueprint. All have been overtaken by events. As a result, in 1992, several allies declined to confirm promised national force contributions; and during 1993 the new peacetime order of battle, though less than two years old, was undergoing 'revision'. At the same time, the Alliance – chastened by the experience of powerlessness in the Bosnian crisis – began belatedly to consider how its politico-military apparatus might be applied to curb (and punish) peacebreaking, tackle peacemaking, and organise peacekeeping.

Put bluntly, NATO is in disarray. It is saddled with an outdated Strategic Concept and an unsuitable force structure blueprint (*pace* Mr Rifkind). It has gone a long way in planning provision for eventualities that are unlikely to occur, but has taken only 'the first tentative steps', according to officials (speaking in May 1993), towards redirecting the Alliance to deal with what has actually been threatening the stability of Europe lately.[22]

The significance of this for the present analysis is obvious. As things stand, neither the United Kingdom nor any other country re-examining the scope of its defence effort can look to NATO for sound guidance concerning what it should or should not retain (in the collective interest). Not until the Alliance has given further consideration to its rôle in the post-Cold War world and articulated a new 'new model' force structure can member nations do that.

The Alliance Context

What NATO must do – and what should be done as a matter of urgency precisely in order to allow member nations to make wise domestic choices – is to look afresh at

- what Allied governments will really want armed forces for in the mid-to-late 1990s (and beyond);
- how best to design a functional and sustainable force structure for the future; and
- who should contribute what capabilities to the revised set-up.

Furthermore, in addressing these matters, it should consider a redefinition of the relationship between the North Atlantic Treaty signatories and their neighbours to the East (all of them now candidate members of the European Community).[23]

Such a fundamental exercise is necessary because events since 1990, when the initial Alliance review of strategy and concepts of operations began in earnest, have invalidated the assumptions that underlay that scrutiny, and hence the prescriptions that emerged from it. The idea of a serious 'residual threat' from the East had been rendered implausible long before NATO formally adopted its revised strategy (Rome, November 1991). Even the modified notion – a 'regenerated threat' from Russia – was scarcely credible then and has become progressively less so since. Few people now believe, therefore, that NATO needs substantial main defence forces sufficient to counter any hostile concentration on the Alliance's eastern boundary, with augmentation forces to back them up, plus the ability to reconstitute military power rapidly in the event of a spectacular deterioration in East–West relations.

During 1992 European nations made their lack of faith in this formula very apparent. The Germans announced swingeing defence cuts, and warned that there might be more to come. The Dutch and Belgians opted to halve the strength of their forces and told NATO they would not be fielding lead contingents for two of the 'main defence' corps in ACE. The United Kingdom trimmed its spending projections (Table 1), foreshadowing perhaps a diminished or diluted contribution to the ARRC. More examples could be cited. Meanwhile the Americans elected a new president pledged to scaling-down his country's forward presence in and around Europe. Implicit acknowledgement that the 1991 blueprint was a dead letter came at the December 1992 meeting of the Alliance's DPC. The Committee's communiqué says:

> a number of planned force reductions will have an effect on the future size and capabilities of main defence forces and we initiated a *review of the implications of changing force levels for the new force structure* (emphasis added).

What the words mean is 'we will see what can be rescued from this shambles'. It would have been better to have said 'back to the drawing board'.[24]

New Military Demands
Disenchantment with, and unwillingness to commit resources to, a set-up geared to 'counter-concentration' (with provision for 'augmentation' and 'reconstitution') reflected NATO members' perception that such arrangements were already an anachronism, decorated with yesterday's buzzwords. But it owed a lot also to their awareness of new military demands, for none of which would they want forces configured and equipped for (possibly protracted) manoeuvre warfare in north-east Europe with troops trained to fight in standard field formations observing a standard concept of operations. (The single exception would be a full-scale assault on a numerous and well-armed adversary, as in the final phase of the 1991 Gulf War.)

Because of the Bosnia fiasco, no task is more urgent than sound intellectual and practical preparation for such 'new military demands': protection of humanitarian relief (where the relief agencies cannot do their job without it); sanctions enforcement (with no loopholes and no half-measures); ceasefire or disengagement monitoring and relatively passive peacekeeping, if protagonists can be persuaded to stop fighting; and policing actions in support of constraints on belligerents (like 'no fly' zones) and more active peacemaking/peace enforcement (to include dealing promptly and effectively with peacebreaking and peacebreakers). Hitherto, such operations have generally been mounted ad hoc, with little prior thought about what criteria should govern whether to act and with performance entrusted to troops diverted from normal duties without extensive prior training. That is not good enough if, as seems probable, demands like these are going to multiply and local operations – often small-scale and low-key, and typically short-term – are going to become the armed forces' primary stock-in-trade. All military people are good at improvisation, but they do it better if they know what the score is.

The military are also generally very good at working with their counterparts from other nations, especially Service-to-Service. However, they do that better, too, with well-understood ground-rules; and they do it best of all if liaison is routine and peacetime co-operation, including regular exercises, is well established. Thus while there is no alternative to composing a unique, and hence ad hoc, coalition for any given peacekeeping or other operation, the benefits that would accrue if any such entity consisted of units accustomed to working together are self-evident.

Coalition-in-Waiting?
This last consideration is the key to what NATO should be doing now. It should be preparing to be the coalition-in-waiting for contingency operations in and around Europe, enriching the military-to-military relationships among member nations' forces, and further developing habits of co-operation, so that coherent and broadly interoperable capabilities are available in times of crisis. It should be thinking imaginatively about this, not worrying about whether it will ever be more than a shadow of its former self. It should also be thinking about how to liaise with, and organise participation in peacetime training by, selected non-NATO countries.

The new defence review authorised by the DPC in December 1992 provides an opportunity to give practical expression to the coalition-in-waiting concept. The exercise should be more than an emergency examination of 'implications of changing force levels for force structure': indeed it will serve no useful purpose, and be of no lasting value, if it simply yields an amended version of the original structural blueprint. That has been comprehensively overtaken by events. The need now is for a definitive post-Cold War prospectus for allied military dispositions. This implies promoting provision for contingency operations (and competence in contingency warfare) as the main objective. That is what governments will want armed forces for in the mid-to-late 1990s and beyond. It implies drawing-up a force structure template with this in mind: specifying the inventory of capabilities from which governments will be able to compose tailored multinational force packages for particular operations (and emphatically not prescribing a unique order of battle optimised for the single and remote possibility of an attack from the East). It implies, further, deciding on participation (existing 'members only' or not), devising a training and exercises policy and, of course, eliciting national contributions to this 'Alliance 2000' model.

The objective should be provision for contingency operations because there is now no threat to European security, in the well-understood sense that underpinned Cold War military arrangements. What governments will want armed forces for are the 'new military demands' or contingencies. For each broad class of contingency – and for each variant within each class – there will be an appropriate 'force package' (almost certainly an eccentric composition to the military traditionalist). The business of NATO's military headquarters should be contingency planning, in a broader-than-usual sense of that expression, covering specification of the 'mix' of capabilities required for each eventuality. The job of military formations should be joint training to develop and hone contingency warfare skills and techniques, engender habits of co-operation and cultivate robust working relationships. Put briefly, what is required is the same professional preparation for diverse post-Cold War demands as Allied forces made, from 1949 to 1989, to counter the monolithic Soviet threat.

Each imaginable contingency would call for a different 'mix' of forces. So deciding what capabilities to maintain year-in-year-out has to be done on the basis of a force structure template rather than a familiar peacetime order of battle. A few small warships plus maritime patrol aircraft might be enough for sanctions enforcement in one setting, a flotilla of fast patrol boats plus light aircraft in another. Surveillance assets might suffice for monitoring a 'no fly' zone, with some (or many) interceptors on standby if there were the occasional (or persistent) infringement. Peace enforcement would require the commitment of ground forces plus tactical air power, the precise make-up of the force depending on its exact mission, the capabilities of the opponent(s), terrain, climate and so on. A tailored composite force – including airlift/sealift, assets to provide tactical mobility, and logistical support – would have to be provided for each deployment, with provision for rotating units and for augmenting the package as necessary.

To allow governments to adopt this approach to contingency force composition, the structural requirement is for a stock or 'supermarket shelf' of capabilities, intrinsically compatible, incorporating adaptable troops with a diverse repertoire of skills, and featuring versatile and interoperable equipment (to generally lighter scales than for manoeuvre warfare in central Europe). The basic planning requirement is to devise the template for this stock, i.e. to define *what* is required on the 'supermarket shelf' if governments are to have choice in the composition of customised packages.

As for participation, or *who* might subscribe to the inventory, clearly NATO members would offer what they could, the Alliance's collective force planning apparatus would declare what it would like, and the machinery of Ministerial Guidance, Force Goals, and so on would operate, as it has for years, aiming to match the one to the other. If the objective were, as arguably it should be, the creation of a grand 'coalition-in-waiting' for contingencies in and around Europe (and further afield), to operate under the aegis of the CSCE or the UN, then provision could be made to accommodate subscriptions from interested Central European countries and the traditionally non-aligned – all of whom are, of course, both CSCE and UN members – through some form of association. (If Swedish involvement could be arranged, the approach to contingency force composition could become the *smörgesbord* rather than the 'supermarket shelf' approach.)

It would have to be clearly understood, in my judgement, that participation – and association – would be possible, even welcome, on the basis of specialised inputs: a country would certainly not have to put all its forces on the shelf (or *smörgesbord*). This would encourage some degree of rôle specialisation based on unique capabilities and strengths, much as NATO's DPC envisaged in 1988. Though thus allowing some 'division of labour' among participants, the coalition-in-waiting concept does not lend itself to extreme specialisation – meaning reliance on one, or even two, nations for key capabilities. That is because it would be necessary to provide for rotation of units in long-running contingencies and prudent to provide for redundancy. There are several imaginable deployments for which the coalition-in-action would have to exclude certain nations' units. There are some countries – Germany and the Nordic states spring to mind – which would find it difficult to accept a commitment to make forces available for all eventualities.

Given these considerations, training and periodic exercises, involving not only NATO members but also 'associates', would have to be conducted in a way that would facilitate, and emphatically not foreclose, the composition of alternate force packages. The co-option of 'associates' would pose no insuperable problems: it could proceed initially on the basis of existing ties (including the general agreement to promote co-operation in peacekeeping and related tasks which NATO has concluded with its partners in the North Atlantic Co-operation Council). Nor would meeting the redundancy requirement be difficult, as I see it: all participants would understand the importance of preserving some real choice for governments in putting together an appropriate force for a specific operation.[25]

Would it be possible, though, to obtain national force contributions to a new 'new model' NATO force structure thus designed according to the contingency warfare template? I believe it would. Certainly an inspection of European countries' forward plans suggests that a satisfactory construct is feasible, even allowing for some further diminution in most states' defence efforts. Nor should that be surprising. For one thing there would be places on the 'supermarket shelf' for all those parts of the old 'new model' structure to which nations have indicated they *will* subscribe. It could accommodate what are currently designated Immediate Reaction Forces (for in-area missions), viz. the Standing Naval Forces and the ACE Mobile Force. It could accommodate the British-led ARRC, with a revised mandate but a virtually unchanged organisation chart. This alone yields a Headquarters and Corps assets, plus a pool of 10 assigned divisions, made up of troops from half-a-dozen countries, which can either deploy as a four-division corps for 'high-intensity conflict in major warfare' or provide smaller but balanced force packages for less demanding contingencies – in effect, a store within a store.[26]

There would be a place also for one (or more) Eurocorps, if that were the framework within which France, Germany, Spain and other continental countries would find it convenient to place their main contingency warfare capabilities.[27] However, instead of the 'main defence' corps that feature in NATO's initial post-Cold War blueprint – the element for which 'the implications of changing force levels for force structures' have proved problematical – Alliance members would be invited to nominate alternative formations or specialist units, reflecting their own unique capabilities and strengths, to fill-out the collective force planners' template. 'Associates' could do the same.

Enumeration of such European contributions to the coalition-in-waiting, incorporating some redundancy, would provide the basis for seeking an appropriate American contribution. This might feature (1) a corps or independent brigades of forward-based ground troops with a small tactical air arm, plus (2) certain specialist force components which, for the time being, only the United States can provide (space-based surveillance and communications assets, strategic and some tactical airlift, stealthy combat aircraft, for instance). It ought to be possible to elicit such a contribution from the Americans, not least because its essential rationale would be rooted not in a perception of the United States as superpower patron of the Western bloc but rather in recognition of the fact that the nation is both the most powerful member of the CSCE and the most powerful of the permanent members of the Security Council.[28]

This entire prescription requires refinement and elaboration. The 'coalition-in-waiting' concept itself needs clarification. The feasibility of a 'supermarket shelf' or *smörgesbord* force structure needs detailed investigation. If it were not only feasible but also acceptable, at least in principle, the crunch question is: would the 'right' contributions be forthcoming? One thing is clear, however. Exploring these ideas, which address the real needs of the 1990s (and the next century), would be a far, far better use of the energies and talents of NATO's policy-makers and planners than expending further effort on amending concepts of operations and patching-up a force structure whose time has obviously gone.

Choices for Britain

The more things change, the more they stay the same. In the mid-to-late 1980s the British MOD might have — in my judgement should have — tackled its underfunding problem by practising concentration of effort, guided in its choices by the NATO-wide endeavour to promote a rational sharing of rôles and responsibilities that was then getting underway. In the mid-to-late 1990s the country is going to be in a similar domestic bind. Indeed it is in trouble already. Another 'funding gap' looms. Of the alternative courses of action available, that old stand-by of cheese-paring all round is to be avoided. Undernourished armed forces are a poor investment (except when only appearances count). Nor is scaling-down all round much better: this quickly leads to a position where, while you may have something of everything, you may not have enough of anything. Concentration of effort, conserving and nurturing unique capabilities and strengths, should be the preferred course now as it was before.

In one crucial respect, though, things are not the same now as they were in the 1980s. The United Kingdom still recognises that its security is best safeguarded by defence provision in a NATO context, implying a preparedness to take the Alliance interest into account when making force structure choices. But whereas in the later 1980s NATO knew where it was going as regards influencing national subscriptions — it wanted to promote 'rationalisation and division of labour' through task specialisation — latterly it has lost its way, not only in this connection but generally. Strategically, the Alliance is floundering in a no-man's-land between what it used to be and what it now ought to be: between the old-style alliance-in-being to deter and if need be defend against a direct, immediate and palpable threat from the East, which rôle it performed successfully for 40 years; and the new-style coalition-in-waiting for contingency operations in and around Europe or further afield for which there is such an evident need, which it has the potential to become, and which is the post-Cold War rôle that so obviously beckons. Practically, therefore, what is happening at present is that member nations looking to NATO for clear and confident guidance in making their domestic choices receive nothing or, what is worse, false steers (which, fortunately, several countries have had the sense to reject).

In these circumstances the temptation is for each nation to go its own way. Whether this is because that is what it has always wanted to do or because there appears to be no alternative is sometimes hard to assess. Either way, the result is movement towards a 'renationalisation' of West European (and Atlantic) defence. Such a trend is already apparent; and, if it persists, it will assuredly diminish rather than enhance European security.[29] It could not only damage NATO beyond repair but also put paid to any idea that Community Europe's pursuit of a common foreign and security policy might in time lead to a common defence policy.

To forestall this tendency, and indeed reverse it, the important thing is that NATO should sort itself out, and the sooner the better. In the meantime, the best that national decision-makers can do is to behave as though the Alliance were already doing this, actively preparing to be the regional coalition-in-waiting for post-Cold War eventualities which threaten European security. If British defence planners proceed, as I have argued they should, to make concentration on selected tasks their aim as they strive to cut the MOD coat according to the cloth the Treasury looks like making available over the next several years, then the criterion for selection should be what the United Kingdom can best contibute to the 'supermarket shelf' of capabilities that a NATO thus reformed would wish to have.

What might that include? Consideration of mission priorities suggests that, on the naval side, assets of value for so-called littoral warfare will be at a premium in the post-Cold War world, while the need for 'blue water' anti-submarine warfare (ASW) ships is fast diminishing. An appropriate British contribution might therefore comprise:

- one carrier, to provide command facilities, plus a platform for Sea Harriers and helicopters, which would mean keeping two of the Invincible-class ships in commission;

- a high-quality amphibious warfare capability, more or less as envisaged in the post-'Options' programme for the Royal Navy/Royal Marines;
- a diverse collection of those 'minor war vessels' – minesweepers/minehunters, offshore patrol ships, fast patrol boats and such-like – that have proved their worth in contingency operations more than once of late;
- a small number of escorts, from a national stock reduced to 'about 30' destroyers and frigates (a majority of them of the air-defence rather than the ASW specialism) and maybe a few submarines from a national stock reduced to, say, 10–12 boats.

There are risks associated with thus abandoning the national preference for a balanced fleet. But the principal one is apoplexy among the admirals.

So far as ground forces are concerned, things are less straightforward. A reformed NATO would clearly want:

- what the United Kingdom currently provides for the AMF;
- the unique capabilities of the country's special forces;
- a major contribution to the 'store within a store' which the ARRC represents.

What is not clear is whether the last of these elements should be precisely as currently envisaged.

There is a real dilemma here. The ARRC is NATO's boldest structural innovation. Its incorporation of national, 'framework' (single nation-led) and multinational divisions shows the way in terms of organisation for contingency warfare. The United Kingdom should do nothing that might sabotage the experiment. However, the powers-that-be have set the direction of the Corps' main development as preparation for high-intensity conflict in a major European war. They clearly regard 'peace support' as a secondary or 'lesser included' rôle. The ARRC is configured accordingly. Its three national divisions are all armoured divisions (British, German, American). There are armoured brigades in three of the four 'framework' mechanised infantry divisions (including the British 3 Division, which may take Italian armour under command). Yet the Corps has only a single air-mobile division and a single infantry division (the two multinational formations). On paper it has Spain's quick reaction force also, but this may find an alternative home in the nascent Eurocorps (in another part of the *mercado*, so to speak). Clearly there is more than enough heavy armour here, but not enough of the lighter, more mobile, more adaptable force components most likely to be needed for contingency operations.

One way in which this imbalance could be corrected would be for Britain to subscribe not a national armoured division but a second mechanised infantry division – or even independent infantry, armoured reconnaissance and artillery units – leaving the Germans and the Americans as the dominant providers of heavy armour. What then, though, of redundancy?

This issue will, I suspect, resolve itself in the not-too-distant future. Because of the demands of Northern Ireland, including provision for unit *roulement* that avoids 'overstretch', there is a floor below which the Army's infantry strength cannot fall. One can argue about whether the figure is 40 battalions (as in the revised post-'Options' programme) or 38 (as in the original plan) or some lower number (as canvassed by those who want an even bigger 'peace dividend' than the United Kingdom has already taken). The point is that, in the longer run, this is what will determine the size and shape of the Army and hence the form of the British contribution to the ARRC and the coalition-in-waiting generally.

Turning finally to air power, a remodelled NATO would obviously wish to have on its 'supermarket shelf':

- all those contingency warfare assets which the RAF has but many other air forces lack, *viz.* its E-3D Sentry aircraft, transports/tankers, heavy-lift helicopters and long-range maritime patrol aircraft;
- several squadrons of interceptors, offensive support and attack aircraft, but not necessarily cover for the full spectrum of tactical air missions.

Concentration of effort on air defence, reconnaissance, electronic warfare, suppression of enemy air defences and deep interdiction would make sense. Intra-service rôle specialisation commends itself here because in organising a European *smørgesbord* of tactical air power, there is scope – always allowing for some redundancy – for each nation to observe the 'complementarity' principle *vis-à-vis* others' force contributions.[30]

In fact, since in future the United Kingdom is only likely to conduct military operations in conjunction with allies, this principle should be applied generally. In practising concentration of effort, the MOD should shape the national force structure in such a way as to complement the efforts of others, maintaining only those force components in the provision of which Britain has a clear comparative advantage. The aim should be to make a quality contribution to NATO in what one must hope will be a new-found post-Cold War rôle as the coalition-in-waiting for future European and extra-European contingencies.

Notes

1. See *Hansard*, 25 July 1990, cols.470–473 (and, for commentary, *The Times*, 26 July 1990 and *The Economist*, 28 July 1990).
2. Statement on the Defence Estimates 1991: *Britain's defence for the 90s*, Cm 1559-I (London: HMSO, July 1991) and the complementary *Britain's army for the 90s*, Cm 1595 (London: HMSO, July 1991).
3. For further detail, see Cm 1559-I, Chapter 4.
4. Statement on the Defence Estimates 1992, Cm 1981 (London: HMSO, July 1992), p.8. The purpose of defence policy is 'to contribute to maintaining the freedom and territorial integrity of the United Kingdom and its dependent territories, and its ability to pursue its legitimate interests and activities at home and abroad'. Quite.
5. Cm 1981, p.9. Philip Sabin has written an excellent critique of the policy formulations in 'British defence choices beyond "Options for Change"', *International Affairs*, 69, 2 (1993), pp.268–73.
6. Cm 1981, pp.5–6.
7. Cm 1981, pp.46–48, and Autumn Statement 1992, Cm 2096 (London: HMSO, November 1992). See also Sabin, *op. cit.*, pp.273–76.
8. The Army's contraction will be slightly *less* than originally envisaged, because of a February 1993 decision to axe two fewer infantry battalions, leaving 40 (see *The Times* and *The Herald* (Glasgow), 4 February 1993, also *Defense News*, 8–14 February 1993). However reductions in the strength of both the Navy and Air Force will be *greater* than first planned (see *The Sunday Times*, 11 April 1993 and *The Herald*, 11 June 1993).
9. Although foreshadowed in articles in *The Times* during 1983–84, the first formal analysis introducing the 'funding gap' concept is to be found in the present writer's 'Managing the defence programme and budget', *The Three Banks Review*, 142, June 1984, pp.26–36. See also my Memorandum in House of Commons Defence Committee (HCDC), Session 1984–85, *Defence Commitments and Resources ...*, Vol.II (Minutes of Evidence), House of Commons Paper 73-II (1984–85) (London: HMSO, 1985), pp.288–98, plus Oral Evidence at pp.307ff. Note, though, that I am using the expository device here simply to highlight the difference between estimated future appropriations and the original budgetary projections accompanying the post-'Options' rundown plan. If defence inflation consistently exceeds the general rate of inflation through the 1990s, the 'volume squeeze' on the MOD's programme will be even more intense.
10. Statement on the Defence Estimates 1985, Cmnd 9430-I (London: HMSO, 1985), p.35.
11. David Greenwood, 'Expenditure and Management' in Peter Byrd (ed), *British Defence Policy: Thatcher and Beyond* (London: Philip Allan, 1991), p.59.
12. Cm 1981, p.28 and p.22 (para.132).
13. David Greenwood, 'Economic Constraints and Defence Choices' in Martin Holmes and others, *British Security Policy and the Atlantic Alliance: Prospects for the 1990s* (Washington: Pergamon-Brassey's, 1987), pp.73–74 and p.77.
14. Two citations are relevant. The first is my article 'Towards Rôle Specialisation in NATO', *NATO's Sixteen Nations*, 31. 4 July 1986. This summarises research done in 1984 with Steven Canby assisted by Clive Archer and Ciro Zoppo, for

the US Department of Defense. We had examined 'alternatives to that distribution of rôles and responsibilities among NATO members which is enshrined in present plans and programmes ... to illustrate options for task specialization other than that de facto 'division of labour' which is already beginning to occur'. The second is an oral presentation that I gave NATO's SHAPEX 88, subsequently published as 'Making better use of resources in NATO', *Defence Minister and Chief of Staff*, 2, 1988. In this I urged force *structure* planning to 'provide a collectively-decided framework for task specialisation', (p.8).

15. *Enhancing Alliance Collective Security: Shared Roles, Risks and Responsibilities in the Alliance*, Report by NATO's Defence Planning Committee, December 1988; and General Galvin's article in *NATO Review*, April 1989, which is quoted at greater length in the Annex to my paper in Brian Holden Reid and Michael Dewar, *Military Strategy in a Changing Europe* (London: Brassey's (UK), 1991), pp.77–78.
16. Analytical work continued, however: see my piece entitled 'Refashioning NATO's defences', *NATO Review*, December 1990, pp.2–8 (also based on work done with Steven Canby, specifically a Report entitled *Reshaping NATO's Defences* prepared for the Strategic Concepts Development Center, National Defense University, Fort McNair, Washington DC and submitted on 15 September 1990).
17. For a rather different view, see Philip Sabin, *op. cit.*, pp.277–86.
18. Cm 1981, p.9.
19. Treaty on European Union including the Protocols and Final Act with Declarations, Maastricht, February 1992: Treaty, Article J.2; and Declaration on Western European Union, *passim*.
20. Cm 1981, p.9.
21. For imaginative analysis and prescription on what might follow from this, see Malcolm Chalmers, *Biting the bullet: European defence options for Britain* (London: Institute of Public Policy Research, 1992).
22. See *Defense News*, 10–16 May 1993. West German Defence Minister Volker Rühe called for revision to NATO's Strategic Concept and the Alliance's 'command and force posture' in his 1993 Alastair Buchan Memorial Lecture to the International Institute for Strategic Studies. See 'Shaping Euro-Atlantic Policies: A Grand Strategy for a New Era', *Survival*, 35, 2, Summer 1993 (esp. p.137).
23. The argument in this section is broadly that presented in a piece of mine 'Towards a new prospectus for NATO' that has appeared in the journal *Enjeux Atlantiques* (July 1993).
24. Defence Planning Committee Communique, 11 December 1992, para.9 (reprinted in *NATO Review*, 40, 6 December 1992, p33). For elucidation, see the One-to-One interview with the Chairman of NATO's Military Committee in *Defense News*, 5–11 April 1993.
25. On the co-option of East European countries for contingency operations, see the Report to Ministers by the North Atlantic Co-operation Council (NACC) Ad Hoc Group on Co-operation in Peacekeeping (Brussels: NATO, June 1993).
26. The ARRC was 'inaugurated' on 2 October 1992 (see *Defense News*, 5–11 October 1992). On its rôle and organisation see 'Standing Together with Multinational Forces', *Military Technology*, XVII, 4, 1993, pp.48–51 (an

interview with the Corps Commander).
27. Rene van Beveren, *Military co-operation: What Structure for the Future?*, Chaillot Papers No.62, January 1993 (Paris: WEU Institute for Security Studies, 1993) contains much useful discussion on the practicalities of military co-operation.
28. On the military requirements for coalition peace enforcement/peacekeeping see R.M. Connaughton, *Peacekeeping and Military Intervention*, Occasional Paper No.3 (Camberley: Strategic and Combat Studies Institute, 1992), especially pp.30–44, and Michael Brenner's perceptive 'Multilateralism and European Security', *Survival*, 35, 2, Summer 1993, pp.138–55.
29. See Jan Willem Honig, 'The "Renationalisation" of Western European Defense', *Security Studies*, 2, 1, Autumn 1992, pp.122–38. (I am indebted to my colleague Chris Smith for bringing this excellent analysis to my attention.)
30. Relus 'ter Beek, the Netherlands' Defence Minister, commended this principle in a speech to the Dutch Society for International Affairs, The Hague, 31 March 1992. (Steven Canby and I had developed the notion of mutual complementarities in *Reshaping NATO's Defences* (cited at note 16 above), partly because the term 'rôle specialisation' carried connotations of extreme specialisation, e.g. total reliance on one ally for an entire capability.)

11
The Future of the British Army

Colin McInnes[1]

One of the key features of Options for Change was a substantial reduction in the size of the Army. Indeed in many respects, cuts in the Army were central to the whole Options for Change exercise. There was a certain logic behind this: for the 25 years since Denis Healey's reviews of the 1960s, the main rôle of the Army had been its contribution to the defence of Germany. As the Soviet threat on the Inner German Border receded, so it was perhaps inevitable that the Army, and particularly its forces based in Germany, would be cut. This Chapter suggests that substantial cuts may have appeared appropriate in the immediate aftermath of the Cold War – though some even then argued that euphoria was misplaced and that conflict might be more prevalent in the new Europe;[2] but by 1993 it was clear that this approach was mistaken. The Army is as important as ever, though its priority rôle has changed from high-intensity warfare on the north German plain to a more mobile, interventionist rôle ranging from humanitarian relief to peacekeeping to direct military action as in the Gulf. Rather than losing in importance relative to the other Services, the Army has if anything gained in importance.

This change in priority rôles also requires a change in the Army's structure. During the Cold War, and particularly during the 1970s and 1980s, the Army had been primarily designed to fight a high-intensity war. This required large numbers of tanks, mechanised infantry, mobile artillery and highly sophisticated support services. Since other rôles were largely secondary to this, it was believed that the Army designed for fighting a high-intensity war in Germany would suffice for other rôles. Now that high intensity warfare is less important, there is a pressing requirement to review the Army's structure. But under Options for Change the Army was to retain roughly the same balance of forces as during the 1980s. This fails to reflect the new priorities of medium–low intensity warfare. More damningly, many if not all of the high-intensity, heavily armoured forces are incapable of being moved any distance quickly and promptly due to the lack of strategic transport; and once in a new theatre of operations they cannot be sustained for any length of time due to inadequate stockpiles. This Chapter therefore suggests that the Army of Options for Change is little more than a scaled-down version of the Army of the 1980s; it is not an Army designed to meet the challenges of the 1990s.

The Army and Options for Change

On 6 February 1990 the Secretary of State for Defence, Tom King, told the House of Commons that the Ministry of Defence (MOD) was examining 'Options for Change' in the wake of the dramatic events which had swept over Europe in the previous few months. The implication appeared to be both that there were a variety of options to choose from, and that a wide-ranging debate over the future of British defence policy was imminent. Also of interest was the omission of the term 'review'. If federalism was the 'f'-word for the government's European policy, then review was the 'r'-word for its defence policy. John Nott's defence review of 1981 had left a sour taste, whilst the budgetary squeeze of the late 1980s had forced the MOD into a Canute-like position of denying the imminence of a defence review. Nevertheless it was clear that a review of defence policy was under way.[3] The major aspect to be revealed was whether the review would be as radical and far-reaching as the changes in European security which preceded it, and which continued beyond it.

As Richard Mottram, the civil servant at the heart of Options for Change, made clear, developments in European security and particularly East–West relations were only one of three factors driving the 'exercise' as it became known (civil servants followed their political masters' squeamishness about using the 'r'-word). The two other factors were developments in NATO and resource constraints.[4] But developments in European security were clearly the more important set of factors, not least because the other two were to a greater or lesser extent products of these developments – changes in NATO followed from the collapse of the Warsaw Pact, whilst it was the consequent pressure for a 'peace dividend' which affected defence resources. NATO was at that time reviewing its future direction and strategy, though the British government does not appear to have worried that the Alliance's existence or relevance was under threat. Thus British defence policy was being reviewed at the same time as NATO policy. This had obvious advantages in that the two could interact to provide a mutually satisfactory outcome. But the danger was that the two could become unsynchronised.

Since Mottram explicitly identifies developments in NATO as one of the factors driving Options for Change, it is interesting to note that the general outlines of Options were announced a mere handful of days after the London Declaration, and over a year before NATO's Rome Summit when the Alliance's new Strategic Concept was agreed. This suggests that developments in NATO were of only peripheral concern to Options for Change. It has, however, been suggested that since NATO's Strategic Review was in large part the work of Sir Michael Alexander (the UK Permanent Representative on the North Atlantic Council, and a close friend of Mottram's) informal links were close, and that more importantly Options for Change was not inconsistent with the direction in which NATO planning was moving.

The impact of future resource limitations on defence planning and force structure was in part a product of the so-called 'peace dividend'. More important, however, was the squeeze on defence spending as a result of higher than expected inflation. By 1990–91 this had led to a 10 per cent real cut in defence expenditure compared to 1985–86. To this were added concerns over manpower. The size of the key age group from which Service personnel are recruited (late teens to early twenties) was projected to fall by some 32 per cent by the mid-1990s. Since many units (especially infantry battalions) were already under strength, a recruitment crisis appeared to be looming, prompting a reconsideration of the size and structure of the armed forces.[5] Therefore, although Options for Change was in large measure a *British* response to the end of the Cold War, other factors were involved including developments in NATO and a tightening budget.

The Options for Change exercise was conducted in two stages. The first stage involved a small group of Ministers and advisers, and centred around a committee of six (the 'Six Wise Men') chaired by Richard Mottram. Each of the Services was represented by a senior officer (Major General Thomas Boyd-Carpenter, Air Vice Marshal John Willis, and an as yet unidentified Rear Admiral), with two, more junior civil servants accompanying Mottram. Although the Six Wise Men requested a number of papers from within the Ministry, the authors of these papers were kept very much on the periphery of the exercise. With the exception of ministers, the only people who were kept informed on the exercise's progress were the Chief of the Defence Staff and the three Service Chiefs, and even then they appear to have been merely informed, rather than being party to the deliberations.

The first stage established the general framework for future defence policy and culminated in a statement to the House of

Commons on 25 July 1990 by the Secretary of State, Tom King. This stage was in many respects the most important: it set the framework for future defence policy, and later, more detailed studies would work within this framework. It was also the stage at which the various 'options' were discussed. But they were discussed not in a full, frank and open debate, but behind closed doors, excluding even the most senior military advisers. The process was therefore marked by secrecy, ostensibly to avoid both the sort of damaging leaks which were beginning to characterise other areas of government policy, and the inter-Service politicking which had featured in John Nott's 1981 defence review. This secrecy however led to claims of a lack of consultation, particularly from the Army. The small group approach had precluded a wide-ranging debate, even within the Ministry. This touched a raw nerve. In an exchange of letters in the *RUSI Journal*, the generally bland and inoffensive Armed Services' journal, the Ministry of Defence (and Mottram in particular) was strongly criticised for excluding military advice from the exercise.

> Was there full consultation with the appropriate staffs ... or were they asked just to respond to specific cut-backs? In short, has there been a defence review with a full military input or has the MOD only sought to meet Government (?) or Treasury (?) dictat? Who had the luxury of 'Options'? Might the choices be debated? Will the military have a voice? Or, is it all cut and dried, except for an election?[6]

In response Mottram stated:

> Emerging proposals from this working group [the Six Wise Men] were looked at by top management below Ministers, involving on the military side the Chief of the Defence Staff, the Vice-Chief of the Defence Staff and the single-Service Chiefs of Staff. They were, of course, also subsequently consulted by the Defence Secretary in reaching his decisions on the best way ahead.[7]

Nevertheless concerns continued to be expressed by, amongst others, David Bolton, who, as Director of the Royal United Services Institute for Defence Studies, was well connected with military sentiments.

> ... voices are still raised concerning the military involvement in the whole process ... It is asked if the Chiefs of Staff were actively involved from the outset and central to the whole process, or even if they should have been? *It is now being suggested*, as doubtful as it may seem, *that they were only kept informed and, thereby, deemed to accept the direction they were being given.* (emphasis added)[8]

Similarly General Sir John Akehurst wrote:

> It is now clear that the Tories have handled the so-called 'Options for Change' (what options?) with a lack of strategic clarity, manifest insensitivity, and obvious political expediency, to say nothing of Treasury domination, and have thus put the country's security in jeopardy.[9]

The overall impression is therefore one of frustration, even betrayal, over Options for Change: that the military were not allowed sufficient influence in the process, and that the Ministry was overly influenced by Treasury pressure. To a certain extent complaints were inevitable: like any bureaucracy, the military has a clear sense of its own value and importance, not to mention a vested interest in retaining its current size and structure, and therefore reductions on any but a minor scale were almost certain to produce howls of outrage in some quarters. But what is of interest here are both the widespread nature of the protests, suggesting that something more than a head-in-the-sand resistance to change was at work, and the strong suspicion that the exercise was driven less by a military assessment of future requirements than by financial exigencies and the pressure for cuts.

In his statement to the House of Commons on 25 July 1990 concerning the broad framework of Options for Change, Tom King revealed few details about the Army other than a reduction in manpower from c.150,000 to c.120,000. Neither was it apparent at this stage that the changes to the Army were the key feature of the exercise. Nevertheless the Six Wise Men, and particularly the Army's representative on the committee, Major General Thomas Boyd-Carpenter, appear to have realised at an early stage that the future of the Army lay at the heart of the review. But this was not made clear to Parliament, nor in the early debates which followed King's statement.

The second stage of the exercise followed fairly quickly, and was concerned with a more detailed working through of the changes. This inevitably involved more people and allowed a greater Service input. But Mottram was emphatic that the exercise was driven not by Service requirements, but by the requirements to meet defence-wide tasks.

> Outcomes had, of course, to be translated into single-Service structures, and the implications identified for support and manpower levels; but the driving force was not the allocation of savings targets by Service.[10]

For the Army this second stage resulted in the publication of the White Paper *Britain's Army for the 90s*.[11] The publication had been delayed until July 1991, ostensibly because of Operation Granby (the

British contribution to the war in the Gulf) and to allow consultations with NATO allies. There is, however, no evidence as yet to suggest that the White Paper's contents were substantially affected by either of these factors. Also of interest is the fact that the Army White Paper was not matched by similar documents for the Royal Navy and Royal Air Force. This then was perhaps the first official indication, albeit more implicit than explicit, of the Army's centrality to the review.

The Not-So-New Defence Policy?

Tom King's July 1990 statement made it clear that the Ministry of Defence was not going to outline a variety of options for public discussion; rather the government had made its decision which it then proceeded to defend if and when necessary. This traditional approach seemed to contradict the implication of King's earlier, February, statement that there was a variety of options to choose from. The February statement had raised expectations, wittingly or not, of a wide-ranging, public debate, expectations which were not to be met. For this the government was criticised, not least by the House of Commons Defence Committee. The Defence Committee considered the changes in European security to have been so fundamental as to require a public debate of the options available. That the reality was merely a 'promulgation of decisions' was not simply unfortunate in the Defence Committee's eyes, but unsatisfactory.[12] But to expect the Ministry of Defence to change its well-established pattern of announcing decisions rather than alternatives was perhaps a touch optimistic. This approach is deeply ingrained in British strategic culture, where the Ministry of Defence considers itself the sole authority on defence matters. Moreover, given the proximity of a general election the government presumably wanted to avoid the sort of damaging row on defence policy which an unstructured, free-ranging debate might have engendered. Therefore the 'options' open to the government had been examined by the Six Wise Men and their conclusions passed on to ministers for comment and approval; they had not been outlined to Parliament, nor even within the Ministry of Defence generally.

At first glance, the new defence policy announced in 1990–91 appeared little different from what had gone before, with the exception that there was to be less of it. Forces were to be cut, but rôles were retained. In particular the four-and-a-half defence rôles which had emerged in the 1970s continued to be emphasised.[13] These were:

1. The nuclear deterrent.
2. Direct defence of the UK.
3. A contribution to NATO's defence of mainland Europe.
4. A contribution to NATO's maritime defence of the Atlantic and Channel.
5. Non-NATO commitments, including the defence of dependent territories such as Hong Kong and the Falkland Islands, and the capability for intervention outside the NATO area (half-rôle).

This tended to suggest a conservative approach to change, and indeed a continued focus on the Soviet Union (or its successor) as the major threat to British security. What this list obscures, however, is the reordering of priorities which had occurred. It is here that radical changes had taken place, changes which affected principally the Army. British defence reviews come in two types. The first is to change defence rôles, the second to change the balance between various rôles. Denis Healey's reviews of the 1960s are an example of the first type in that they abandoned commitments east of Suez; Options for Change, however, appeared to fit into the latter category by reducing the emphasis placed on the contribution to NATO's defence of mainland Europe.

For the past decade this rôle, along with the independent deterrent, had held centre-stage in British defence policy. It had centred around the deployment in Germany of BAOR (British Army of the Rhine) with a peacetime strength of three divisions and 55,000 men, to be boosted to 150,000 men in the event of war. This was supported by the deployment of some 12 RAF squadrons in Germany. Under Options for Change the strength of BAOR was to be cut to 23,000 troops and a single division, while RAF support was to be halved to six squadrons at two air bases in Germany.[14] Whereas the overall strength of the Army was to be cut by around 25 per cent, BAOR was to be cut by 60 per cent. The 50 per cent reduction of the RAF in Germany was similarly disproportionate to the overall cuts in RAF strength. What appears to have happened therefore is a reordering of priorities within existing defence rôles; away from the mainland defence of Europe and towards the direct defence of the UK.

This impression is reinforced by the 1992 Statement on the Defence Estimates, under which the four-and-a-half rôles are reconstituted into three rôles, each with a number of components.[15]

1. Protection of the UK and dependent territories. This rôle includes:
   - Direct defence of the UK.
   - Northern Ireland.
   - Other counter-terrorist tasks.
   - Bomb disposal.

The Future of the British Army 205

- Defence of dependent territories (Hong Kong and the Falkland Islands).

2. The defence of the UK against a major external threat. This rôle includes:

    - Contribution to the defence of mainland Europe.
    - Maritime operations in the NATO area.

3. Wider security interests. This rôle includes:

    - Overseas intervention.
    - Overseas garrisons in Belize and Brunei.
    - Naval deployments outside European waters.
    - Peacekeeping.
    - Disaster relief.
    - Military assistance.
    - Antarctic ice patrol.

How much should be read into this change to three rôles was at first unclear: for example, the government had made it clear that the independent strategic deterrent remained a central element of British defence policy, but it was not mentioned in this new list of defence rôles. Increasingly, however, it became clear that this was a fundamental reformulation, one which had been at the heart of the Options process, but which had only been presented at a later date. It governed the deliberations of the Six Wise Men, and may even have originated with them, and constituted the British government's new approach to defence policy in the post-Cold War world. No commitments or rôles had been abandoned, but the manner of approach had changed. Thus is one sense it was less a review of defence policy than a reformulation of rôles and priorities. Nevertheless, one of the implications of this reformulation was the reduced importance of the contribution to European mainland defence compared to the direct defence of the UK. Given the past significance of the European mainland defence rôle to the Army, this reordering of priorities would have a major impact upon the Army's size and structure.

Britain's Army for the 90s: Size and Structure

Tom King's July 1990 announcement contained few details concerning the Army other than a cut in strength from around 150,000 to around 120,000, and a halving of BAOR's strength. By late 1991, however, considerably more details had been made available with the publication of both the Army White Paper and the House of Commons Defence Committee inquiry into the future of the Army.[16] The White Paper revealed that the Army would in fact be cut to a trained strength of 104,000 (total establishment 116,000) compared to its strength on 1 April 1991 of 144,000 trained soldiers, 156,000 total strength.[17] As the Defence Committee noted, this represented a slight change from Tom King's July statement, but one which could be satisfactorily explained by the initial figures being merely estimates which required a more detailed working through, and by changes in the contribution to NATO's land forces.[18] Most interest, however, focused on the cuts to the various arms, and particularly the infantry. The Army White Paper announced a cut in infantry strength from 50 UK battalions and five of Gurkhas, to 36 UK battalions and three of Gurkhas by 1995, with a further Gurkha battalion to be lost once Hong Kong was handed over to the Chinese in 1997.[19] The three Royal Marine Commando units which act as rather specialised infantry were retained in full, giving an overall infantry strength of 42 battalions in 1995. The Ministry of Defence, however, made it clear that they intended to keep these 42 battalions at full strength. Most battalions in 1991 were well under strength due to recruitment problems, so that the real infantry strength was closer to 50 battalions than the 55 on paper. The reductions produced by Options for Change would, in the Ministry's view, solve this recruitment problem.

The cuts proposed by Options for Change required a number of the large infantry regiments to lose one or more of their regular battalions, but more controversially it required the amalgamation of a number of smaller, historic regiments – a process shared by the armoured corps. The amalgamation of certain county regiments, in particular, produced something of a public outcry, and a number of vociferous protests. Although the Minister of State for the Armed Services publicly accepted responsibility for these decisions, he nevertheless made it quite clear that it was the Army which had decided which regiments were to amalgamate, not politicians, thus removing some of the blame from the political masters in the MOD.[20] The public outcry was a mixture of sentiment, military NIMBY-ness (the Not in My Back Yard syndrome) and outright scepticism over the rationale behind some of the amalgamations. If cuts were to be made, it was clear that a number of regiments would have to be amalgamated. Given the history and sentiment bound up with many regiments this was never going to be easy, and some form of public outcry was perhaps inevitable on these grounds alone. More worrying, however, was the suspicion that a number of regiments which recruited well and had demonstrated their effectiveness and efficiency were being cut for no good reason.

TABLE 1   COMBAT STRENGTH OF THE ARMY IN 1995, AS PLANNED UNDER OPTIONS FOR CHANGE

A. Household Cavalry and Royal Armoured Corps (11 regiments)
   8 – armoured regiments
   2 – armoured reconnaissance regiments
   1 – training regiment
   (1 – mounted regiment – ceremonial duties)

B. Royal Regiment of Artillery (16 regiments)
   9 – field regiments (AS 90)
   3 – MLRS regiments
   4 – air defence regiments (2 – Rapier, 2 – Starstreak)
   (1 – King's Troop – ceremonial)

C. Corps of Royal Engineers (10 regiments)
   7 – engineer regiments
   1 – RAF support regiment
   1 – explosive ordnance disposal regiment
   1 – engineer regiment resident in Northern Ireland

D. Royal Corps of Signals (11 regiments)
   10 – signal regiments
   1 – electronic warfare regiment
   5 – independent signals squadrons

E. Infantry (38 battalions – 31 March 1998*)
   8 – armoured infantry battalions
   4 – mechanised battalions
   2 – airmobile battalions
   2 – parachute battalions
   21 – general purpose battalions
   1 – ACE Mobile Force (Land)

F. Army Air Corps (6 regiments)
   2 – anti-tank regiments
   2 – airmobile regiments
   1 – general aviation regiment
   1 – general aviation regiment resident in Northern Ireland
   4 – independent flights

*Increased to 40 battalions in February 1993.
Source: Cm 1595, pp.13–15.

Although the infantry cuts received much of the attention, the Royal Armoured Corps was to undergo equally dramatic reductions. Its April 1991 strength of 19 regiments (including four armoured reconnaissance regiments, one for each of the four divisions) was to be cut to 11 regiments, including two armoured reconnaissance regiments. Moreover a higher percentage than previously would be based in the UK rather than Germany, whilst the order for the new Challenger II tanks was dramatically cut to just two regiments (127 tanks, including spares). Artillery strength was also to be cut, from 22 to 16 regiments, though the new AS90 self-propelled gun was to be supplied as standard to the field regiments. The Royal Corps of Signals and the Corps of Royal Engineers were also to be cut in line with the other arms, as were the support services. Only the Army Air Corps survived intact, retaining all six of its regiments in an explicit acknowledgement of the increased importance of the helicopter to the modern land battle (for details see Table 1).

The Ministry of Defence argued that the resulting force structure would create a smaller but better-equipped army for the future. New equipment would include Challenger II, the upgrading of Challenger I to II standards, a new model of Rapier, Starstreak, AS90, and possibly even a replacement for Clansman. This list was met with open scepticism even at the time. Leading critics such as retired commander of BAOR General Sir Martin Farndale replied that the promise of 'jam tomorrow' had been all too frequent over past years, but that the reality tended to be that such promises were rarely realised.[21] With the squeeze on public expenditure in late 1992, the chances of increased funding for new Army equipment were even less likely, making the promise of 'smaller but better' appear even more hollow.[22] But two other problems also faced the Army in terms of its size and structure. The first was whether it had enough forces to meet its commitments – what is referred to as the problem of overstretch; the second concerned the balance of forces.

(i) Overstretch
In planning the size of Britain's future Army, the government had little to work on. Although a number of existing commitments and responsibilities likely to remain for the foreseeable future could be identified, future risks and commitments were difficult to envisage. Might the Army find itself being used more extensively now that the Cold War was over? Or did the relaxation of the threat of major aggression mean that it had only secondary tasks to fulfil? How many simultaneous crises should the government plan for? And of what sort? After all, the forces and skills required for high intensity operations in the Gulf and humanitarian relief in Bosnia were quite different. The Ministry's answer seems to have been based upon the capability to meet the following commitments:

- support for the civil authority in Northern Ireland;
- defence of the UK (to which the Territorial Army would also contribute substantial forces);

- overseas garrisons;
- NATO commitments;
- training
- and one emergency, in Northern Ireland or overseas.

Given the uncertainty surrounding future commitments, the Minister of State for the Armed Forces assured the House of Commons Defence Committee that the Army's size and structure would be re-examined should any future commitments emerge.[23] This occurred almost immediately with the deployment of a reinforced infantry battalion to Bosnia. The pressure created by this deployment forced the new Defence Secretary, Malcolm Rifkind, to announced a reprieve for four regiments due to be amalgamated – effectively increasing the number of infantry battalions ultimately available from 38 to 40. In addition Rifkind announced that a further 2,000 personnel would be transferred from support to front-line duties. This was all to be accomplished within existing budgetary guidelines, and the opportunity cost would therefore be in equipment budgets (particularly for the Navy and Air Force).[24] This reprieve suggested that the planning assumption underpinning Options for Change – that the Army would be relatively less important in the future and could therefore be cut disproportionately – was being revised, and that Army strength would become an increasingly important issue.

The lack of flexibility within the planned future Army structure to react to the unforeseen had created twin suspicions: that the cuts were driven less by a realistic (or pessimistic) appraisal of future risks and dangers than by Treasury pressure; and that the Army would be overextended. One of the sternest critics of the cuts was General Sir Martin Farndale, who argued that the Army of the future would be too small to react independently to any but the most minor of crises. Moreover, the Army's ability to fight independently at the operational level – the key level in modern warfare – was practically non-existent. As a result Britain would be dependent upon the active support of friends and allies in protecting its overseas interests. Furthermore, the strain on Army units would become unbearable as the time between tours of duty was reduced, creating major problems in terms of morale and retention.[25] Similar concerns over cuts were expressed by the House of Commons Defence Committee, most forcibly in its 1993 report on the Army.[26]

Although Farndale raises some important points, they should not be overstated. Existing capabilities for independent operations overseas are already extremely limited. Deployment in the Gulf revealed not only how difficult it was to send heavily equipped forces any distance, but how the entire BAOR had to be raided to equip just one comparatively small division (three armoured regiments, three infantry battalions, plus support). Moreover, it was clear that the British were reliant upon friends and allies for the provision of key support assets such as strategic reconnaissance/intelligence – a situation similar to that in the Falklands a decade earlier. Therefore, although Farndale is correct to state that Britain will be unable to react independently in the future, that is nothing new. Rather it reflects existing limitations, a position which a medium power such as Britain might reasonably expect to find itself in. Further, it is difficult to see what sort of international crises might require a substantial British commitment without requiring other powers to react similarly. A crisis is likely to be either sufficiently serious as to affect a number of powers, generating a coalition response (such as the Gulf), or insufficiently serious such as to question the wisdom of a major British involvement. Although there may be grey areas where an independent capability might allow the British government greater freedom of manoeuvre, the cost of this, not just in terms of forces but transport and support, would be disproportionately high.

Finally, and somewhat ironically, the cuts in the Army theoretically relax the pressure on the Emergency Tour Plot (ETP, the scheduling of infantry battalions for unaccompanied tours). It is the infantry which bears the brunt of the ETP, and so it is here that overstretch is most likely to be felt. But the infantry have actually benefited from reduced commitments (particularly with BAOR), and from the more extensive scheduling of armoured and artillery regiments for use as infantry in Northern Ireland (though whether this is a proper use of specialised forces whose expensive equipment will have to be put into store is a moot point). The infantry should also benefit from battalions being at full strength, eliminating the current situation where, to make up numbers, troops are borrowed from other battalions which might have only recently been on a tour of duty. Thus while the number of infantry battalions has been reduced by 17, the number of commitments has been reduced by 19 battalions, and the Ministry hoped for a 24-month gap between tours on the ETP.[27]

Nevertheless, there is a fear that the margin for error is slight. The Minister of State, Archie Hamilton commented:

> I do not think it is any good holding enormous numbers of forces just in case one of the vast new hefty commitments comes up ... I could produce any justification you like for any numbers of troops in the British Army that you like to mention. There is almost no limit to the number of people whom you could have in the British Army and you could say these are covering this eventuality, that eventuality, 16 different things all happening at the same time.[28]

This is obviously a fair point, but there must be some additional capacity to meet the unexpected. The suspicion is that the cuts provide only a thin layer of additional capacity. Heavy demand on this may lead to opportunity costs in other commitments, or to an inability to respond adequately. If the deployment in Bosnia of a single infantry battalion with support – less than two per cent of the Army's strength – created sufficient pressure to force the Defence Secretary to reprieve a number of planned amalgamations, there can be little confidence in the Army's ability to react to other international crises. Options for Change appears to have assumed that, with the end of East–West hostilities, the Army would lose its major rôle (the defence of West Germany) and would not acquire any new rôles. As new conflicts emerge in Europe and beyond, conflicts in which Britain may acquire some responsibility through its permanent membership of the Security Council,[29] so the Army may acquire new, long-term commitments unplanned for under Options for Change.

(ii) Balance
The second, less widely debated, issue concerns the Army's structure and the balance of forces. This is more a package of issues than a single issue, however, involving three areas: the balance between forces based in the UK and overseas; the balance between the four main fighting arms; and the balance between regular and reserve forces. On the first issue, with the withdrawal of over half of BAOR, proportionately more forces will be based in the UK than at any time since the end of the Second World War. Although this effect has been moderated by cuts in the overall size of the Army so that the actual increase in numbers of troops stationed in the UK is quite small, nevertheless increased accommodation and in particular training areas will have to be found. This is especially problematic for armoured and mechanised forces, which require large areas of land on which to exercise. Almost all of the armoured corps was based in Germany during the Cold War. This will no longer be the case, but finding suitable, non-environmentally sensitive land may not be easy. Accommodation may prove to be less of a long-term problem, but in the short term, accommodation may have to be built or refurbished to meet the needs of troops returning from Germany, reducing the prospect of short-term savings in the defence budget.

The second issue of balance concerns the relative strength of the four main fighting arms (the infantry, armour, artillery and the air corps). Somewhat surprisingly the balance between these four arms was barely changed, the Army Air corps being slightly increased relative to the other arms, and the Royal Armoured Corps slightly reduced (see Table 2). If the British Army envisaged fighting a similar war in the future to that which it trained for in Germany for 40 years, then this balance might be understandable. But it doesn't. Instead it foresees a variety of possible tasks, mostly at the low-medium intensity level. In other words the Army's balance of arms reflects the requirement to be able to fight a high-intensity war in some strength, whereas the situations it is most likely to encounter are somewhat different. The key issue is the infantry. This is the most useful force for low-medium intensity warfare, but its future strength fails to reflect the increased demands likely to be made of it (even with the February 1993 reprieve for two infantry battalions). On the other hand, the armour and artillery are more useful for high-intensity warfare, a less likely scenario.

Most damning of all, armour and artillery cannot be moved in strength due to the lack of strategic transport, while the deployment of forces to the Gulf in 1990–91 demonstrated serious shortfalls in equipment and weapons stockpiles. The British Army was severely stretched to move and supply three armoured regiments, three armoured infantry battalions and six artillery regiments for a 100-hour war; under Options for Change it will have 11 armoured regiments, 16 artillery regiments, and 12 armoured/mechanised infantry battalions, only a small number of which can be moved from where they are based, and which can be supplied for only a very limited period of time. In contrast, the 21 general purpose battalions of infantry are already severely stretched to meet existing commitments. By retaining a similar balance to that of the 1980s, the Army appears ill-prepared to meet the challenges of the 1990s.

TABLE 2 BALANCE OF FIGHTING ARMS UNDER OPTIONS FOR CHANGE

	Infantry	Armour	Artillery	AAC
Nos Battalions etc 1991	58*	19	22	6
Nos Battalions etc 1995	42**	11	16	6
+/–	–16	–8	–6	0
% Total fighting strength 1991	55%	18%	21%	6%
% Total fighting strength 1995	56%	15%	21%	8%
+/–	+1%	–3%	0	+2%

* Includes 5 Gurkha battalions + 3 Royal Marine Commandos.
** Includes 3 Gurkha battalions + 3 Royal Marine Commandos. To be reduced by a further Gurkha battalion 1997–98. Two regimental amalgamations were reprieved in February 1993, increasing the number of battalions by two.
Source: CM 1595.

The final question of balance concerns that between regular forces and reserves (particularly the Territorial Army – TA). There was an initial belief that as the regular Army was cut, so reserve forces would become more important, and possibly even increase in size. The argument for this rested on the belief that reservists allowed a greater margin for error in calculating regular force size. The Army White Paper however dispelled this illusion. Although it produced no definitive figures, it suggested a cut in strength from 75,000 to 60–65,000. On 10 December 1991 the Secretary of State announced that the TA would be reduced to 63,500, a cut of some 15 per cent. The public reason for this was the poor level of recruitment – the TA was already well under strength. But equally there appeared to be little enthusiasm for the TA playing an increased rôle in British defence policy. Although its rôle was altered somewhat – less emphasis being placed on leg infantry, more on specialised combat skills, less on static home defence and more on a flexible general reserve – and although it was cut by a mere 15 per cent compared to 25 per cent for regular forces, there is nevertheless the feeling that even if there had been no recruitment problems, the TA would still have been cut quite substantially. It was not going to 'take up the slack' from the regular Army.[30]

Rôles

Four main rôles have been identified for the future Army:

- Northern Ireland.
- direct defence of the UK.
- contribution to NATO.
- overseas interests, including garrisons and peacekeeping.

Forces committed to each of these rôles are identified in Table 3. The most significant change here concerns the contribution to NATO. The dramatic cut in BAOR's strength seems to imply a major reduction in the importance of this rôle. But at the same time the British Army has been given command of the most important and newest NATO force, the Allied Command Europe Rapid Reaction Corps (ARRC). This new force serves two main purposes: politically it shows that the Atlantic Alliance is moving beyond its Cold War roots and devising a new force structure to meet the challenges of a new Europe; militarily it offers a flexible force which can be adapted for a variety of scenarios and deployed wherever necessary. It is difficult to underestimate the importance of the ARRC to NATO. As the risk of major aggression disappears, so NATO had to develop the means to respond effectively to a variety of lesser crises. The ARRC is the means by which it hopes to do this. Although large armoured forces are to be retained in Western Europe for collective defence purposes, these are increasingly seen even within NATO as dinosaurs: relics of the past with no rôle in the new Europe. It is the ARRC that will carry NATO's standard into the post-Cold War world, and on which NATO's hopes of survival are pinned.[31]

Some 10 divisions have been committed to the ARRC, and up to four may be used depending on the scenario (from peacekeeping and crisis management to full-scale military intervention). The British Army provides not only the leadership of the Corps and the majority of its headquarters staff, but two full divisions (one armoured and one mechanised) and an airmobile brigade as part of a multinational airmobile division. Since a number of the 10 divisions committed to the ARRC have little substance at present, the British Army is therefore making a very substantial contribution. Since this comes at a time when the Army is reducing the number of forces it contributes to NATO, both in real terms and even more dramatically as a percentage of the Army's strength, this situation is somewhat ironic and requires some explanation.

TABLE 3 THE ALLOCATION OF FORCES TO ROLES

Role	Forces
1. NATO (ARRC)	HQ and Corps troops; 1st (UK) Armoured Division; 3rd (UK) Division**; 24 Airmobile Brigade. Plus: one infantry battalion for ACE Mobile Force.
2. Defence of UK	15 infantry battalions with combat support.
3. Northern Ireland	6 infantry battalions on regular tours (2 year duration); 4 infantry battalions on short tours (6 month duration).*
4. Overseas Garrisons	5 infantry battalions (2 in Cyprus, 2 in Hong Kong, 1 in Brunei).**

* Forces drawn primarily from defence of the UK, though battalions committed to the ARRC may be included in the Emergency Tour Plot. Figures are current strength and may vary over time.
** Garrisons for the Falkland Islands and Belize will be found from forces in UK, Germany and Cyprus (as is current practice). 3rd (UK) Division is double-hatted as a strategic reserve division for use outside NATO, either to reinforce garrisons or to act in support of British interests worldwide.
Source: Cm 1595.

The command of the ARRC was assigned to the British Army in 1990 by NATO's top military commander in Europe, SACEUR. This decision seems to have been prompted by the realisation that for political reasons the ARRC would have to have a European commander, that the commander would have to be drawn from one of the major European powers, and that only the British had the necessary experience of, and willingness to undertake, expeditionary operations. This produced something of a political storm within NATO, with the Germans in particular lobbying hard for a German commander rather than a British one. In response the Secretary of State, Tom King, put his full weight behind SACEUR's original decision, and succeeded in gaining political ratification for British command of the ARRC in the June 1991 meeting of the North Atlantic Council. In other words the Secretary of State went out of his way to secure this command, reflecting the importance attached to it. It enabled Britain generally, and the Army in particular, to maintain and even improve its position within NATO. At the same time it provided protection from further Treasury cuts by implicitly requiring the Army to contribute substantial forces to the ARRC. As a result the importance of the ARRC for the British Army cannot be overestimated: not only does it give the Army a rôle with considerable status within NATO, but it offers a degree of cover from further Treasury cuts.

This new rôle does not come problem-free, however. Aside from the question of whether the ARRC can ever be used due to political limitations,[32] the British Army faces two particular problems. Firstly, British forces committed to the ARRC may be double-hatted, leading to possible problems of prioritisation and overstretch. In particular, 3rd Division is identified as the force for independent action outside of NATO, while a number of battalions from both 1st Armoured Division and 3rd Division will be involved in the ETP at any one time. Thus the actual strength of these units will be somewhat less than their strength on paper, while a conflict in priorities may arise through double-hatting. Secondly, command of the ARRC may provide a degree of cover from further cuts, but it does not provide an impermeable shield. As the pressure for cuts in public expenditure mounts, so the Army may find itself vulnerable. But if the Army is cut yet further, forces committed to the ARRC look the most vulnerable. There appears to be general consensus that there is little room for further cuts in the general purpose infantry, particularly given the continuing commitment to Northern Ireland. It is therefore the armoured/mechanised infantry, armour and artillery which look most vulnerable – in other words, the very forces committed to the ARRC. Command of the ARRC implies a responsibility to provide substantial and capable forces to the Corps, but the pressure for further cuts in defence expenditure may seriously threaten this.

In addition to the ARRC, the British Army may find itself more heavily involved in peacekeeping and related activities than has previously been the case. Bosnia may be but the first of a series of such operations for the Army, some of which may have to be conducted simultaneously. The Army's ability to fulfil these responsibilities is extremely stretched at present – indeed there are indications that the Army was unable rather than unwilling to assist US forces in Somalia. In the future the situation will be worse, not better. This is a product not simply of the cuts under Options for Change, but also of a balance of forces which places the infantry under increased pressure and of the demands placed on the Army (especially the infantry) by Northern Ireland. The problem of overstretch is therefore looming.

Conclusion

Options for Change constituted a defence review in all but name. A key feature of this review – perhaps the most important feature – was the changes to the British Army. Over the years the Army in Germany (BAOR) had become very much a central element of British defence policy, and by the 1980s it was arguably second only to the independent deterrent in terms of defence priorities. 'Options' changed that, and reoriented the Army to the home defence rôle, a limited intervention capability, overseas garrisons, and a much reduced contribution to NATO. Ironically, however, at the same time the Army secured command of, and a disproportionate rôle in, the newest and most important NATO formation, the ARRC, and an increased commitment to intervention and peacekeeping (particularly in Bosnia). It remains to be seen whether or not command of the ARRC, increased peacekeeping responsibilities and Options for Change are mutually exclusive. Certainly the February 1993 reprieve of two battalions suggests that problems exist. But as pressure mounts for further cuts in public expenditure, and particularly defence, even the force levels outlined under Options for Change appear vulnerable.

The cuts in the Army also raised questions over balance and overstretch. The government's figures suggest that demands made by the ETP will actually be reduced in the future as commitments are dropped (particularly to BAOR). But it is also clear that the margin for error is slight, and that future commitments – such as peacekeeping or an increased presence in Northern Ireland – may require an increase in the Army's strength. Indeed the limited deployment in Bosnia has already demonstrated the lack of flexibility in current plans. Whereas the question of overstretch received considerable attention, that of balance received rather less. Perhaps surprisingly the balance between the various fighting arms and between the regulars and reserves has been only marginally altered.

The only major change has been in the balance of forces stationed in the UK. Whether this balance is still appropriate may be questioned. The relative and real increase in forces in the UK has led to substantial resettlement and relocation costs in the short-term, but in the longer term may create major problems in terms of exercise areas.

Finally the government promised a 'smaller but better' Army, with an extensive list of new equipment to be purchased in the next few years. The scepticism with which this promise was received appears to be justified, with pressure on public expenditure threatening future equipment purchases and further damaging the Army's already fragile morale. The 1992 Autumn Statement on public expenditure, in the wake of the ERM crisis, revealed that defence spending was to be cut by 10.5 per cent in real terms in the period 1993–96. This was twice as much as had been planned in the July 1992 Statement on the Defence Estimates. The Chancellor of the Exchequer stated that these extra savings would be 'consistent with the policies which underlie [Options for Change]'. Since a much reduced Army was a key element of Options for Change, further Army cuts cannot therefore be ruled out. Most of the speculation in late 1992 considered that the most likely candidates for cuts were equipment and training.[33] In spring 1993, however, reports began to appear in the press concerning a further substantial review – dubbed 'Grievous Bodily Harm', or GBH – to deal with a £4 billion 'hole' in the defence budget over the next three years.[34] The reports suggested that 'virtually every single equipment programme is either being delayed or having specifications reduced'.[35] In addition the RAF and Navy were to have their regular strength cut quite dramatically, and the TA was to lose a further 9,600 men (or the equivalent of 12 battalions). Interestingly the one area which does not appear to have been targeted for further deep cuts is the strength of the regular Army. This is highly suggestive that the thinking behind Options for Change – that the Army was relatively less important in the post-Cold War world – was being reversed, and that the demands already made on the Army had prompted something of a rethink.

Options for Change came after a relatively fallow period for the military in the late 1980s, and hit the somewhat demoralised Services a body blow. In particular, morale in the Army suffered badly as it was targeted for the heaviest cuts, and as the prospect of compulsory redundancies loomed. But in a sense it is difficult to be particularly sympathetic. The Army is a public service and cannot and should not be divorced from the financial pressures experienced by other public services. If the economy cannot sustain high public expenditure, then public services will be cut. Defence was shielded from some of these pressures in the 1980s due to the reluctance of the Conservative Party to cut defence spending, and the belief in a real threat to British security from the Soviet Union. As that threat disappears, so the remaining threats appear much less direct and less significant. So it is that Options for Change, a review undertaken when the Soviet Union still existed and maintained large forces in Europe, may prove merely a temporary measure before further, deeper cuts. What is questionable, however, is the structure of the Army. The balance of the Army appears little different to that of the 1980s, but the demands likely to be placed on it in the 1990s are very different. Large numbers of shop-window armoured forces, incapable of being moved any distance quickly and unable to fight for any length of time, are not what the Army requires in the more unpredictable and multi-faceted security environment of the post-Cold War world.

Notes

1. This paper would not have been possible without a series of interviews conducted over the summer and autumn of 1992 and spring 1993. I am most grateful to all those who assisted me but who, for reasons of confidentiality, cannot be named. This Chapter first appeared as 'The Future of the British Army', in *Defense Analysis* 9/2 (August 1993). Although I have made a number of changes, much remains the same and I am therefore most grateful to Martin Edmonds, UK editor of *Defense Analysis*, for permission to reproduce this piece.
2. Perhaps the most (in)famous being John Mearsheimer, in 'Back to the Future: instability in Europe after the Cold War', *International Security* 15/1 (1990).
3. House of Commons Defence Committee report on *Defence Implications of Recent Events*, HC 320, p.vi. HMSO, London (1990).
4. Richard Mottram, 'Options for Change: process and prospects', *RUSI Journal* 136/1 (1991) p.22.
5. Mottram, pp.23–24.
6. Col. Henry Lowe, letter to *RUSI Journal*. *RUSI Journal* 136/2 (1991).
7. Richard Mottram, letter to *RUSI Journal*. *RUSI Journal* 136/3 (1991).
8. David Bolton, 'Defence in transition: options for change', (emphasis added). *RUSI Journal* 136/3 (1991) p.2.
9. Gen. Sir John Akehurst, letter to *RUSI Journal*. *RUSI Journal* 136/3 (1991).
10. Mottram, 'Options for Change', p.24.
11. *Britain's Army for the 90s*, Cm 1595. HMSO, London (1991).
12. HC 320, p.vi, and the HCDC report on *Options for Change: Army, Review of the White Paper Britain's Army for the 90s*, HC 45, p.vi. HMSO, London (1992).
13. Statement on the Defence Estimates 1991: Britain's Defence for the 90s, vol.1, Cm 1559–I pp.40–7. HMSO, London (1991). HC 320, pp.xxxvi–xxxviii. Mottram, 'Options for Change', p.24.
14. Cm 1559-1.
15. Statement on the Defence Estimates 1992, Cm 1981, pp.26–43. HMSO, London (1992).
16. Cm 1595, HC 45.
17. Cm 1595, p.4.

18. HC 45, p.xii.
19. HC 45, pp.xii–xiii.
20. HC 45, pp.xxix–xxx and 35.
21. Gen. Sir Martin Farndale, 'The British Army: implications of change', *RUSI and Brassey's Defence Yearbook 1992*, Brassey's, London (1992) p.45.
22. Ian Kemp, 'UK defence cuts bite deeper', *Jane's Defence Weekly*, 21 November 1992, p.12.
23. HC 45, p.ix.
24. *The Independent*, 4 February 1993. *Jane's Defence Weekly*, 13 February 1993.
26. Farndale, *op. cit.*
26. HCDC report on *Britain's Army for the 90s: Commitments and Resources*, HC 306. HMSO, London (1993).
27. Cm 1981, p.32. HC 45, p.xxiii.
28. HC 45, p.x.
29. This point was made by the Defence Secretary Malcolm Rifkind. See Malcolm Rifkind, 'Peacekeeping or peacemaking? Implications and prospects'. *RUSI Journal* 138/2, p.2.
30.. Cm 1595, p.6. Cm 1981, p.35. Maj. Gen. Murray Naylor, 'The challenge of the 90s for the Territorial Army'. *RUSI Journal* 137/3 (1992).
31. Colin McInnes, *The British Army and NATO's Rapid Reaction Corps*. Brassey's/Centre for Defence Studies, London (1993).
32. *Ibid.*
33. See for example Ian Kemp, 'UK defence cuts bite deeper'. *Jane's Defence Weekly*, 21 November 1992, p.12.
34. *The Sunday Times*, 4 April 1993, 11 April 1993.
35. *The Sunday Times*, 4 April 1993.

12
Britain and Nuclear Weapons

Lawrence Freedman

In July 1980 the British government announced that Britain's nuclear deterrent of four nuclear-powered submarines each carrying 16 Polaris missiles was to be replaced by a similar number of missiles on a similar number of submarines, but the new missiles would be the most modern in the American arsenal – the Trident C4 – and they would be accommodated on new and larger submarines. In March 1982 it was further announced that American policy was being followed and that instead of the C4 version of Trident, Britain would acquire the even more modern D5.[1] This would allow for a longer range – up to 6,000 miles – and even more warheads, although the government took care to stress that it was not anxious to maximise the warhead potential.

The discussion document which accompanied the July 1980 decision was widely praised at the time for its full discussion of all elements of nuclear weapons policy and the thorough discussion of all the options for Polaris replacement, yet it did not contain any discussion of the changing political context. The only hint that history might move on was a vague reference to a Soviet leadership 'much changed in character from today, perhaps operating amid the pressures of turbulent internal or external circumstances'.[2] As the first of the new submarines, HMS *Vanguard*, is preparing to enter service, the Soviet Union no longer exists and Britain's strategic environment has been completely transformed.

The end of the Cold War came too late for the nuclear sceptics. If the government had had to make the case for the investment in a new nuclear force in 1990 it would have been hard pressed. Much has changed since those harsh days of the summer of 1980, when the decision to purchase a new generation of submarine-launched missiles from the United States was announced. Then the headlines were of Soviet troops in Afghanistan, arms control on hold, mass demonstrations against cruise missiles, and Ronald Reagan about to obtain the Republican presidential nomination. There was a keen sense of an intensifying Cold War. Now the Cold War is history, the Soviet empire is in fragments and the Warsaw Pact has evaporated. The United States and Russia are engaged in co-operative disarmament and President Yeltsin has promised not to target British cities any more. My concern in this Chapter is to discuss the impact of these changes (up to the middle of 1993) on Britain's nuclear policy.

The impact of such change is often expected to be expressed through arms control, as the method by which an improved political climate can most reliably have a long-term influence on armaments policies. However, for that to be possible in this case, there would have to be a change in Britain's basic attitude towards strategic arms control, about which, despite a professed enthusiasm in principle, it has always been wary in practice. Pre-1989 this was explained as follows:

> The US and the Soviet Union between them have about 95 per cent of the world's nuclear weapons. The clear priority is to get these huge stockpiles reduced. Even when the UK's nuclear deterrent is modernised with Trident, it will remain less than 3 per cent of the Russians' nuclear potential — at the minimum level for effective deterrence. But the British government has never said 'never' to including UK nuclear weapons in the negotiations. If Soviet and American strategic arsenals are very substantially reduced, and if no new significant changes have occurred in Soviet defences against them, we will be ready to consider how the UK can best contribute to arms control talks in that new situation.[3]

Once substantial reductions in numbers were scheduled for the rest of the century, the government was forced to be somewhat more candid about seeing slight room for manoeuvre:

> We have always made it clear that the United Kingdom would deploy only the minimum deterrent required for our security needs. These are not determined by the scale of the offensive capabilities of the superpowers. We did not seek to match them in the large build-up in their strategic forces in the 1970s and 1980s, and the reductions they have now agreed — though very welcome in themselves — are not a determinant in sizing our own deterrent.
>
> The superpowers have now charted a course which, if all goes well, will lead after another seven to eleven years to substantially smaller strategic stockpiles, reflecting a much improved strategic environment. We very much hope that this improvement will continue; but the course of international events cannot be predicted with certainty. At the same time there is increasing interest in the improvement of ballistic missile defences, and their deployment on a limited basis.[4]

Such statements suggest that the transformation of the European security scene is of slight relevance to Britain. If it had a minimum deterrent before, then it cannot go further down if it is to have any deterrent at all. The reductions in numbers being implemented by the United States and Russia do not mean that either of these countries are denying themselves a deterrent. Even if Russia, in particular, intends to go down to a minimum force, it still has *some* force and so unilateral deterrence by Britain, or even a contribution to a NATO deterrent, also still requires *some* force which will not be below the practical minimum. There is even a suggestion in the above statements that the required level for a minimum could grow rather than decline – should Russia develop effective ballistic missile defences.

The number of warheads in the British strategic nuclear arsenal is liable to rise over the 1990s. However this will not be as great a rise as had been anticipated. The lower warhead numbers reflect both a readiness to make an informal response to the changing political climate and also a recognition of production problems with the warheads themselves. In this Chapter I will argue that here, rather than in submarine or missile numbers, is to be found the major area of flexibility in the nuclear force. In addition, I will argue that the pressures for a minimal deterrent are being reflected much more in the non-strategic than the strategic arsenal. Lastly I will suggest that, if anything, the pressure is growing for a broader rationale for Britain's nuclear forces. The rationale for sustaining a national nuclear capability has always had a large political component. This remains the case. The strategic rationale has always depended as much on uncertainty over the future as on tailored responses to a specific threat. This, too, will remain the case, except that now it can be claimed that the uncertainties are far greater than ever.

The Strategic Nuclear Force

(i) Capabilities
The Trident force is scheduled to enter service more or less on time and at a lower cost than originally expected. When the final shape of the programme was confirmed in March 1982 the bill was put at £7,520 million over 20 years in September 1981 prices. At September 1992 prices and exchange rates this would come to £13,500 million. As it is, the most recent estimate puts the cost at £10,676 million.[5] Many of the savings have been found on the American side as the price of the missiles has come down. On the other hand, this does not take account of all the overruns on some associated building programmes, most notably at Faslane and Aldermaston, only part of

which is attributed directly to the Trident programme.

By the summer of 1993, some two-thirds of the programme cost had been spent, leaving another £2.5 billion to be spent in the United Kingdom and another $1 billion in the United States. Much of this has already been committed.[6] Thus, Britain has already largely made its investment in Trident, which is why there is not the pressure, which might have developed if the Cold War had ended sooner, for the programme to be abandoned. The fact that the programme has not exceeded budget, despite some gloomy informal estimates,[7] has also helped it survive. The costs of running the programme over the lifetime of the submarines will be some £185 million per annum, barely higher than the costs of running Polaris.[8]

After *Vanguard* enters service in late 1994/early 1995 the Trident force should build up steadily for the rest of the decade. The second of the new submarines, HMS *Victorious*, is scheduled for launch in late summer 1993 and should enter service around 1996. However, delays in the ordering of HMS *Vigilant* and the fourth boat – for which the contract was not signed until July 1992 – mean that it may be early next century before the force is complete.

The old Polaris submarines will thus continue to play an important rôle until the last boat is over 30 years old. These are now showing wear and tear and are steadily being phased out as they become due for long refits. If problems do develop, it is not inconceivable that in the months preceding the entry of Trident into service the deterrent will depend on a Polaris submarine stationed at its Faslane base rather than on ocean patrol, though the government remains confident that the tradition of uninterrupted patrols can be sustained.

With the greater efficiency of the new propulsion units, each Trident submarine will last longer than its Polaris counterpart without a long refit (which can take boats out of service for around two years). Assuming three-month patrols (and then three months at port) a four-boat Trident fleet should be able to ensure two/three boats on station at any given time as opposed to one/two with Polaris. It has been suggested that this could give scope for only a three-boat Trident fleet, but the view in Whitehall is that the current problems in sustaining Polaris patrols indicate the dangers of being over-dependent upon single submarines.[9] At any rate the fourth boat has now been ordered. There has been no suggestion that two boats would be viable, as would be required to match a 50 per cent superpower cut, because that would mean long periods when no boat was on station.

(ii) Warhead Requirements
One estimate for British nuclear warheads – revealed in 1989 – suggested a total of 120 for Polaris/Chevaline.[10] As it is assumed that

Chevaline involves only two re-entry vehicles (RVs), plus a substantial number of decoys to confuse ballistic missile defences, this figure appears realistic. Prior to the introduction of Chevaline, each Polaris A-3 missile carried a shotgun warhead comprised of three 200 KT RVs.

When in 1982 it was decided to opt for the D5 version of the Trident missile instead of the C4 as originally envisaged, the government stated explicitly that it would not need extra warheads – that is it would stick with a maximum of eight warheads per missile or 128 on each 16-missile SSBN. In terms of arms control, where the total number of deployable warheads tends to be counted, the maximum under declared policy is 512 warheads. Should START II be implemented, by 2003 those warheads would be equivalent to about 15 per cent of the American total and nearly 30 per cent of its submarine-launched arsenal.

By early 1993, 44 missiles had already been purchased from the United States, which means that there is no longer any risk to the programme from changes in American plans for the D-5.[11] However, even with a full complement of missiles there is a basis for considerable variation in warhead numbers. This means that Trident's relative contribution to the world's total stockpile will probably be far less. However, before considering the factors likely to bring the numbers down, we need to address the one which might push it up – the possibility of improved strategic defences.

Strategic Defences

Russia's current ballistic missile defence system covers an area around Moscow. It has recently been upgraded with the longer-range Gordon interceptors in 36 silos in an outer defence ring and with 64 shorter-range Gazelle missiles in an inner ring. In 1992 George Bush and Boris Yeltsin agreed that Russia might accept possible changes in the ABM Treaty in return for access to US defensive technology. This represented a major shift in Moscow's declaratory policy, though one that was not surprising given Russian vulnerability to third-country missile forces.

Even a limited Global Protection against Limited Strikes (GPALS) system – a system capable of dealing with 200 incoming warheads was mentioned – might have been assumed to pose some problems to Britain and France with their limited arsenals. Although such problems would have been more apparent than real as UK or French warheads would still be able to saturate any Russian GPALS, Britain did not see why the Americans should be prepared to make its offensive task *vis-à-vis* Moscow any harder when the future political philosophy of the resident government could not be assumed to be friendly. Nor was it sympathetic to the philosophy of attempting to engineer a universal shift to the strategic defence. The British view remained that for European states, GPALS was extremely expensive, especially in the current harsh financial climate, and of doubtful effectiveness. The programme was thus damned with faint praise, and evidence of American half-heartedness was highlighted:

> The United States Administration has made very clear that it will not take any action which might prejudice the credibility of the European nuclear deterrents, and is proceeding on a sensible step-by-step basis.[12]

Under President Clinton, the strategic defence initiative has been officially declared over and it is now less likely than ever that a major strategic defensive system, as opposed to a limited form of theatre defence, will be deployed. While this may fit Britain's deterrence thinking it does have the effect of removing one of the concerns which were used to justify a reluctance to engage in strategic arms reductions.

Problems at Aldermaston
There are three reasons to suspect that warhead numbers may be kept lower than eight per missile. First, though it is hard to judge the influence of this factor, the United States now only intends to carry four warheads per D5 missile. Second, fewer warheads means less use of plutonium and other special materials, and so a lower cost. Third, it may not be possible to build warheads to the maximum.

There have been a series of major problems at Aldermaston relating to both recruitment and construction, which have led to a private company being given responsibility for the management of the plant. Of particular concern have been the delays in the construction of the A90 and A91 plants which are required for warhead production. As a result, Trident warhead production has come to rely on the older and smaller facilities, A1-1 and A45, which were supposed to have been replaced by now. This is sufficient for a load for the *Vanguard*, but has been considered to be insufficient for subsequent boats.[13] Given the reduced current pressure to carry full loads of warheads, it may well make political as well as practical sense to spread *Vanguard*'s load with *Victorious*. It would be ironic if the modern plants at Aldermaston only became available at the point where the old plants they were scheduled to replace had met most of the requirements. However, the delays to *Vigilant* should allow the development of the warhead production facilities to catch up with the production of new submarines.

Tom King, when Secretary of Defence, refused to hint at how low the total number of warheads might go, but did confirm that 'we're not going to carry the maximum'.[14] In confirming this in early March 1992, the Prime Minister observed that there would be flexibility to tailor the size of the force to conditions. 'What would be irresponsible', he added, 'would be to decide in advance to limit ourselves to a lower figure'.[15] Thus the objection is to fixed numbers (which would be a natural feature of an arms control regime). The official formulation now is that:

> We have long emphasised that each Trident submarine would carry no more than 128 warheads. This has always been an upper limit, not a specification: the number to be deployed in the mid-1990s onwards will be decided in the light of circumstances at the time.[16]

Assuming that the US and Russian cuts continue as planned and that no enhanced ballistic missile defence is deployed around Moscow, it is possible to speculate that UK warheads will be around a third or at most a half of this maximum.

The Sub-Strategic Nuclear Force[17]

At its most recent peak Britain's sub-strategic capability was described as follows:

> The British free-fall nuclear bomb can be delivered by RAF Tornado GR1 and Buccaneer and Royal Navy Sea Harrier aircraft; options to replace it with a tactical air-launched missile are currently being studied. British nuclear depth bombs can be delivered by Royal Navy anti-submarine helicopters; RAF Nimrod maritime patrol aircraft can deliver US nuclear depth bombs. An Army artillery regiment equipped with short-range Lance missiles and four regiments of artillery in the Federal Republic of Germany are capable of firing nuclear warheads supplied by the United States.[18]

However, since then this capability has been cut back significantly. In the future, it will 'consist solely of RAF Tornado, and until 1994 Buccaneer, dual-capable aircraft and the WE-177 free-fall bomb'.[19] Short-range land-based systems (which were dual-key) are being abandoned. These included four batteries of three Lance short-range missiles,[20] plus 16 M-110 203mm self-propelled howitzers and 101 M-109 155mm self-propelled howitzers.[21] In 1987 it was reported that 16 203mm guns would be withdrawn completely from the nuclear rôle so that resources could be concentrated on the 155mm gun. Modernisation here would have involved deployment of the US W-28 shell.[22] However, following the NATO decision to abandon short-range nuclear forces in Germany, it was announced that 50 Missile Regiment and 56 Special Weapons Battery Royal Artillery were to disband by 1 April 1993.

Britain no longer retains a maritime tactical nuclear weapons capability. Nuclear depth-bombs were carried on board the three Invincible class light aircraft carriers, to be used with Lynx and Sea King helicopters, even though many frigates were also allowed to carry them. Only 20–30 were produced, and their yield was put at 5-10KT.[23] The weapons designated for this rôle are being destroyed. RAF Nimrod maritime patrol aircraft were able to carry American nuclear depth charges. These patrols have been terminated.

It was in the autumn of 1991 that Tom King, then Secretary of State for Defence, announced that nuclear weapons would no longer be carried on Royal Navy ships 'in normal circumstances'. Making this more permanent in June 1992, King's successor, Malcolm Rifkind, explicitly described this as 'a further indication that we live in a changed world', though he stressed that the cuts were not part of any treaty obligation. 'It is a decision that we ourselves have taken.' Certainly there was no pressing economic reason. There would be savings in the training of crews and detailed certification of equipment, and in the storing and maintenance of the weapons. But the weapons would be returned to Aldermaston to be dismantled, where they involved a substantial extra workload.[24]

The only sub-strategic weapons being maintained are air-delivered. Even here there are to be reductions. There is to be a reduction from 11 Tornado and two Buccaneer squadrons to four Tornado GR 1/1a squadrons based in the United Kingdom and four GR 1 still based in Germany. The number of WE-177 free-fall bombs available for these aircraft is being cut by half.

The WE-177 was one of 'a family of weapons of different characteristics having come in at different dates', including the Navy's nuclear depth-charge (WE-177C) as well as the RAF's free-fall bomb (WE-177A and B).[25] A 1989 estimate put the number of WE-177 free-fall bombs and depth bombs at 180.[26] Tornados are normally assumed to carry two WE-177 bombs.[27] One source gives the yield of these weapons as around 20KT;[28] another suggests a variable nuclear yield between five and 200 kilotons.[29] Both IISS and SIPRI suggest that there is a variant with a yield of 400 KT.[30] The yield varies according to the amount and condition of the Tritium in the bomb. In practice the bombs kept have yields well below 200 KT and probably as low as 10 KT.[31] The original yield may have been reduced at the request of SACEUR, out of deference to German concerns over high-yield weapons being used over their territory.

A major question mark now hangs over the issue of a possible new stand-off missile to succeed WE-177. Instead of requiring the aircraft to operate at the limits of their range and penetrate Soviet air defences, an air-launched stand-off missile would have given the aircraft more space to manoeuvre, allowing them to avoid the most dense concentrations of air defences or to extend their effective range. As security policy was reassessed in the wake of the December 1987 US-Soviet INF Treaty, interest in a stand-off missile revived. This led to a debate in Whitehall over the comparative merits of collaboration with France or the United States.

In May 1988 there were indications that a decision on the WE-177 replacement would be taken by the end of 1990, with a planned in-service date at the end of the 1990s. Almost at the end of 1990 it was reported that a decision had been taken that a Tactical Air-to-Surface Missile (TASM) should be approved, but the question of whether this should be Anglo-American or Anglo-French had yet to be decided. The requirement was believed to be for a weapon with 400–600km range, with high accuracy and some 'stealthy' features. Some 100–200 missiles would be built. Estimates of potential costs, especially in collaboration with the French, have reached £3bn (compared with just over £10bn for Trident).

When President Bush cancelled the SRAM T programme in September 1991 he removed the cheapest of the three options being considered by the Ministry of Defence for the British TASM. It has been suggested that it was only with UK prompting that he included a reference in his announcement to the need to 'preserve an effective air-delivered nuclear capability in Europe'.[32] Internal UK studies have since looked at other US programmes, including the joint Anglo-American Tactical Integrated Rocket Ramjet Missile, and the possibility of working with the French to develop their ASLP D. Studies are reported to have then turned to the possible sub-strategic use of Trident warheads.[33] In the July 1992 Defence Estimates there was no specific mention of a stand-off missile,[34] and this was generally taken to mean, probably correctly, that the political logic of the situation was to abandon this programme.

Nonetheless, £1.5 million is said to have been spent during 1992 looking at the various options for the WE-177 replacement, including a tactical warhead for Trident and submarine-launched Tomahawk cruise missiles, as well as a free-fall bomb. In March 1993 Malcolm Rifkind told the House of Commons:

> We are looking at a series of replacements for the WE177 which could either be an alternative free-fall bomb or other means of achieving a sub-strategic capability.

The free-fall bomb would not meet the RAF's desire for a stand-off missile, while a new submarine-based weapon would involve considerable additional costs. The use of Trident in a sub-strategic rôle, though an enormously expensive means of delivering a small warhead, may well end up as the simplest option, perhaps combined with a free-fall bomb.[35]

A new warhead is under development by Aldermaston, and being tested in the United States, although the programme is not yet complete. It may therefore be vulnerable to a nuclear test ban. A test ban could not have an effect on Trident because the warhead development programme is now complete.

A Test Ban

The 1992 Defence Estimates observed that Britain's underground nuclear test programme had been very much smaller than those of other nuclear powers, 'with a strictly limited number of tests to enhance safety and to establish the effectiveness of new generations of weapons'. There had been only 21 tests since 1963. 'We shall continue to conduct only the minimum number of tests necessary and to recognise a comprehensive ban on nuclear tests as a long-term goal.'[36] However, the UK depends on the Americans being willing to allow it to continue to use the Nevada test site, since Britain lacks its own facility. As regards the cost of testing, the only published information is that it is 'significant': the government refuses to disclose precise figures.[37]

In September 1992, Congress, against the wishes of President Bush, enforced a nine-month moratorium on US nuclear testing, which was intended (at least by Congress) to lead to a complete ban by 1996. Britain would be allowed one test per year up to 1996, and the Pentagon was reported to have made provision for this number (that is three out of 15 in total).[38] The British Embassy lobbied against the moratorium on the grounds that 'we still need to carry out our minimum test programme for reasons of safety, reliability and effectiveness'. The Ministry of Defence's response to the prospect of a complete ban after September 1996 was that it would 'use the intervening time to ensure our deterrent is in good order for the 21st Century'.[39]

The Clinton administration came to power under considerable pressure to accept a complete ban on nuclear testing. As a candidate, Bill Clinton had supported the Congressional move. This threatened to put Britain in a difficult position, especially as the Labour Party saw this as one defence issue where it was safe to attack government policy as being 'out of kilter with the American government'. John Major denied that the issue was discussed with President Clinton when the two met in late February, though he hinted that Britain's position on testing was under review. Officially the position remained that tests were necessary to 'maintain the safety and credibility of our deterrent'.[40] As with a number of issues, President Clinton did not find the test ban issue as straightforward as had candidate Clinton. The Department of Energy, responsible for testing, claimed that nine tests would be needed up to 1996, largely for safety purposes, though the Pentagon argued that these would be unnecessary.

On 3 July Clinton announced that he had decided to maintain the moratorium so long as no other nation tested first. The British were reported to be frustrated, as one test had been ready to go when the moratorium had first been imposed. Three tests were planned, of which one was probably for a single warhead Trident and another was said to be to add safety features to the existing WE177, and now had to be abandoned. Policy shifted towards improving computer simulation capabilities.[41]

Pressure for Further Cuts

This Chapter has argued thus far that plans for Britain's future nuclear arsenal have been scaled back in response to the changing environment, but flexibility has been retained, at least in the strategic area, by keeping the nuclear force out of formal arms control.

This has not been a major issue in Britain. It only tends to get debated around election times. However, with an anti-nuclear policy blamed for two election defeats, the Labour Party trod exceedingly softly around the issue in April 1992. An election-eve launch of the first of the Trident submarines, HMS *Vanguard*, might have been expected to spark some argument, but in practice it helped explain why the debate was so half-hearted. Much of the investment in the coming generation of submarines and missiles had been made, and so the economic case for abandoning the deterrent, which was the basis for the Labour challenge in 1983 and 1987, was weak.

The point at which the government became most vulnerable on this issue was January 1992, just before the election, when Boris Yeltsin visited London as the head of the newly-independent Russian Federation. Both the Labour and Liberal Democrat parties were calling for a commitment to limit the number of British warheads on the Trident missiles to the levels currently held on Polaris. Labour also indicated that it would be prepared in office to negotiate a further reduction in the number of warheads, though it was taking care in this election not to commit itself to negotiating away the whole nuclear deterrent.[42]

An understanding had just been reached with George Bush that the processes of strategic arms reductions would be accelerated. Yeltsin had called for Britain, along with France and China, to put their nuclear forces into international disarmament talks. John Major had insisted that this path would not be followed. Downing Street dismissed the call as 'the standard Russian line'. Part of the pressure was expected to be a repetition to Britain of a promise that Yeltsin had just made to the United States, namely that its cities would be spared Russian nuclear targeting. Indeed this pledge was made. Standing outside 10 Downing Street, Yeltsin said:

> In the past, the United States, Britain and Europe in general were regarded as our potential enemy. That doctrine has to be changed, and the missiles retargeted.

A degree of scepticism was expressed with regard to the retargeting of Russian missiles – they could be retargeted back again. One British official was reported to have remarked: 'Targeting can be punched in and out at will. Weapons can easily be retargeted. Most of them simply point up into the sky.'

However, the Prime Minister had clearly had some success in persuading Yeltsin not to push the question of British participation in a disarmament regime. When pressed by reporters, Yeltsin played down the issue:

> The number of nuclear weapons at Britain's disposal is not comparable with ours, and therefore the matter is not really worth discussion.[43]

This effectively removed the issue from the domestic political agenda.

Meanwhile, the government sought to reinforce its arms control credentials by drawing attention to initiatives outside the strategic arms area, such as chemical weapons and arms transfers.[44] In claiming credit for the cuts in sub-strategic forces, the benefit was described in terms of the objective of confidence-building rather than 'stability' or 'balance':

> All these measures to reduce nuclear force levels not only have obvious attraction for tax-payers and for finance ministers: they also reduce, as a matter of simple mathematics, the risk of an error or accident; and they contribute to the building of greater confidence, facilitating the development of co-operative relations.[45]

Britain has always been more sympathetic to proposals for confidence-building measures that do not impinge directly on force structure. Thus London has its own 'hot-line' with Moscow, and there has been considerable sympathy for the American effort to add to the locks and safety catches safeguarding nuclear arsenals by strengthening command and control procedures, ending quick-reaction alerts, dismantling warheads and separating nuclear weapons from general purposes forces. Measures have been taken to encourage the nuclear successor states in the former Soviet Union to act responsibly by putting their weapons into Russian territory and under Russian control and promising to abide by the strictures of the Non-Proliferation Treaty – (achieved by offering a say in the ratification of START – which is more than the British ever got).[46]

Rationales

While Boris Yeltsin offered to remove British cities from the Russian target list, it was difficult for John Major to reciprocate. The introduction of Chevaline, which began operational service in the summer of 1982,[47] did not commit Britain to an attack on the Moscow area as the only targeting option. However, it may be that it committed Britain to an attack on a few, and possibly no more than one, large target(s). In 1980 it was acknowledged officially that:

> There is a concept which Chevaline makes clear, that Governments did not want to have a situation where the adversary could have a sanctuary for his capital and a large area around it.[48]

Whereas with the old A-3 warhead all missiles would have to be committed without complete confidence of success, with Chevaline a similar number of missiles would be launched but with a much greater chance of success. Until Trident becomes operational in late 1994 or early 1995 Britain therefore will have little flexibility in targeting.[49]

With Trident, each submarine can carry up to 16 missiles, each with up to 8 independently-targetable warheads. In addition, more boats could be on station at any given time. With a maximum of three boats on station, this would allow maximum coverage of 384 targets.

However, as already noted, the likely number will be less than 200. There is considerable flexibility on the number of warheads carried. This number can be varied according to the perceived strategic situation.[50] In an individual boat, some missiles could carry loads geared to a strategic exchange with Russia while others would carry smaller packages geared to 'sub-strategic' use.[51]

The old rationale for the nuclear force depended on the threat to Moscow. NATO had determined that it needed the threat of nuclear war to deter Moscow from unleashing the Warsaw Pact's massive conventional armies in a drive to the channel. The United States obviously provided the bulk of the deterrent force, but it was important that one European country made a contribution (with France sitting on the sidelines outside the Alliance's integrated command). Furthermore, because there was unavoidable doubts over whether the United States would put itself at risk for the sake of Europe, it was helpful if Moscow had to consider the possibility that London would respond even if Washington held back. It may have been hard to think of occasions on which this might happen, but then the great virtue of nuclear deterrence lay in awareness of the large consequences of slight miscalculations.[52]

In one sense the case for a national nuclear force has been strengthened, in that previous justifications always played on doubts over the durability of the US nuclear guarantee. There is now nothing like the old preoccupation with the US umbrella – which is just as well, as many of the old standards set for extended deterrence can no longer be met. In the past it has been assumed that only the stationing of US nuclear systems on allied territory can provide tangible evidence of the nuclear umbrella. Apart from SLBMs in European waters, whose mobility allows for a speedy withdrawal, this will now at most depend on forward deployment of nuclear-capable aircraft. The number of US nuclear warheads in Europe is set to come down to 700 – almost 10 per cent of those at peak deployment. The target set has obviously changed, but the dramatic reduction in warheads reflects the level of visible commitment now considered adequate both in the United States and Europe, especially now that the most dire contingencies seem remote.[53] Whether or not the numbers would be seen to be sufficient should one of these contingencies actually arise is a difficult question, as is the general credibility of a 'reconstitution' policy for a nuclear umbrella. Once the weapons have been marginalised, will it be possible to give them a revived rôle without aggravating the crisis that occasioned the reappraisal? Bringing weapons out of store, putting others back on alert, coyness about deployment and targeting plans will appear provocative.

Even though the local presence of US systems may become an untenable basis for extended deterrence, for the moment NATO countries have little option but to accept US declaratory assurances that extended deterrence is still in place. This is unlikely to be formally withdrawn but it may not be sustained over the years because it will rarely be a high political priority and so will lapse. There may be a break in the US institutional memory, and no tangible reminders of the nature of the nuclear commitment.

The uncoupling of the US nuclear arsenal from European security is now a much more serious prospect than it has ever been, but precisely for that reason, the British government does not want to start talking of American disengagement as a foregone conclusion. In his most important restatement of British nuclear policy, Malcolm Rifkind observed that it was not in Britain's security interest to encourage any tendency towards thinking that there could be a major conflict in Europe in which the question of nuclear use arose which did not involve the vital interests of all the allies including the US.[54]

On this basis it is not surprising that he also indicated that the old second-centre of decision-making theory retained 'validity'.

Nor has there been much support for the view that an alternative guarantee can be based on France and Britain. It has always been assumed that such a guarantee would lack credibility – in part because of French policy, which remains a problem, and in part because of the balance of forces, which may become less of a problem. There has been no indication that other allies see an Anglo-French guarantee as a serious alternative to an American guarantee, so long as the latter is on offer.[55] Furthermore, the major project which could symbolise revived Anglo-French co-operation – the Tactical Air-to-Surface Missile (TASM) – still seems likely to fall by the wayside as a result of budgetary stringency.

There has always been a private rationale for the nuclear force less convoluted than the 'second-centre of decision-making' but also more nationalist and so inappropriate for NATO gatherings. According to this Gaullist view, a nuclear capability means that Britain still carries international weight, deserving its permanent place on the UN Security Council and at other 'top tables'. The ability to devastate any potential enemy provides the 'ultimate guarantee of security' were the country ever again forced to 'stand alone'. In a cruel and uncertain world, who knows what threats might emerge in the future?

With the Alliance rationales now looking distinctly dated the rationale for Trident is tending to revert back to the private view, which was probably always the most credible to public opinion. Although Rifkind in his September 1992 speech in Paris reaffirmed loyalty to concepts of extended deterrence, the latest Statement on Defence Estimates defined the essence of national strategy in much narrower terms:

> Our defence strategy will continue to be underpinned by nuclear forces as the ultimate guarantee of our country's security. Nuclear weapons guard against any attempt by an adversary to gain advantage by threat or coercion. They are also uniquely able to ensure that aggression is not a realistic option, by presenting to a potential aggressor the prospect of a cost that would far outweigh any hoped-for gain.[56]

Rifkind also acknowledged that nuclear use would only be credible, justifiable and proportionate when 'vital national interests were at stake', and that the most vital of interests were narrowly national – 'the most obvious hypothesis being a direct homeland threat from an aggressor equipped with weapons of mass destruction'.[57]

It is rather difficult to put too much stress on prestige arguments for a nuclear arsenal at a time when Ukraine, Belarus and Kazakhstan are being told that they have very little to gain by clinging on to pieces of the old Soviet arsenal still residing in their territory and when a major plank of policy towards the Third World is to prevent the further acquisition of weapons of mass destruction. Britain may feel that it is so much more stable and mature, but that does not tend to be an argument that commends itself to potential proliferators.

In fact the risks of Third World proliferation are now being used to reinforce the case for the British deterrent. This rarely goes further than the rhetorical 'what if [whoever happens to be the most menacing dictator at the time – Galtieri, Gaddafi, Saddam, etc] had nuclear weapons and we did not?'[58] The rôle of a nuclear capability in future regional crises would be at most to neutralise any threats of mass destruction being made by a rogue country in the course of an Iraq-type challenge to international law. This is a serious rationale, but it should be noted that it implies a readiness to make nuclear commitments to other countries that go well beyond anything contemplated in recent years. Trident is not especially well suited to this rôle. However, if the only sub-strategic use of nuclear weapons that might still be contemplated is a warning-shot function, any strategic weapon could be used for this purpose, the 'sub-strategic' nature of the shot being made clear by the choice of target.

On the basis of past practice and international declarations it will be no part of Western policy to use nuclear weapons to intimidate non-nuclear powers armed with only conventional forces,[59] although policy is ambiguous with regard to states armed with other terror (i.e. chemical and biological) weapons.

The Gulf crisis raised the question of the readiness to use nuclear forces to deter chemical/biological attacks. In this case at least, a capacity for defensive measures and for severe retaliation with conventional air power, plus a deterrent threat based on the extension of political objectives to threaten the Iraqi regime, appeared sufficient, and that should be the pattern in the future. When John Major was questioned on nuclear use in retaliation for Iraqi chemical use while visiting troops just before the start of the war, he replied: 'We have plenty of weapons short of that. We have no plans of the sort you envisage.'[60]

Rifkind has shown little enthusiasm for nuclear threats in such circumstances. If deterrence relies on rationality and caution in an aggressor, would it, he asked, work with a 'tyrant with little regard for the safety and welfare of his own country and people? If he is a gambler or an adventurer? If his judgement is unbalanced or clouded by isolation'. He also expressed concern that public opinion would always think nuclear use disproportionate against a 'small country, or an economically weak one ...' Nor would more 'usable' low-yield nuclear weapons be effective as a deterrent: 'There is a horror associated with nuclear weapons which we should not attempt to mitigate'. The hope here must therefore be placed in non-proliferation regimes, plus the use of conventional weapons with precision technologies and also precision intelligence. In addition:

> Pre-emptive conventional strikes against clearly-identifiable targets under appropriate international sanction are a conceivable option, given the capability of modern conventional weapons, and given the availability of good intelligence.[61]

Other than this, the critical focus remains on the former Soviet Union. The CIS will be an unstable region, perhaps for decades to come, where the potential for authoritarian (albeit non-Communist) regimes is considerable. The key state is the Russian Federation. Even taking into account reductions to 3,500 warheads by the early years of the next century, Russia will still have a capacity to inflict unacceptable damage on Western nations, and its integration into the Western economic and political systems is likely to be at best tenuous. Thus Rifkind argued that: 'Our strategy makes military recidivism by any future Russian leadership a pointless option for them'.[62]

However, with much reduced overall military power, there is no obvious dynamic leading towards total war with the West. The dominant strategic issue is now more the fragility of the former Soviet Union than the old fears of brilliantly-executed first strikes. There are still grim forebodings of nuclear weapons getting tangled up with chronic political instability. The possibility of a renegade nuclear power emerging out of the wreckage of the Soviet Union should not be overstated but it is no less fanciful than many others which have sustained nuclear policy over the years. Moscow may be ruled by someone less benign, while the Americans may allow their past guarantees to European security to lapse. In a harsher security environment, the non-nuclear powers of western Europe, and in particular Germany, may be grateful that Britain and France have held onto their arsenals.

Conclusion

The British government does not see its nuclear arsenal as being of great relevance to strategic arms control, even assuming that strategic arms control itself has a future. It has moved unilaterally to remove the bulk of its sub-strategic arsenal, and even what is left of this is unlikely to be modernised significantly in the near future. The argument that if Britain believes that it should be allowed to maintain a nuclear arsenal, why not other countries, will tend to get the riposte that other nuclear arsenals might be tolerable if they were in the hands of mature democracies of honourable intent and kept as no more than insurance policies. The problem with nuclear proliferation, according to this view, is not the spread of the technology *per se* but the purposes for which it is acquired and the unsettled strategic environments of the proliferators.

For Britain, nuclear weapons remain little more than a hedge against an uncertain future. The inclination is to keep them well clear of any conflicts in which it is likely to be involved where the future of western Europe is not directly at stake. Within Europe, the possibility of a revival of a Russian nuclear threat can be acknowledged even though it remains difficult to describe the circumstances which might bring it about. With a substantial premium having already been paid on this particular insurance policy, it is unlikely to be casually abandoned.

This is in many ways a much simpler strategic environment in which to develop a national nuclear policy than the one which it replaced, though in every other respect the current environment is much more complicated. The easiest nuclear doctrine is one geared to the deterrence of another's nuclear use against national territory. This was always difficult for Britain to adopt because of its loyalty to the Alliance and to the associated strategy of flexible response, which depended on the threat to use nuclear weapons on behalf of allies who could not be defended in the face of a superior conventional force.

Given the small size of its force it was never clear why Britain would take such a step on its own and, if it would only initiate nuclear war in concert with the United States, exactly what it was adding to the American nuclear clout. However, for the moment, there is no pressing need to worry about deterring conventional threats or worrying about the vulnerabilities of close allies. The residual threat may be remote and defy precise identification, but nuclear strategy has always been geared to remote scenarios.

Nuclear weapons can play the rôle that they have always played – of reminding of the folly of total war – but in circumstances less demanding than before. Providing a further reminder may be at best a marginal rationale for Trident, but with most of the money spent or committed, perhaps that is all that it now needs.

Notes

1. *The United Kingdom Trident Programme*, Defence Open Government Document 1982/1. (London: Ministry of Defence: March 1982).
2. *The Future United Kingdom Strategic Deterrent Force*, Defence Open Government Document 80/23. (London: Ministry of Defence, July 1980). I noted at the time: 'There is no discussion of the possibility that the superpowers' strategic relationship might undergo a critical transformation before Trident is in service, or that the dispersion of the relevant technology around the world will lead to the emergence of new nuclear threats'. Lawrence Freedman, 'Trident: Will it still work in 2020 AD?', *The Sunday Times*, 20 July 1980.
3. Questions on Arms Control, Foreign and Commonwealth Office and Ministry of Defence: February 1988, cited in John Poole (ed), *Independence and Interdependence: A Reader on British Nuclear Weapons Policy* (London: Brassey's, 1990), p.261.
4. Statement on the Defence Estimates 1992, Vol.1, Cmnd 1981, (London: HMSO, July 1992), p.22.
5. HCDC report on *The Progress of the Trident Programme* HC 549, (London: HMSO, June 1993) p.vi.
6. *Ibid*, If the programme were cancelled now there would be substantial cancellation costs which would further negate any potential savings.
7. David Greenwood, *The Trident Programme* (Aberdeen Studies in Defence Economics, No 22: Summer 1982). Greenwood suggested that the cost could be up to 25 per cent higher than the original estimate.
8. HC 549, p.vii.
9. For a discussion of this issue see the colloquy involving Rear Admiral Ian Pirnie in House of Commons Defence Committee, Fifth Report of session 1991–92, *The Progress of the Trident Programme*, HC 337, March 1992, Minutes of Evidence pp.4–7.
10. *The Independent*, 23 June 1989. President Mitterrand of France observed in 1987 that Britain had '90–100 [strategic] weapons'. Cited in Richard Fieldhouse, Robert Norris and William Arkin, 'Nuclear weapon developments and unilateral reductions initiatives', in Stockholm International Peace Research Institute. *SIPRI Yearbook 1992: World Armaments and Disarmament*, (London: Oxford University Press, 1992), p.80.
11. HC 549, p.xiv.
12. Secretary of State for Defence, Rt. Hon. Malcolm Rifkind MP, Intervention in Paris Symposium, (30 September 1992), p.13. Hereinafter referred to as Rifkind Speech.
13. HC 549, p.xix.
14. *Financial Times*, 10 February 1992.
15. *The Independent*, 4 March 1992.
16. Statement on the Defence Estimates 1983, Vol 1, Cmnd 1981–I (London: HMSO, July 1992), p.22.
17. 'Sub-strategic' is the preferred British nomenclature to the alternatives – pre-strategic or non-strategic.
18. Statement on the Defence Estimates 1990, Vol 1, Cmnd 1022–1 (London: HMSO, 1990), para 201.
19. Defence Estimates 1992, p.28.
20. Lance has a range of 130km, and an accuracy of 0.4 to 0.45km, with a yield

ranging from 1 to 100 kilotons.
21. The M-110 launched a shell of 2 kilotons to a distance of 14 kilometres with an accuracy from 0.04 to 0.17km depending on the range. The M-109 had a comparable accuracy and a slightly longer range with a yield of 2 kilotons.
22. *Financial Times*, 25 July 1987. *Official Record*, 23 July 1987, col 390.
23. *The Independent*, 23 June 1989.
24. *Financial Times*, 16 June 1992; *The Independent*, 16 June 1992. The non-UK weapons were returned to the United States.
25. The weapon was developed in the early 1960s. The first WE-177s were delivered to the RAF in 1966–67. Thereafter more than 180 were produced up to 1982, of which 20–30 were C variants. Production continued at Aldermaston and Burghfield until 1978, when manufacturing lines began to produce warheads for Chevaline. The line was interrupted earlier for Polaris production. *The Independent*, 16 May 1988; 23 June 1989.
26. *The Independent*, 23 June 1989. Fieldhouse et al, *SIPRI Yearbook 1992*, p.80.
27. *SIPRI Yearbook 1992*, pp.79–80.
28. Shaun Gregory, *The Command and Control of British Nuclear Weapons* (University of Bradford School Of Peace Studies, Peace Research Report Number 13, December 1986).
29. Duncan Campbell, 'Too Few Bombs To Go Round', *New Statesman*, 29 November 1985.
30. SIPRI Yearbook 1992, p.80; The International Institute for Strategic Studies, *The Military Balance: 1992–1993*, (London: Brassey's for the IISS, 1992), p.232.
31. *The Independent*, 16 May 1988.
32. For text see *Arms Control Today* (October 1991), pp.3–5.
33. *The Independent*, 23 June 1992.
34. 'The RAF will continue to make a major contribution to sub-strategic forces in support of NATO and to provide a national sub-strategic capability. We are currently studying possible replacements for the WE-177 free-fall bomb which will approach the end of its service life around the turn of this century', Defence Estimates 1992, p.22.
35. *Jane's Defence Weekly*, 6 March 1993; *Independent*, 15 April 1993.
36. Defence Estimates 1992, p.22.
37. HC 549, p.xii. The costs include 'payments covering arrangements for the management and disposal of radioactive wastes associated with the test, but none are made specifically in respect of environmental issues'. Legislation has been introduced to the US Congress to make Britain pay for its share of a decontamination project at the Nevada test site. Australia has also been requesting further payment for the Maralinga test site used in the 1950s. *The Observer*, 14 March 1993.
38. The nuclear testing moratorium was adopted against President Bush's objections as part of the FY 1993 Energy and Water Appropriations Bill, a measure otherwise eagerly sought by the President. It provided for a moratorium on testing until July 1993. Testing can thereafter only start again under strict conditions, including a plan for a comprehensive test ban, and then there can be no more than five tests a year or 15 over four years. According to one clause: 'The President may authorize the United Kingdom to conduct in the United States within a period covered by an annual report one test of a weapon if the President determines that it is in the national interests of the United States to do so. Such a test shall be considered as one of the maximum number of tests that the United

States is permitted to conduct under that period ...' *Congressional Record*, 18 September 1992, S13949.
39. *The Times*, 26 September 1992; *The Independent*, 3 October 1992.
40. *The Observer*, 14 March 1993. The shadow cabinet agreed on 3 March 1993 'that no further testing is needed for Britain's Trident programme and that any further work can be adequately conducted under laboratory conditions'. *The Times*, 4 March 1993.
41. HC 549, p.xii; *Arms Control Reporter*, 1993.
42. *The Independent*, 30 January 1992.
43. *The Independent*, 31 January 1992; *Financial Times*, 31 January 1992. There was no pressure from the United States for Britain to get involved. A few days later speaking in Washington, General Colin Powell, Chairman of the Joint Chiefs of Staff, observed that the strategic arms negotiations had always been bilateral and should remain so. He was 'not inclined' to pull the allies in 'and I don't suspect they wished to be pulled in ... We don't believe that the Russians should feel any particular concern over these non-US systems but they do, and that's a matter for them to take up with the other Western nuclear powers.' *Arms Control Reporter 1992*, 408.B.137.
44. See statement by Prime Minister John Major after Bush proposals of September 1991, *The Guardian*, 28 September 1991.
45. Rifkind Speech, p.7.
46. Britain sent to Russia 250 special containers and 20 vehicles for the safe transport of nuclear warheads, and offered consultancy assistance in various fields, including nuclear accident response techniques, conversion of fissile material for civil use, environmental restoration and the implementation of IAEA safeguards.
47. Statement on the Defence Estimates 1983, Vol 1, Cmnd 8951-I (London: HMSO, 1983), p.7.
48. HC 36 of 1980–81, p.107.
49. The nature of the Chevaline concept is to rain a series of warheads and decoys simultaneously over the target so as to swamp the target area. Its effect does not come from the contents of a single missile but from the combined contents of a number of missiles – probably the complement of one SSBN! It is now difficult to disentangle the system to take on a number of targets at once.
50. HC 549, p.vi.
51. *Ibid*.
52. The old rationale is discussed in Lawrence Freedman, *Britain and Nuclear Weapons* (London: Macmillan, 1980).
53. Thus Secretary of State for Defence Malcolm Rifkind interprets the 'reduced reliance' on nuclear weapons in NATO's strategic concept as meaning that one can get away with 'very significantly lower levels of forces'. Rifkind Speech, p.6, Interpretations of the meaning of 'reduced reliance' vary. In December 1990 the Nuclear Planning Group clearly saw reduced reliance as influencing both 'Alliance nuclear force levels and structures'. It stressed the promise of 'further dramatic reductions in the number of NATO's nuclear weapons retained in Europe', but also that the

> remaining nuclear forces, for which we seek the lowest and most stable level commensurate with our security requirements must be sufficiently flexible, effective, survivable and broadly based if they are to make a credible

contribution to NATO's overall strategy for the prevention of war. We will develop our future nuclear posture in conjunction with the new strategic concept reflecting the principles and new directions for nuclear forces set out in the London Declaration.

Nuclear Planning Group, Final Communique (7 December 1990), para 14.
54. Rifkind Speech, p.17.
55. There have been discussions in the past over the possibility of collaboration with regard to patrol areas and targeting. The problems with a joint force were summed up in the 1987 White Paper:

> If one were considering a fully integrated, jointly controlled Anglo-French nuclear deterrent, significant problems would arise. Our two countries would need to agree on the criteria the force would have to meet, the targets that would be put at risk, the details of complementary refits and patrol cycles and, by no means least, the problems of consultation leading to the launch of a nuclear weapon and the authority for the actual firing of a weapon. And if a jointly controlled force were contemplated, which country would change its defence philosophy? For certainly there would have to be a change. British nuclear forces are committed to NATO, and the Alliance would unquestionably be weakened in military and political terms if they were removed. France, on the other hand, although a member of the Alliance, is not part of the NATO military structure, and her forces are therefore independent of the Alliance.

Statement on the Defence Estimates 1987, Vol 1, (London: HMSO, 1987). Rifkind has taken this a bit further. While not suggesting that Anglo-French co-operation could be a basis for an alternative nuclear deterrent, he has proposed that the 'more closely we can concert our policies, the more weight we shall carry', citing issues of nuclear testing as an example where both suffered the consequences of a failure to work together. Rifkind Speech, pp.18, 20–21.
56. Defence Estimates 1992, p.9.
57. Rifkind Speech, p.14.
58. E.g. Rifkind Speech: 'The thought of what might have happened had Saddam Hussein been able to build a nuclear weapon before the invasion of Kuwait is a sobering one indeed'.
59. In 1978 the Head of the UK Delegation to the UN Special Session on Disarmament made the following statement:

> I accordingly give the following assurances on behalf of my Government to non-nuclear weapon States which are parties to the Non-Proliferation Treaty or other internationally binding commitments not to manufacture or acquire nuclear explosive devices: Britain undertakes not to use nuclear weapons against such states except in the case of an attack on the United Kingdom, its dependent territories, its armed forces or its allies by such a state in association or in alliance with a nuclear weapons State.

Annex Q, *The United Nations Special Session on Disarmament*, Cmnd 7267 (London: HMSO, 1978).
60. *The Independent*, 9 January 1991.
61. Rifkind Speech, pp.10–12.
62. *Ibid*, p.5.

Index

In the interests of discrimination, this index does not include mere passing references to subjects or individuals. References to specific defence forces or programmes such as EFA are not detailed separately but are listed under Army, Royal Navy, Royal Air Force or Nuclear forces, as appropriate.

Aid spending 110–113, 140–143
Akehurst, John 202
Allies, dependence on 94–97, 113–116, 126–127, 136–137, 155–158, 162–163, 209–210
Amphibious forces *See* Royal Marines
Arms control 132, 221–222, 230–232
Army, British xvii-xx, 16–17, 44–45, 59, 95, 99–100, 108, 118–121, 132–134, 162–163, 165–166, 171–172, 193–194, 198⎯⎯⎯9199, 202–203, 205–218
ARRC xvii, xx-xxi, 16–17, 108, 120–121, 154, 166, 190, 193–194, 213–215

Ballistic missiles 122
BAOR *See* Germany, British forces in
Barnett, Correlli 35, 48
Belize 22
Bolton, David 201
Bosnia *See* Yugoslavia, former
Brunei 22
Burden sharing 102–116, 127–127, 153–154
Bush, George 228–229

Cambodia 40
Chemical & biological weapons 95, 235
Chamberlain, Joseph 51–52
Clarke, Michael 52
Clinton, Bill 229–230
Collective security 34–36

CSCE 7–10, 18, 27, 34–36
Cyprus 45

Defence budget 60–61, 74–80, 86–87, 93, 104–105, 108, 118, 177–179
Defence exports 61, 85
Defence industry 61, 82–85, 156–157
Defence, meaning of xv-xvii, 50–59
Defence priorities 17, 44–45, 65–66, 97–100, 133–137, 149–174, 211–212
Defence programme 80–82
Defence reviews 54, 170, 199, 203–205
Defence roles xxi-xxii 51, 55–56, 62, 80, 175–176, 203–205, 213–214
Denmark xviii
Derby, Earl of 51
Dulles, John Foster 53

EC xiv, 10–12, 18, 24–25, 28–29, 113–115, 157
Eastern Europe 6–7, 15, 27
Economic burden of defence 93–94, 96–97, 102–104, 110–112, 141–143
Economic constraints xiv, 31, 67, 73–80, 144, 168, 171–172, 177–179, 200, 217–218
Environmental threats 137–141

Falkland Islands 22, 60, 117
Farndale, Martin 209
Flexibility 159–163
France 24–25, 106, 158, 162–163, 234

242

Index

Franco-German Corps 12, 25, 163
Freedman, Lawrence 40

Germany 11, 14–15, 106, 112–114, 158, 162
Germany, British forces in xvii-xviii, 16, 100, 108, 119–124, 204, 211
Global security 137–145
Gulf crisis 34, 63, 164

Hamilton, Archie 210
Heath, Edward 38
Heseltine, Michael 179–180
Holsti, Kalevi 64
Hong Kong 57
Hopkinson, William 58
Humanitarian intervention 36–49
Hurd, Douglas 37, 45–46, 48

Intervention 21–22, 31–49, 62–66, 97, 100
Italy 106
Iraq 116

Japan 63
Jenkins, Simon 37–38

King, Tom 175, 199, 225, 227
Kurds 41–42

Long Term Costings 81–82
Lowe, Henry 201

McInnes, Colin 16
Major, John 235
Mearsheimer, John 4
Merchant shipping 166
Mobility 163–167, 212
Mottram, Richard 199–202

NATO xiv, 12–19, 23, 27–28, 51–58, 92, 114–115, 153–154, 158, 183–192, 199–200
Neutrality 58–59
News media 37–39
Northern Ireland 42–43, 59, 80, 97, 117
Nott, John 159, 164
Nuclear forces 20, 30, 60, 95, 117–118, 123–124, 135, 181–182, 220–241
Nuclear proliferation 5, 132, 235
Nuclear testing 229–230

Oil *See* Resource supplies
Options for Change xvii-xxi, 16, 33, 51, 104, 132, 150, 159, 170, 175, 199–203
Overstretch 154, 208–211

Parliament xviii, 39, 51, 54, 104–105, 150, 203, 230
Peacemaking & peacekeeping 9, 26, 37, 116, 133, 186–187, 215–216
Personnel, civilian xviii, 74–76
Personnel, service xvii-xx, 59, 74–76, 168-169
Population growth 137–141

Quality of forces 167–170
Quinlan, Michael 160

Reconstitution of forces xv, 65, 132–133, 154–155
Reserve forces xviii, 154, 213
Resource supplies 63
Rifkind, Malcolm 35, 45, 160, 176, 225, 227–228, 231, 233–236
Role specialisation 16–17, 45–46, 94–96, 126–127, 133–134, 162–163, 182–185, 189–194
Royal Air Force xviii-xx, 60, 98, 108, 121–124, 134–135, 159, 162–163, 165–167, 194, 226–228
Royal Marines xvii-xix, 60, 98–99, 136, 193
Royal Navy xviii-xx, 20, 59–60, 98–99, 108, 124–126, 135–136, 159, 162, 192–193, 226–227
Russia *See* Soviet Union, former

Security, definition of xv-xvii, 36–38, 112, 130, 137–145
Sharp, Jane 38
Smith, Steve 38
Somalia 37
Soviet Union, former 5–6, 13–14, 64–65, 91, 105, 116, 153, 230–232, 236
Special forces 60, 94
Strategic defences 224–225

Television *See* News media
Ten Year Rule 64–65, 151
Territorial Army *See* Reserve forces
threats 56–58, 64–65, 106, 130–132, 138, 151–153
Trident *See* Nuclear forces
Turkey 12

UN 18, 26–27, 34–35, 39, 46–47, 61, 161
USA 13, 24, 91, 96–97, 106, 114, 157, 160, 228–230, 233
Underfunding 167–170, 178–181

WEU 10–12, 18, 25, 28, 110–111, 116

Yeltsin, Boris 230–231
Yugoslavia, former 6–7, 10–11, 36, 38, 62